# BUDGETARY CONTROL

By

## JAMES O. McKINSEY, A.M., LL.B.

Certified Public Accountant; Member of the
firm of Frazer & Torbet; Assistant Professor
of Accounting, University of Chicago

NEW YORK
## THE RONALD PRESS COMPANY
1922

# PREFACE

Although much has been written of budgetary control as applied to particular phases of a business, this is the first attempt, so far as the author is aware, to present the subject as a whole, and cover the entire budgetary program. It is to be regarded as an effort to state clearly the problems involved, rather than to offer full solutions. It is hoped that the discussion will stimulate thought, and constructive criticism will be gladly received.

One obvious difficulty has been the problem of what to include and what to omit. The budgetary procedure involves administrative policies on the one hand, and administrative routine on the other. The discussion might easily cover the whole field of business administration, ranging over a wide variety of topics about which no one individual can be expected to have expert knowledge. In the present work, however, the reader is addressed throughout, not as a technical expert, but rather as a student of the broad problem of administration. The advertising man, for example, may be aided in handling his own problems through understanding the method of applying budgetary control to the operations of all other departments of the business, as explained in the other chapters of the book. So with the other departmental executives; it is hoped that each of them will be helped by a comprehensive picture of the problem as a whole. The discussion has been kept sufficiently elementary, it is believed, to be easily understandable by those who are not experts on the technical subjects discussed.

With this thought in mind, there has been no effort to prescribe an arbitrary procedure. In some cases, assumptions have been made and definite procedures discussed, but

iii

only for the purpose of making the treatment concrete; the
definite procedures given are intended to be suggestive only.
Similarly, the various forms given are merely indicative.
All of them have been used by the author at some time in
his professional practice, but he by no means regards them
as standard forms.    He has found it necessary to design
forms to meet each particular case.

Finally, no attempt has been made to discuss in detail
the many problems which may arise in the installation and
operation of budgetary control.    To do so would be to make
the volume less useful to those for whom it is primarily intended.    It is thought that the reader who has a comprehensive picture of the entire problem will be able to make
his own applications and to work out the special adjustments required for his own situation.

The text is based primarily on the rather wide experience
of the author in professional work, but material assistance
has been received from various business men, accountants,
and instructors.    Particular acknowledgment is due to the
following: Mr. W. V. Lindblom, executive in charge of the
budgetary procedure of the Walworth Manufacturing Company, and Mr. Albert S. Keister, Lecturer on Business
Finance, University of Chicago, who have read all the
manuscript and given many useful suggestions; Mr. N. L.
McCully, executive in charge of the budgetary procedure of
the Lewis Manufacturing Company, who prepared the
chart on budgetary procedure given in Chapter XXIII; and
Mr. George E. Frazer, C.P.A., the author's partner, to
whose counsel and assistance the author is especially in-
debted.

JAMES O. MCKINSEY

Chicago, Illinois,
June 20, 1922

# CONTENTS

v

# ILLUSTRATIONS

vii

A Trust Company Budget System (Appendix C)

# BUDGETARY CONTROL

# CHAPTER I

## THE MEANING OF BUDGETARY CONTROL

### Planning of Business Operations

That comprehensive planning is necessary for efficient administration may be regarded as an axiom of the present-day philosophy of business administration. Business executives have come to realize that they can perform properly the tasks of today only if they have already planned those tasks yesterday, and planned also the tasks of tomorrow. There are many who do not yet plan scientifically, but there are few who will deny the merits of the system.

The planning which may be done in connection with any particular business may be classified into three broad overlapping groups:

1. That which deals with the operations of the separate departments, such as production, sales, and finance. Such planning has been described loosely in the past, as "industrial engineering."
2. That which deals with the coordination of the operations of the several departments to the end that a well-formulated program may be made, for the business as a whole. Such planning may well be termed "budgetary control."
3. That which deals with the determination of future conditions as reflected in the business cycle and the shaping of the plans of the business to meet these conditions. Such planning is known as "forecasting" or "business predicting."

While the discussion in the following pages is restricted primarily to a consideration of planning of the second kind, it must be realized of course that these various kinds of plans are all very closely related and must be coordinated if proper results are to be obtained. The budgetary plans are vitally affected by the business cycle, and the departmental plans are equally affected by the budgetary plan. The reader will notice that in the following pages it will be necessary to discuss to some extent all three kinds of planning.

## Popular Conception of Budgetary Control

In the past, budgetary control has been considered primarily in connection with governmental units. There has been much discussion of the "budgets" of cities and states, and during recent years much interest has been manifested in the budget of the national government. This interest has been greatly increased by the passage of the National Budget Act and the submission to Congress of the first budget prepared under this act. The budgets of governmental units are discussed frequently in the daily press and by aspirants for political office, and are thus called constantly to the attention of the public. As a consequence many people have come to think of budgetary control as an instrument for governmental administration. Not only is this the popular view but practically all the literature on budgetary control is confined to a discussion of governmental budgets.

Although practically all people who have given thought to the subject will admit that there should be budgetary control of public finances, very few have thought of budgetary control with reference to the individual business unit. It is the purpose of these chapters to show that the principles of budgetary control are as applicable to the individual business unit as to the governmental unit, and to explain the method by which these principles may be applied. As a first step it is necessary to see (1) what budgetary control is, and (2) why it is needed in business administration. The present chapter and the chapter immediately following will be devoted to a consideration of these topics.

## Procedure for Budgetary Control

Probably the best way to show "what budgetary control is" is to outline how it operates. The procedure to be followed by a business firm in the installation and operation of budgetary control will of necessity vary, depending primarily on the organization of the business and the nature of its operations. A possible procedure, stated briefly and in outline form, is as follows:

1. Each department prepares an estimate of its activities for the budget period. The method of stating these activities depends on the nature of the operations of the department, the sales department stating the sales it expects to make and the estimated expenses it will incur in making these sales; the production department stating the estimated production for the period and the estimated requirements in materials, labor, and manufacturing expenses to meet this estimate; the service departments, such as the personnel department, the traffic department, the accounting department, and the office manager's department, stating the estimated expenditures of their departments. Because of the interdependence of these departments, some will need to use the estimates of other departments in making their own estimates. For instance, the production department must know the estimated sales before it can estimate the production necessary to meet the sales demands; the treasurer must know the plans of all the departments before he can estimate his cash receipts and cash disbursements. Consequently a procedure must be set up which provides for a proper scheduling of the estimates with reference to preparation and distribution.

2. The departmental heads will transmit the departmental estimates to an executive who has supervision of the budgetary procedure. Sometimes the controller acts in this capacity, while in many cases the duty is delegated to a

member of the staff of the general manager or president. Since many businesses do not have a controller, it will be assumed during the present discussion that an assistant to the president acts in this capacity. This official combines the estimates of all the departments into a proposed financial budget for the business. In preparing this estimate he will be assisted by the treasurer, though in some cases this budget is prepared by the treasurer alone. The proposed financial budget should show the estimated receipts from all sources and the estimated expenditures by all departments of the business.

3. The executive in charge of the budget procedure makes a comparison between the estimated receipts and the estimated expenditures as shown by the proposed budget. If the estimated expenditures exceed the estimated receipts, one of the following courses of action must be taken:

(a) The departmental expenditures may be reduced. In making such reductions a problem arises due to the fact that the reduction of expenditures may result in a reduction of receipts. For instance, if the expenditures of the advertising department are reduced, this may result in a reduction of sales, with a consequent reduction of receipts from collections. In the same manner, a reduction of the expenditures of the production department may result in a reduction of production, with a consequent lack of goods to meet sales demands which will result in a reduction of receipts from sales. Care must be taken, therefore, in the reduction of expenditures to see that receipts are not reduced more than proportionately.

(b) Additional receipts may be secured. It may be possible by speeding up operations and securing more efficient administration to secure additional receipts without incurring a proportionate increase of expenditures.

(c) Additional capital may be secured. If it is not

deemed wise to reduce expenditures, plans must be made
to secure additional capital with which to finance the excess
of expenditures over receipts. It is understood, of course,
that this condition cannot continue for long, otherwise the
business will find it necessary to liquidate.

The executive in charge of the budgetary procedure may
make recommendations with reference to possible procedures, but he is usually not invested with authority to
determine the plans to be followed.

4. The executive in charge of the budgetary procedure
prepares from the departmental estimates an estimated
balance sheet and an estimated statement of profit and
loss, showing respectively the anticipated financial condition at the end of the budget period and the anticipated
result of the operations of the period.

5. The departmental estimates, together with the proposed financial budget, and the estimated financial statements, are submitted by the executive in charge of the budgetary procedure to a budget committee, composed of the
principal executives of the company and presided over by
the president. This committee considers the proposed estimates and makes such revisions as it thinks necessary. In
case the proposed budgets involve important changes in the
company's policy, or require the securing of additional
capital for a material amount, it may be necessary to submit
them to the board of directors for consideration. Indeed,
in some businesses all budgetary plans are submitted to the
board of directors for approval. After the proposed estimates have been approved, they constitute the working
program for the budget period. The budgets as adopted
set limits upon the expenditures of all the departments, and
these limits cannot be exceeded without the permission of
the budget committee. The budgets also set up standards
of performance for certain departments. For instance, the

sales budget states the sales that are to be made by the sales department, and the production budget states the estimated production of the production department.

6. Each department makes plans which will enable it to carry out its program as outlined by its budget. For instance, the advertising department makes contracts for advertising space; the sales department sets quotas for its salesmen; the production department sets up schedules of production.

7. Records are established so that the performance of each department may be properly recorded and comparisons made between the estimated and the actual performance. Periodic reports, showing a comparison between the estimated and the actual performance of each department for the budget period, are made to the executive in charge of the budgetary procedure and are by him transmitted to the budget committee and in some cases to the board of directors. On the basis of these reports the budget committee or board of directors may make such revisions of the budgetary program as it may deem desirable.

### Essential Features

The foregoing procedure is intended to be suggestive only. Each organization must adopt a procedure which is fitted to its particular needs. The purpose of the foregoing outline is to indicate what budgetary control is by suggesting how it operates. From this outline it can be seen that budgetary control involves the following:

1. The statement of the plans of all the departments of the business for a certain period of time in the form of estimates.
2. The coordination of these estimates into a well-balanced program for the business as a whole.
3. The preparation of reports showing a comparison between the actual and the estimated performance, and the revision of the original plans when these reports show that such a revision is necessary.

## Budgetary Control Not a New Idea

All businesses practice budgetary control to a greater or lesser degree although many of them do not realize the fact. The newsboy estimates his probable sales before making his purchases, and every business man must do likewise if he is to continue to operate long. Even the farmer, who usually scorns the use of formal methods of control, estimates the probable returns from land used for various kinds of crops and the cost of producing each, and on this basis decides upon the crop which he will plant. During the war the Red Cross, the Y.M.C.A., and Liberty Loan committees used the budgetary idea in their "drives" by setting up *quotas* for each territory. These quotas were based on estimates of the sales possibilities in these territories. Budgets for governmental units have been in use for many years, and the "family budget" has long been a matter of discussion.

Many business firms which deny that they operate a budgetary program will be found to make and use estimates. In this connection the author recalls a visit he made to the merchandise manager of a large wholesale store several years ago. This executive derided the idea of preparing a sales estimate and stated that he did not care to discuss such an academic question. A few minutes later the author inquired if the merchandise manager permitted his buyers to use their own judgment in deciding on the quantity of goods to purchase. He emphatically replied that to permit the buyers to purchase all they desired would bankrupt the firm in six months. In response to the request to explain how the buyers' purchases were controlled, he stated that the executives of the firm first obtained the average sales for the past three years and added to this average the percentage of increase which they expected during the next year. After they determined in this manner their "expected" sales, they "calculated" the purchases necessary to meet these sales and instructed the buyers accordingly. It took the author some minutes to show the manager that his firm was preparing both a sales estimate and a purchases estimate. Further investigation showed that it was the practice of the treasurer of the company to obtain a copy of the sales estimate and purchase estimate and to use these as a means of making estimates of cash receipts and disbursements. In other words, the company had an informal and imperfect system of budgetary control.

Similar investigations will show that all other profitable businesses make plans for future operations, and however informal these plans may be, they are in essence budgetary control.

## Modern Tendency Towards Budgetary Control

Modern business administration tends more and more to become a standardized routine. In a large organization such standardization is essential to the maintenance of a unified business policy and to the coordination of the activities of the several departments; and coordination means subordination to a common head. Business men are gradually coming to realize that this can best be accomplished by the formulation of plans submitted for approval in black and white, if indeed coordination can ever be accomplished in any other way for a great length of time. Not that plans have not always been made, but they have commonly been carried around in someone's head. Because of the increase, however, in the volume of business performed by the typical industrial unit, with the corresponding complexity in business organization, it is coming to be less and less possible to maintain a business organization that depends upon the intuitive faculties of a single individual developed by years of experience, faculties which perish with the individual.

The organization must be independent of any single individual in it. All of which goes to show that there should be some systematic method of gathering information from the past and formulating on this basis plans for the future, and of subsequently reporting how these plans have been carried out. Such an accounting and statistical organization we may call a budget system.

# CHAPTER II

## THE NEED FOR BUDGETARY CONTROL

### Why Budgetary Control Is Needed

In the preceding chapter it has been explained that budgetary control has long been practiced in an informal way but that only in recent years has it been introduced as a formal and comprehensive procedure. In fact the firms are largely in the minority which have formally adopted budgetary control at the present time. It is the belief of the author that the delay of business firms to adopt budgetary control as a definite part of their administrative methods is due to one of two causes: Either they do not fully realize its need, or they do not understand how to install and operate it.

It is the purpose of the present chapter to explain its need as an instrument of administration, while the remaining chapters of this book are devoted to an explanation of its installation and operation.

Budgetary control is urgently needed in administrative control for two purposes:

1. As a means of coordinating the activities of the various functional departments.
2. As a basis for centralized executive control.

Perhaps its use for these purposes can best be shown by sketching the method by which administrative control is exercised in the modern type of business organization, the problems which arise therefrom, and the need for a comprehensive method of planning ahead as a basis for solving these problems. Much that is said in the remainder of this chapter, though perhaps more or less familiar to the reader, is stated here in order to present a comprehensive picture of the problems which give rise to a need of budgetary control.

## Interdependence of Business Activities

It is the author's experience that executives often become so engrossed with what they regard as the larger administrative policies of their business, that they fail to give sufficient attention to many of the administrative problems to realize their significance. They are easily impressed with the value of a sales campaign which will result in a large increase in the volume of sales, but they may fail to realize the importance of working out methods by which to coordinate the sales campaign with the production program so that the goods sold will be ready for delivery at the proper time. They are keenly interested in the enlargement of manufacturing facilities and the increase of production, but may fail to realize the significance of maintaining a careful check on inventory to avoid the accumulation of unsalable merchandise.

It is worth while for the executive to make a comprehensive survey of the whole problem of administrative control from time to time to see that he is not overemphasizing some phases of the problem at the expense of others. If this chapter serves to impress upon the reader the interdependence of all the activities of a business, it will have served a useful purpose regardless of his reaction to the argument presented in behalf of the need for budgetary control as a means of coordinating these activities.

## Functional Activities—Their Coordination

The operations of businesses vary widely and the variations in operations produce a divergence in organization, but in every business there are certain functional groups of activities which must be performed. These functions are:

1. The sales function
2. The production or purchasing function
3. The personnel function
4. The finance function
5. The standard and record function

Since these functions are found combined in a single business unit, it is fair to suppose that there must be a close relationship between them.   A very brief study will show that there is such a close interrelation that it is impossible to perform one of them unless the others are also being properly performed.   It is true that some businesses emphasize one of these functions and other businesses emphasize another, but in no business can any of these functions be safely neglected.   A few illustrations of the interrelationship will make this clear.

### Balancing Production and Sales

Goods are purchased or produced in order to be sold. It is unwise and unprofitable to purchase or produce more goods than can be sold within a reasonable time after their purchase or production.   To do so results in tying up capital in a non-income producing investment, for excess inventories yield no profit.   A second danger arising from this procedure is the deterioration which may take place in the surplus stock due to time or obsolescence.   It is obvious, therefore, that wise administration will take into consideration sales expectancies in planning purchases or production. The failure to limit purchases and production to correspond with sales possibilities has caused many firms heavy losses during recent years.

On the other hand, it is unwise to sell goods in excess of the possibilities of supply.   To sell more than can be purchased or produced leads to an unnecessary expense both in securing the sale and in handling the inevitable complaints

which arise from failure to fill orders.    An additional loss
may arise from the ill-will of the disappointed customer.    It
is better to refuse an order in the beginning than to accept
the order and fail to satisfy it.    Many firms lost prestige by
such actions during the years 1918 and 1919.    It is necessary,
therefore, to consider production or purchasing possibilities
in planning the sales campaign.    In other words, the sales
function and the production or purchasing function are so
closely interrelated and interdependent that they must be
considered jointly in planning executive policies.

### Planning for Equipment and Personnel

Not only must sales and production be correlated, but
this correlation must be planned sufficiently in advance of
the time when it is to be effected to make possible the securing of the necessary equipment and personnel to produce
the goods required.    In a manufacturing business plant and
equipment are essential to the production of goods, and in
considering increased production the possible increase in
plant and equipment requirements resulting thereform must
be taken into account.    But the quantity of production is
determined by the volume of sales; so in the end the sales
campaign determines the plant and equipment program.
The relation between these two functions can be easily seen.
Loss will result from the sale of more goods than the present
equipment can produce or than it is possible or profitable to
purchase equipment to produce.    In this connection three
questions must be asked:

1. Can the desired amount of goods be produced with the present
   plant and equipment?
2. If not, can additional plant and equipment be secured in time to
   produce goods to supply the present demand?
3. If so, can such plant and equipment be secured and operated
   profitably?

It is equally unwise to secure plant and equipment beyond that needed to satisfy the present or the anticipated demands of customers.   Consequently the plant and equipment program is closely related to both the sales and production programs.

But equipment cannot be operated without workers and it is necessary to know the production requirements sufficiently in advance of the time of their fulfilment to make possible the securing of the necessary amount of personnel. Where skilled labor is employed the securing of the proper personnel is a problem of major importance.

### Planning of Finances

The making of sales, the producing of goods, and the securing of equipment and personnel, all involve an expenditure of funds.   All these operations must be financed and they can be carried on only to the extent to which the financial resources of the business will permit.   It is unwise indeed for a business to plan a sales campaign with the consequent production requirements without considering the financial possibilities of the business.   A lack of coordination of the sales and production programs may lead to loss, but a lack of coordination of the various departmental programs of the business with its financial program will lead to bankruptcy.

### Coordination—Special Problems

The foregoing illustrations point out the interrelationship of the primary functions of the business and show the necessity for their correlation.   But in the securing of this correlation many things must be considered.   For instance, emphasis has been placed upon the desirability of not producing beyond sales requirements because of the consequent loss arising from the capital invested and the possible de-

terioration of the goods. There may be other factors, however, which make it desirable to produce beyond sales capacity for a certain period of time. For instance, if the sales
fluctuate from period to period, it may not be desirable to
have the production fluctuate accordingly. There are several reasons for this, one of the principal being the problem
of maintaining a proper labor supply if wide fluctuations in
production take place. If production fluctuates it is necessary to discharge laborers whom it may be difficult to replace
later, especially in the case of skilled labor, or it is necessary
to retain laborers not employed for full time, which is undesirable and uneconomical. It may be preferable to maintain a uniform production and thereby accumulate in a
period of slack sales an inventory which may be used to
meet the excess demands during the rush period. The loss
of the excess capital tied up in the inventory may be less
than the loss which would result from fluctuating production. This is but one illustration of the many problems
which arise in planning coordination of the operations of
the functional departments. Many more will undoubtedly
occur to the reader.

## Cooperation among Functional Officers

From the few illustrations given, the interrelation of the
various functions of the business should be evident and the
necessity for the coordination of these functions should be
apparent. But business administration can be discussed
only in terms of business organization, and "functions" of
the business can be discussed only in terms of the "functionaries" who are responsible for them. The discussion of the
coordination of functions, therefore, resolves itself into a
discussion of the coordination of functionaries, and a brief
study of the prevailing conditions in large business establishments will show that such coordination is the most

2

urgent need for effective business organization at the present
time.   A conservative estimate would attribute a majority
of the business failures of the present time to a lack of coordination of the functions of the business due to a lack of
cooperation on the part of the functional officers.   That this
lack of cooperation is not intentional and is due primarily to
a lack of information which would make such cooperation
possible, does not change the situation.

### Reason for Present Lack of Coordination

It is quite easy to see how the present situation came
about.   When the business enterprise was small, with a
simple organization and its activities local, the owner, who
was also the manager, was able to exercise direct control of
all the functions of the business.   He acted as the executive
head of each of the functional departments; he was sales
manager, production manager, treasurer, and controller,
all in one.   Because of this condition he was able to bring
about the proper correlation without difficulty.   In his capacity of sales manager he knew the sales which he estimated
possible, so that he knew what purchases to make when he
was acting as merchandise manager or purchasing agent.
As treasurer he knew the funds which were available so that
he could make his sales and purchasing plans accordingly.

When the business unit increased in size and its organization became more complex, the executive was forced to
delegate certain of his duties to assistants, and the present
plan of functional organization developed, with a separate
executive in charge of each function.   The change in conditions is apparent.   The sales manager devotes his entire
time, thought, and energy to the securing of sales, and he
has no direct contact with the production department.   The
production manager has become engrossed in the problems
of production and has little or no means of becoming

familiar with the operations of the sales department.    The treasurer secures the needed funds as best he can and has little information upon which to make his plans.    And thus the coordination which formerly was brought about by the centralization of control in the hands of the chief executive is lacking.

## Mere Study of Past Records Inadequate

During the past few years the functional staff officers of many large businesses have realized the necessity for a co-ordination of the activities of the various departments of a business and have attempted to bring about this coordina-tion by studying past results and trying to correct the worst evils which were revealed.    For instance, the production manager may find that on certain articles large inventories have been carried, so that he plans to cut down the produc-tion of these articles during the coming year, thereby reduc-ing the inventories.    The treasurer may find that during certain months his bank balances are very low because of the demand on the part of the purchasing or production de-partment for funds, consequently he may plan to increase his bank loans at that time during the coming year.    In the same manner each department may study its past activities and plan to correct the difficulties of the past.    In some cases the departmental heads may go farther and study the past operations of the other departments so as to see the cause for the difficulties incurred in their own department.

This method of attacking the problem accomplishes some results; but even if carried out very completely it usually is subject to two serious objections:

1.  It is basing future plans on past results and not taking into con-
    sideration possible changes.    This is almost sure to lead to
    inaccuracies, since a business does not remain stationary; it
    either advances or goes backward.

2. It is a negative rather than a positive program.   It plans to try to remove the difficulties of *last* year; its goal is to try to do *this* year what it should have done *last* year.   It is only an attempt to reach a *past* goal, not an attempt to reach a *new* goal which should have been set for this year.

## New Method Needed

It is contended, therefore, that a new method and a new policy is needed, different from that followed by many firms at present, a policy which will provide correlation and compel progress.   Such a policy will involve dealing with future plans rather than with past results, although plans must of necessity be formed in the light of results.   Administrative control necessitates the use of estimates.   The past is gone and cannot be changed.   It is only future operations over which control can be exercised.

If the departmental estimates are to be used efficiently and effectively, it is necessary that a procedure be developed for their preparation, coordination, and operation.   This procedure when established constitutes budgetary control.

## Centralization of Executive Control

If efficient administration is to be accomplished, it is necessary to provide not only for the making of plans to secure coordination of departmental activities, but also for administrative control of these activities so that the plans made will be carried out.   The tendency in business administration during the past half century has been towards centralization of control in the hands of a few executives and the delegation of duties by these to subordinates who are responsible to the primary executives for the performance of the tasks thus delegated.   This method has important advantages, but it also gives rise to certain significant problems.   In order to see the nature of these problems and the need of budgetary control in their solution, let us sketch briefly the method of exercising administrative control in a typical organization.

Although the tendency during the past several years has been towards the centralization of administrative control, the number of people who exercise influence in the administration of the typical business is quite large. The ultimate control of a business is with the owners, but in the modern corporate enterprise their control in the main is exercised only indirectly. Most of their authority is delegated to a board of directors, who in turn delegate a large part of their authority to the general officers of the corporation. The general officers in turn entrust the execution of

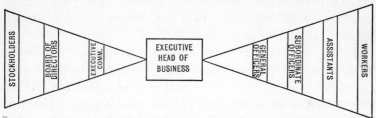

Figure 1. Chart Showing Corporate Form of Organization

many of the policies of the business to subordinates, and these subordinates employ the services of assistants who are directly in contact with the workers. Such a form of organization may be shown graphically as in Figure 1.

From the foregoing graph it can be seen that in the corporate enterprise executive control is exercised through the medium of a number of groups, cooperating in the performance of the administrative function. As showing the problems involved in securing this cooperation, a brief account is given below of the degree of control exercised by each group.

### Control Exercised by Owners

In the corporate type of business organization the ownership is vested in the stockholders. Legally the executive control also is vested in the stockholders. As a matter of practice they exercise this control very indirectly. The stockholders pass upon only a few of the policies of the business, the remainder being left to the jurisdiction of the board of directors which is chosen by the stockholders. The direct control of the stockholders is usually limited to the following:

1. PROTECTION OF PROPERTY INTEREST. The stockholder invests in the corporation for two purposes: (a) to secure the preservation of his capital, and (b) to secure an income from the use of the capital in the business. He desires reports which will show that his property interest is being protected, and in case he realizes that it is being impaired, he may exercise his right to direct actively the operations of the business. Of course, such action is possible only where there is a community of interest with consequent cooperation of a majority of the stockholders.

2. MAINTENANCE OF DIVIDEND RATE. As stated in the preceding paragraph, the stockholder desires to obtain an income from the use of his property in the operation of the business. This income he obtains by means of the dividends which are declared by the board of directors. He desires consequently that the dividend rate be sufficiently high to afford him a proper return on his investment, and he desires that this dividend rate be maintained regularly if possible. He is especially sensitive to a lowering of the dividend rate or the passing of a dividend payment. He desires, therefore, to be consulted about a change of policies which will affect the dividend rate. The chief interest of most stockholders in the board of directors is in the question of its ability to protect their property interests and to maintain a fair and adequate rate of dividend. So long as this is accomplished, the stockholder does not seek to interfere in the administration of the corporation.

3. FINANCING OF EXTENSIONS.   If extensions are to be made on a large scale, it may be necessary to appeal to the stockholders to contribute additional capital or to obtain their permission for the issuance of additional stock or bonds. In either case the consent of the stockholders should be obtained by the board of directors, although in the case of issuing bonds the stockholders' approval is often only formal, since the board of directors works out the plan and submits it for approval.   It is within the province of the stockholders to reject such plan, but this authority is exercised rarely.

### Control by Board of Directors

The preceding discussion has emphasized the fact that the stockholders delegate most of their powers of control to the board of directors.   The board of directors, although they are responsible for the administration of the business, do not as directors participate in such administration.   They content themselves with outlining the general policies to be followed and then delegate the execution of these policies to the general officers of the business.   The method by which the board of directors exercises control may be indicated by the following:

1. They select the general officers of the company and delegate to them certain administrative duties.
2. They outline the general policies of the business for the guidance of these executives, to the end that the desires of the stockholders may be realized; that is, that their property interests be protected and a reasonable dividend rate maintained.   To this end they may set up a dividend rate which is to be maintained, and judge the efficiency of the general officers by their ability to make possible the maintenance of this rate.
3. They consider and approve, modify, or reject the general plans submitted by the general officers.   Such plans include the estimates or budgets which the general officers present to show their proposed accomplishment during the coming period.

4. They receive reports from the executives of the business which show the degree of success they have attained in carrying out the plans which have previously been approved.   Such reports, if properly prepared, show the success of each principal executive, as well as the success which has attended the efforts of the executive staff as a whole.

5. They award bonuses or increases of salaries to the executives on the basis of their performance, and thus encourage efficiency and initiative.

Such are the duties of the board of directors in most cases.   In a corporation where the general officers of the corporation are members of the board, they may exercise a more direct control than that indicated.   It is questionable, however, whether in this case the general officers are not acting in their capacity as executives rather than as directors.   It is not feasible or desirable to consider here in detail the administrative functions of the board of directors.   It is sufficient for our purposes to see that the execution of the administrative policies of the business is left in the main to the general officers of the business.

### Control through General Officers

As indicated by Figure 1, it is customary to have in each business a chief executive who is responsible for the administration of the business.   In a corporation this executive is usually the president, although in some cases the president may be subordinate to the chairman of the board of directors, when the latter assumes active executive duties.   For the purposes of this discussion we will assume that the president is the chief executive officer.

In a small business the president may supervise and direct all of the administrative functions.   In a business of any considerable size this is impossible and it is necessary to employ other officers to assist in the formulation and execution of the executive policies of the business.   The number of such officers who may be employed and the duties which they may perform will depend to a considerable extent on the nature of the operations of the business and consequently on the administrative functions which must be subject to executive supervision.  On a previous page it has been explained that the primary administrative functions are:

1. The sales function
2. The production function
3. The purchasing function
4. The personnel function
5. The finance function
6. The standard and record function

In a business of sufficient size to make advisable a functional organization of the administrative personnel, there is an executive head for each of the foregoing functions and therefore we have the following general officers:

1. Sales manager
2. Production manager
3. Purchasing manager (often termed purchasing agent)
4. Personnel manager
5. Financial manager (usually termed the treasurer)
6. Standard and record manager (usually termed the controller)

The foregoing list of functional managers who assist the president or the general manager in the formulation and execution of the policies of a business is intended to be suggestive rather than inclusive.  The ones mentioned are those which are needed to supervise and control the functions common to all businesses.

## Control Exercised by Junior Executives

As indicated by Figure 1, the general officers delegate a considerable part of their administrative duties to the subordinate or junior executives.  No definite statement can be made with reference to the duties to be performed by these officers, but the modern tendency is to delegate as many details as possible so that the general officers may have more time to give to a consideration of general plans and policies. The junior officers delegate duties to their assistants, and these in turn give instructions to the workers, both manual and clerical.

### Result of the Delegation of Administrative Duties

The foregoing sketchy outline of the process by which administrative control is exercised in the typical business organization shows that it involves a continual delegation of duties from one administrative group to another. The stockholders delegate duties to directors, the directors delegate duties to the general officers, the general officers delegate duties to subordinate officers, and so on. Experience has shown that in such an organization, if rational control is to be exercised, it is essential that there be available information of three kinds:

1. Information which will serve as a basis for the formulation of the general policies of the business and for the delegation by each group of certain duties to the next subordinate group.
2. Information which will enable each group to perform properly the duties delegated to it and to coordinate its activities with those of all the other groups.
3. Information which will enable each group to judge as to the efficiency with which the duties delegated by it have been performed by the subordinate group to which they were delegated.

To obtain this information in an accurate and comprehensive manner it is necessary

1. To maintain accounting and statistical records which will show past performance.
2. To use the information shown by the accounting and statistical records as a basis for preparing estimates of future performance.

3. To obtain from the accounting and statistical records the current performance.
4. To prepare reports showing a comparison between current, past, and estimated performance.

## Judging by Past Performance and by Contemplated Plans

In the past, executives have relied primarily on information with reference to current and past performance. They have judged current results by past results. They have left their subordinates to use their initiative to a large extent and rewarded them on the basis of the success which they attained. To some extent this practice is still followed. As pointed out in the discussion of the control exercised by the stockholders, they judge the success of the directors by their ability to maintain the capital of the corporation and to earn a satisfactory income. It is typical of them to consider the accomplished results of the directors' administration rather than the anticipated results of their contemplated plans. Many stockholders have followed this custom to their sorrow and have found their investment dissipated by actions of the directors which they could not correct after they had been consummated. In some cases directors depend on reports showing the results of the actions of the general officers instead of insisting on reports showing their contemplated plans and the anticipated results of these plans. Officers in turn sometimes follow the same policy in dealing with subordinates.

Gradually, however, stockholders, directors, and general officers are coming to realize that effective administration requires the making of plans and that the formulation of plans necessitates the use of estimates. The preparation and enforcement of these estimates is the purpose of the budgetary program as outlined in the following chapters.

# CHAPTER III

## PRELIMINARY STEPS IN INSTALLATION

### First Steps Towards Budgetary Control

Many business firms which realize the need for budgetary control are at a loss how to proceed to effect its installation. Often an attempt is made to commence its operation without giving proper thought to the formulation of a comprehensive procedure for its execution. In these cases undesirable consequences almost invariably result. In working out the budgetary procedure it is necessary that a logical sequence be followed so that no part of the program may be delayed because of the failure of any other part.

Executives have a tendency to think that the departmental estimates are the essence of the budgetary program and consequently start the preparation of sales estimates, production estimates, and financial estimates without first working out a procedure to govern their preparation and use. Consequently a great amount of data is collected as the result of much labor and expense but is found to be of little use because it is not in form to be correlated and also because the executives do not understand the service which may be obtained from it. They are apt to feel, therefore, that the budgetary program entails useless expense and they seek to secure its abandonment.

It is necessary for the success of the budgetary plans that certain preliminary problems be settled before the budgetary process is commenced. Every professional accountant and industrial engineer who has given consideration to methods of administrative control has seen many well-intended administrative plans fail because attention had not been given to the problems to which they necessarily give rise, or to the method of meeting these problems.    This situation is particularly apt to occur in an attempt to install budgetary control, because most executives have not given careful thought to its operation and consequently are not apt to foresee the problems to which it will give rise.

It is the purpose of this chapter to discuss the first steps which are involved in the installation and operation of budgetary control.    The following topics will be discussed in order:

1. Length of the budget period
2. Responsibility for the preparation of estimates
3. Responsibility for reports
4. Method of enforcing budgets
5. Cooperation of executives and employees

## Length of the Budget Period

One of the first questions which arise in connection with the installation of budgetary control is, What shall be the length of the budget period?    Little or nothing can be done until this question is answered.    Each department must know the period for which its estimate is to be made, otherwise the various departmental estimates will in all probability be for different periods of time and hence cannot be correlated.    For instance, if the sales estimate is made for six months and the production estimate for one year, it is not possible to compare the two.

The length of the budget period is governed by a number of factors, the most important of which are:

1. Length of merchandise turnover period
2. Length of production period
3. The method of financing employed
4. The market conditions
5. The adequacy and completeness of the data with reference to past operations
6. Length of the accounting period

### Length of Merchandise Turnover Period

If a business has a long turnover period and the peak of
the sales comes at the end of the period, it is necessary for
the budget period to be equal in length to the turnover
period. Otherwise it is impossible to obtain a correlation between sales and purchases or production. Such a condition
is apt to exist where sales are affected by seasonal demands.

To illustrate, a publishing company selling textbooks
for use in secondary schools has the principal volume of its
sales in July, August, and September, just before the opening of the academic year. It has a smaller volume in January prior to the opening of the second semester, and has
scattering sales throughout the year. In preparing its budgets it is preferable to make them one year in length but
subdivided by months, so that the total required operations
of each department for the year can be seen and these scheduled by months. It is necessary for the company to have
some books printed throughout the year, otherwise it will
be impossible to have sufficient inventory on hand to meet
sales demands during the rush season. Consequently the
production during any month or quarter will not correspond
with the sales for that month or quarter. During the
period of slack sales the production will exceed the sales,
while during the period of large sales the production will be
less than the sales. It should be easily seen, therefore, that
it is impossible to secure a coordination between the sales
estimates and the production estimates for any period less
than a year. Assuming that a uniform inventory is maintained, the sales for the year will equal the production for
the year, but this equality will not exist for any shorter
period of time. Similarly a proper comprehension of the
financial requirements of the business can be obtained only
on the basis of the year's program, although estimates of cash
receipts and disbursements can be made monthly.

In a business having a long turnover period it is usually preferable to make the budget period of corresponding length. On the other hand, a business like a grocery store which has a short turnover period will find it feasible to have a short budget period. In such a business sales are apt to fluctuate from period to period, and by having a short budget period it is possible to take advantage of these fluctuations in making the budgetary program. If the turnover period is short it is usually possible to purchase additional goods easily and quickly; therefore it is not difficult to replenish the inventory even though sales are estimated for only a short period of time in advance.

**Length of Production Period**

In a manufacturing business producing a commodity which requires a long production period, it may be necessary to provide for a budget period which is at least equal in length. It is necessary to know the sales a sufficient length of time in advance to make possible the placing of orders which will result in an inventory of sufficient size to meet the sales demands. It is obvious that the orders must be placed a length of time equal to the production period in advance of the time when the sales are to be made. This is particularly essential in a business where the sales fluctuate from period to period and there is a corresponding fluctuation in the production. For instance, the X Company, which has a production period of six months, estimates that its sales will increase 50 per cent during the last quarter of the year 1922. The production department should be informed of this expected increase by April 1, if it is to have the inventory available to meet these sales. The reader can probably recall numerous other illustrations which will show the relation between the length of the production period and the budget period.

### Method of Financing Employed

In some cases the financial peak load comes at a time of the year when it is difficult to obtain the necessary funds quickly. Consequently, it is desirable to make financial arrangements some time in advance of the period when the peak load will come. In such cases it may be necessary to make the budget period sufficiently long to make possible the determination of financial requirements some months in advance. If the executive can go to his banker several months before the funds are required and show him the contemplated plans of the business with the consequent demand for funds at the time of the peak load, he is much more apt to get a promise of funds than if he waits until the funds are urgently needed. In the latter case the banker does not see the reason for the sudden demands for funds, while in the first case he has seen months in advance that the plans of the business would result in a need for funds at that particular time.

The treasurer of a young but rapidly growing corporation in New York City has built up a large line of bank credit for his firm by following the practice of taking his financial budget to the bankers at the beginning of each year and showing them the plans for the year and the consequent financial requirements. At the end of the year he shows them a comparison between the budgets for the year and the actual results. By this means he shows them his requirements and convinces them that the credit which he requests is reasonable and justified.

There is a growing tendency among business firms to determine their financial requirements for a considerable period of time in advance and to arrange for the necessary funds prior to the initiation of the program which necessitates the funds. If provision for the necessary funds cannot be made, the program is revised. The advantage of this plan over the far too frequent practice of starting the program and arranging for the procurement of funds when the necessity for them arises should be apparent to the reader.

## Market Conditions

When the market conditions are uncertain and variable, it is desirable to make the budget period as short as possible, in order that revisions in plans can be made more easily. Estimates are always difficult to make with accuracy and in a period of uncertain market conditions this difficulty is greatly increased.

If the sales estimate proves incorrect this will affect all the other estimates, since most of them are based, at least in part, on the sales estimate. For instance, it was impossible for a firm in January, 1921, to estimate accurately its sales for the year, and if correct estimates for the year had been prepared based on the yearly sales estimates, it would have been entirely a matter of accident. Many firms prepared their estimates for 1921 on a quarterly basis and made new estimates at the beginning of each quarter. Even these they found necessary to revise monthly. For the year 1922 similar difficulties exist.

The marketing methods of a business may affect the length of its budget period. For instance, some of the large mail-order houses issue catalogues each six months, which quote prices effective for that period of time. In order to protect themselves they find it necessary to enter into contracts for the purchase of sufficient goods to satisfy the estimated sales demands for the period covered by the catalogue. As a consequence it is necessary for these firms to make their budget period six months in length, since their sales estimates and purchase estimates must be made for this period of time.

3

### Adequacy and Completeness of Data

In a new business, or in an old-established one where adequate records have not been kept, it is impossible to obtain adequate statistics with reference to past results. Hence it is difficult to estimate future operations, for estimates should always be made in the light of past events. In such cases it is better to make the budget period as short as possible so that new budgets can be made as statistics are obtained which will serve as a basis for their preparation.

### Length of Accounting Period

After estimates are made, it is necessary that means be provided for checking their accuracy. This is usually accomplished by preparing reports showing a comparison between the estimated and the actual results. The actual results are obtained to a considerable extent from the accounting records. The information obtained from these records is usually obtainable only at the end of an accounting period. It is necessary, therefore, that the budget period end on the same day as an accounting period. The budget period may include two or more accounting periods, so long as it commences on the first day of one period and ends on the last day of the same or some other period. There is a recent tendency of business firms to secure the information with which to check the budgetary program from sources other than the accounting records. But even in this case, the information so obtained is later checked by the accounting records.

### Usual Length of Budget Period

The usual length of the budget period is for three, six, or twelve months. Some firms state their general plans for one year in advance so as to have a goal to work for, but work out detailed schedules for only one month at a time.

A few firms known to the author make their budgets for one year, and at the end of each month drop the past month and add one month at the other end of the period. By this means they have their budgetary plans made for twelve months in advance at all times. Regardless of the length of time for which the budgets are prepared, they must be scheduled to show monthly expectancies, so that comparisons can be made at the end of each month between the actual and the estimated performance and the necessary revisions put into effect.

### General Conclusions as to Length of Budget Period

It will undoubtedly occur to the reader of the foregoing discussion that some of the factors, which it is suggested must be considered in determining the length of the budget period, afford an argument for a short period while others afford an argument for a long period. This is undoubtedly correct and it is the purpose of the discussion to emphasize this fact. It is desired to suggest to the reader that an arbitrary answer cannot be given to the question, How long shall the budget period be? In each business all the factors suggested should be considered and the length of the budget period determined as a result of this consideration.

In conclusion it may be said that it is important that two things be accomplished by the budgetary program:

1. That the executives obtain a perspective of the plans of the business for a sufficient length of time in advance to enable them to adjust their plans to the general program without too much abruptness. This is especially important in a rapidly growing business or one subject to material changes.

2. That the executives have a definite and concrete program for the immediate future which they can use as the basis of day-to-day operations. Such a program is also necessary as a basis for comparing the actual with the estimated performance, and unless this comparison is made it is impossible to exercise an

effective control of the budgetary program. Such a definite and concrete program can usually be made for only a short time in advance.

For these reasons, therefore, it is desirable to make at least a general program for one year in advance and to make subsidiary thereto a more specific program for a month or a quarter. The latter program can be used as the basis for immediate action, while the former can be used as the basis for future planning. The yearly program can be revised monthly or quarterly as the changing conditions demand. In working out some of the programs of the business—for instance, the advertising program—it may be necessary to make general plans for two or three years in advance.

### Responsibility for Preparation of Estimates

At the very inception of the budgetary program it is necessary to determine the responsibility for the preparation of the various estimates which its installation requires. The practice of business firms in this matter varies widely. In some businesses the controller and his staff prepare the estimates and submit them to the departmental executives for revision or approval. This method may secure satisfactory results if the controller has a well-trained staff and if the fluctuations in the volume of business are small.

It is the opinion of the author that though the controller and his staff may be able to prepare accurate estimates, it is not desirable for this task to be performed by them. One of the important results of budgetary control is the benefit derived by the executives in its installation and operation. If the major part of the work is performed by a central agency such as the controller, those who should benefit most from the budgetary program lose the opportunity of gaining this advantage.

In most businesses the departmental executives are held

responsible for the preparation of the estimates.  The sales
manager is held responsible for the sales estimate, the production manager is held responsible for the production
estimates, and so on.   Each departmental head will usually
delegate his responsibility for the preparation of the estimate of his department to subordinates.   Practice varies
greatly with reference to the subordinates selected for this
task.   If the head of the department has a staff, he may ask
his staff assistants to perform the task.   For instance, the
sales manager may have the sales estimate prepared in his
office by staff assistants, and the production manager may
do likewise.

On the other hand, the sales manager may ask his branch
and division managers to prepare estimates of their sales,
and he may then combine these to get the total estimated
sales.   In this case the sales manager and his assistants will
study the estimates submitted by the subordinates and
make revisions where necessary.   The production manager
may ask his works managers to submit estimates, and these
in turn may ask the advice of their foremen or heads of departments.   The production manager and his assistants
will make such revisions as the evidence they have at hand
indicates to be necessary.

### Responsibility for Performance Best Source of Estimates

It is the experience of the author that as a general rule
better results will be obtained if the individuals responsible
for the performance of the estimate are the ones who origi-
nate it.   This procedure is desirable:

1. Because these individuals should be best able to make the estimate.
2. Because they will obtain the most value from making it.
3. Because if they are required to make the estimate, they will feel
   more responsible for its enforcement.

To illustrate the foregoing by means of the sales estimate, the branch manager should know more about the sales possibilities in his territory than does the sales manager.   If he does not, he ought to be made to study his territory until he does.   If he is required to make the sales estimate, either he will make it more accurately than will the sales manager, or the latter can discover the incapacity of the branch manager and take the necessary steps to correct the situation. In making the sales estimate the branch manager will learn much, because its preparation will force him to study past results and future prospects.   Finally, if the branch manager makes the original estimate he will feel more responsibility for its enforcement than if it is prepared by the general office without consultation with him.   If he fails to meet an estimate to which he has previously agreed, he cannot object to being required to explain the reasons for his failure.   It is of course possible to enforce procedures whether subordinates like them or not, but this is rather destructive of morale, and morale is an important factor in present-day administration.

What has been said in the foregoing paragraph with reference to the sales estimate is equally true with reference to all the other estimates.   Better results will be obtained if the *line* subordinates are consulted in their preparation.

### Responsibility for Reports

After the budgetary program is established, it is necessary to have periodic reports showing the performance of each department so that a comparison may be made between the estimated and the actual performance.   To accomplish this it is necessary that two things be done:

1. That the reports desired be determined.
2. That the responsibility be fixed for the preparation of these reports.

Because of the importance of the reports used in budgetary control, it is desirable that considerable attention be given to their form and content.   It is preferable that they be designed by a central authority so that the information received from all departments will be in proper form for comparison and correlation.   The executive in charge of the budget procedure knows the form in which the information is desired for his use and for the use of the budget committee, hence he is best able to design the necessary reports.

It is advisable that the reports desired be determined at the beginning of the budget period so that provision can be made for collecting the information needed for their preparation.   If instructions for their preparation are not issued until the end of the period, it is very possible that some of the necessary information will not be available.   This not only results in a failure to secure the desired information, but also tends to create ill-will on the part of those who are held responsible for the preparation of the reports.

The departmental heads are responsible for the preparation of the departmental estimates, but in many cases it is not possible to make them responsible for the preparation of the reports showing the actual performance.   In some cases it is more desirable to obtain this information from the accounting department or a central statistical department.

In any case, it is necessary to determine from which department this information should come and fix responsibility therefor, and this determination should be reached very early in the course of the budgetary procedure in order that plans may be made by the department made responsible for the collection of the required data.

### Necessity for Promptness in Preparing Reports

In deciding the responsibility for the preparation of reports, careful attention should be given to the necessity for their prompt preparation after the end of the budget period. Unless they are prepared with promptness so that the actual and the estimated performance can be compared immediately after the close of the period, it is impossible to make the necessary revisions in the budgetary program which the reports show are necessary. To know the variations between the estimated sales and the actual sales of January is of value if the knowledge is available on February 1, but such knowledge is of little value in controlling the budget program for February if not available until February 25.

It will seem on first thought that it is the function of the accounting department to prepare the budget reports. There are certain advantages in this procedure since it eliminates the possibility of duplication of work if another department is required to collect and report data which will later be shown in the accounting records. The reports are also apt to be more accurate if they are verified by the formal methods employed by the accounting department. It has been the author's experience, however, that it is difficult to get the accounting department of most businesses to summarize their records at the end of the period with sufficient speed to make available the desired reports at the time needed. He has found it advisable, therefore, to obtain information regarding actual performance from other sources wherever possible. It is true that the audited reports prepared from the accounting records may differ slightly from those prepared by the operating departments, but these differences are usually not of sufficient amount to affect the conclusions to be drawn from the latter.

## Method of Enforcing Budgets

After the departmental estimates have been approved it is necessary for each department to formulate plans to carry out its estimate. Unless this is done the budgetary program is apt to result in failure. Many firms have made estimates of departmental activities but have failed to formulate a plan for their attainment, with the result that the actual has varied widely from the estimated performance and consequently the executives have tended to feel that the budgets had little or no significance. A well thought-out plan for the enforcement of the departmental estimates should be formulated before the introduction of the budgetary program.

The method by which the departmental estimates will be enforced will vary with the different departments. For instance, the sales department may find it necessary to set up quotas for the different sales units and for salesmen at each unit in order to secure the amount of sales called for by its estimate. The production department will find it necessary to set up balance of stores records so that the inventory schedules called for by the production budget may be maintained, and to operate a planning department so that its schedule of finished goods may be enforced. Other departments will find it necessary to use similar means to carry out their programs.

Some part of this procedure may be developed as the budgetary program proceeds, but it is necessary to remember that it is useless to set up a budgetary program unless means for its enforcement are provided, and it is necessary that the means be developed as early as possible in the installation of the budgetary procedure.

## Cooperation of Executives and Employees

In order that the budgetary program be properly formulated and executed it is necessary that all the executives and employees of the business cooperate to that end; and in order to secure their cooperation it is necessary that they be instructed with reference to the budgetary plans so they may understand the relation of the duties delegated to them to the general plans of the business. Although previous to its installation it is impossible to secure a complete realization by all the executives and employees of what the budgetary program involves, as much as possible should be done to this end before the budget program commences. If diplomacy and tact are used much can be accomplished.

After the budgetary program is installed, it is desirable to have prepared a manual on budgetary procedure outlining the purpose of the budget program and the procedure to be followed by all departments and units of the business in its preparation. If this manual is placed in the hands of all those responsible for the performance of duties in connection with the budget program, it will aid them to see the necessity and desirability for prompt and efficient cooperation on their part. The contents of such a manual is discussed and illustrated in Chapter XXIII.

Much more might be said with reference to the importance of securing the cooperation of executives and employees, but it is thought that the necessity for this cooperation is evident. The method which should be employed to secure their cooperation will depend on the circumstances of each case. Tact, courtesy, and patience are all necessary, and these should be backed up by determination based on confidence in the program and comprehensive knowledge of the method of executing it.

# CHAPTER IV

## ORGANIZATION FOR BUDGETARY CONTROL

### Need for Organization

The preceding chapters have shown that in the operation of budgetary control it is necessary to formulate a comprehensive procedure which will govern the preparation, correlation, and enforcement of the departmental estimates. To insure the carrying out of the budgetary procedure, it is necessary to set up an organization responsible for its enforcement; and it is desirable that this organization be effected before the budgetary program is initiated, for otherwise there will be no fixed responsibility for its enforcement, and delays and errors are almost sure to occur. These errors and delays tend to lessen the interest and enthusiasm of the executives and employees in the budgetary program, and this in turn renders its successful completion more difficult.   It is the purpose of this chapter to indicate the nature of the organization which many business firms have found desirable.

### Head of the Budgetary Program

Previous chapters have emphasized  the interrelation of the activities of the functional departments and the need of a correlation of these activities.   Since it is the purpose of budgetary control to effect this correlation, the budgetary program is as broad and comprehensive as the business itself.   Inasmuch as the budgetary program involves the activities of all the departments, it is not expedient to delegate its execution to any one department.   Rather, it is necessary to set up an organization which, although it must include the executives of all departments, has a central head which is independent and superior to the departmental executives.

In harmony with this conclusion, it is desirable that the president or chief executive of the business should have direct control of all matters pertaining to the budgetary program. He must of necessity delegate most of the duties imposed on him by this program to subordinate officers, but these officers should act as his agents and be directly responsible to him for the proper performance of the duties delegated to them. In case of disagreement between departments with reference to the coordination of estimates, the decision of the president must be final.

### Disadvantages of Not Having Chief Executive at Head

The importance of having the chief executive in direct and immediate control of the budgetary program cannot be overemphasized, for unless this be done two undesirable situations may develop:

1. The departmental executives and their subordinates will fail to realize the importance of the budgetary work and will not give it the time and attention necessary to make it worth while. If they are required to submit estimates and to make reports regarding their execution to some subordinate official, or even to the head of some other functional department, such as the general auditor's, they are apt to resent what they will regard as an undue interference with their activities by one who is not directly concerned with them.

2. Disagreements will arise with reference to the coordination of departmental programs. For instance, the sales department may desire to sell more than the production department thinks it can produce profitably, or the production department may desire to produce articles which

the sales department does not think it can sell, or both the sales and production departments may desire to increase their activities beyond what the financial department thinks can be financed. Obviously the only authority who can decide these questions is the chief executive who is superior to all the executives interested in the controversy. These departmental executives will not accept as final the decision of an officer of equal or lower rank to themselves. Furthermore, if the executives in charge of the preliminary work on the budget are the direct representatives of the chief executive they are apt to be given more consideration than if they are members of a subordinate department.

## Direct Control of Governmental Budgets by Chief Executive

In the preparation of governmental budgets it has usually been assumed that final control and responsibility is vested in the chief executive. Consequently he is usually required to submit to the legislative body the proposed budget with his personal approval, and he is held directly accountable for its contents. In the enactment of the recent legislation creating budgetary control for the United States government, there was much discussion with reference to the relation of the President to the budgetary organization. The Senate desired to place the Budget Bureau in the Treasury Department, while the House desired to make it independent of any department and answerable directly to the President. The *New York Evening Post* discussing the proposed law very ably sets forth the arguments for placing the President in direct control of the Budget Bureau, in the following editorial entitled "The Right Kind of Budget":

> Passage by the Senate of the McCormick budget bill is gratifying as a forecast of the early establishment of a budget system at Washington. But it is highly desirable that we get the right kind of budget system. Otherwise the work will have to be done over.

One of the prime essentials of a proper budget is that it be placed directly under the President. The McCormick bill places the system in the Treasury Department. On the other hand, the Good bill, which has been introduced in the House, places the Budget Bureau directly under the President. This undoubtedly is the course that should be followed. The McCormick arrangement, if not fatal to the right function of a budget system, would greatly hamper it. The reasons lie on the surface. One of the most important duties of the chief budget officer will be to cut the estimates submitted to him by Cabinet officers. It takes no great stretch of the imagination to see the situation that will be created if an official connected with a particular department cuts the estimates that come from other departments. Think of a budget official passing upon the estimates of his chief. Inevitably there will be a feeling that the department to which the budget system is attached is being favored. In order that the system may have a fair chance, it must be in exactly the same relation to all the departments. With respect to it, just as with respect to the President and Congress, the departments must be on the same plane. A budget officer representing the President will be in a very different position from a budget officer representing the Treasury.

The argument is no less strong with reference to the relation between the budget and the President. No matter where the budget system is placed, the President will be the final arbiter in important differences between the budget officer and the department heads. It will be much easier for him to settle these differences if the budget is part of his office than if it is connected with one of the departments. In the latter case appeal would first be taken from the budget officer to the head of the department and then to the President. This would put the President in the delicate position of having to decide between two of his Cabinet officers. With the budget officer a part of the President's Staff, the final conference would consist of the President, the budget officer, the department head and perhaps the head of the bureau affected—a much more promising assemblage for an objective consideration of the case.

The budget officer will not be a mere reducer of figures. To be of the greatest usefulness, he will make it his business to keep the President informed of the activities of the various departments. He will follow up his work on the estimates each year by observing the way in which the appropriations are spent, continually reporting to the President.   This valuable service, it is obvious, can be rendered much better by an officer attached to the President's Staff, than by one attached to a department.   Under the latter arrangement, indeed, it would be rendered at a maximum of difficulty.

As is well known, the Senate and the House compromised their differences by placing the Budget Bureau nominally in the Treasury Department, but with the Director of the Bureau reporting directly to the President.   Since the appointment of the present Director, the President has taken care to emphasize to the departmental heads that the Director is the representative of the President and that his requests should be treated as if the President himself made them.

The arguments set forth in the foregoing quotation apply with slight modification to the organization for budgetary control of the private enterprise.   The chief executive must be both the nominal and active head of the budgetary organization.

## The Budget Committee

In all businesses where a functional organization exists the budgetary program will usually be expedited and benefited by the establishment of a budget committee.   This committee will consist of the principal functional executives, with the president as chairman.   In a manufacturing business it will usually be satisfactory to have it composed of the president, the sales manager, production manager, treasurer, personnel manager, and controller or general auditor.   In a merchandise business the president, merchandise manager, treasurer, personnel manager, and controller may be sufficient.

Under the authority and direction of the president the budget committee considers all departmental estimates and makes changes and revisions as it may think desirable.   No estimate is to be effective until it has received the approval of the budget committee. In case the budget committee cannot agree with reference to any estimate, the question in dispute is left to the president and his decision is final. In case the judgment of the president does not agree with that of the majority of the committee, he has the privilege of overruling them since he is the head of the budgetary organization. A wise executive would take such a step, however, only in extreme cases, for the success of the budgetary program depends to a considerable degree upon the cooperation of the executives.

In the consideration of the departmental estimates the budget committee may call on departmental heads to explain reasons for the variations in their estimates from the estimates for past periods, or to explain why changes cannot be made which the committee thinks desirable. By this means the committee obtains full information on the subject before making its decisions. When the departmental estimates have been approved by the committee and the president, they then become the working budgets for the departments. Of course they may have to be submitted to the board of directors for approval before becoming effective.

At the end of stated periods of time, preferably monthly, the committee will receive reports showing a comparison of the performance for the period with the estimated performance. For instance, it will receive a comparison of the sales for the month with the estimated sales for the month; of the actual production with the estimated production; and of the actual expenses of each department with the estimated expenses. On the basis of these reports it may make revisions in the budgets for the remainder of the budget period if it deems such revisions necessary. The receiving of such reports and the making of such revisions are a very important part of the committee's duties.

It is of little value to make budgets unless a check is maintained on those who are responsible for their execution, and unless such a check is maintained, proper attention will not be given to the preparation or the execution of the budgets. Furthermore, budgets deal with future operations and are therefore apt to be inaccurate. It is essential that these inaccuracies be discovered and corrected as quickly as possible. It is exceedingly unwise to make plans covering any considerable period of time and to follow these plans blindly without taking into consideration the changing conditions which could not be foreseen when the plans were made.

## Executive in Charge of Budgetary Procedure

If the departmental estimates and the periodic reports are to reach the budget committee at the proper time for their consideration, a definite procedure must be established for their preparation and submission; and after this procedure is established, there must be an executive responsible for its execution. Although the president is the head of the budgetary program, he cannot assume responsibility for the direct supervision of the budgetary procedure and therefore must delegate this duty to some other executive. In a business where there exists a controller he may very well be charged with the direct supervision of the budgetary procedure.

In many businesses there is no controller, and in many where there is an executive known by that title he in fact acts only as head of the accounting department and is not a controller in the correct sense of the word. In those businesses where there is no controller the supervision of the budgetary procedure may well be delegated to a member of the staff of the president. This executive may be given a distinctive title or he may merely be termed "staff assistant to the president." Since the businesses which have a

4

controller are by far in the minority, it will be assumed in the remainder of this discussion that a staff assistant of the president is the executive in charge of the budgetary procedure.

### Duties of Executive in Charge of Budgetary Procedure

Under the authority and direction of the president, the staff assistant to the president has general control and supervision over the preparation and execution of the budgetary program. His general duties are indicated by the following summarized outline:

1. To receive from the departmental heads the periodic estimates which will be discussed and illustrated in the following chapters. In order that these estimates may be made in the proper form for his use, he may design forms for the use of the departments in the submission of their estimates.

2. To transmit these estimates to the budget committee with such recommendations as he may think necessary. He may combine and summarize these estimates so that they may be submitted to the budget committee in the form which will make them most useful to it. It is usually his function to prepare from the departmental estimates an estimated balance sheet and an estimated statement of profit and loss for submission to the budget committee and the board of directors. These show the estimated effect of the contemplated program on the financial condition and earnings of the company.

3. To supply the budget committee with all the information available which will assist it in the consideration of the estimates. He should have assistants whom he should use in the collecting of statistical data and the translating of these data into the form of reports and charts which will be useful to both the budget committee and the department heads.

4. To receive from the budget committee the estimates as approved and transmit these to the departmental heads.

5. To receive periodic reports prepared by the operating departments or the accounting department showing the performance of each department during the budget period.

6. To transmit periodic reports to the budget committee showing a comparison between the estimated performance and the actual performance for the period for each department, and to make any recommendations with reference to revisions which he thinks necessary.

7. To transmit to the departmental heads any revisions in the original estimates which have been made by the budget committee.

8. To recommend to the president and to the budget committee any changes in the budget procedure which he may think necessary; and to enable him to make these recommendations, he should be continually making studies and doing research.

The staff assistant usually acts as secretary to the budget committee, and in this capacity is constantly available for consultation with the members of the committee. He has the implied authority to do everything necessary to the proper performance of the duties expressly stipulated for him.

### Importance of Staff Assistant's Work

It is important that the staff assistant in charge of the budgetary procedure should not be regarded as doing work of a clerical nature. His function is something more than the supervision of the budgetary routine. In the operations of the budgetary program many questions of policy will arise. The departmental executives will often differ with reference to these questions. It is the duty of the staff assistant to study these and be able to offer to the budget committee and the president the matured judgment of an impartial observer. His work brings him in touch with all the departments of the business and should enable him to have a more comprehensive view of it than is usually possessed by the line executives. As a result he should be able to make recommendations and suggestions as to new methods and policies which will be beneficial to the business. He should also make a practice of collecting data which will serve as a basis of more accurate estimates.    By these means he can become one of the most important executives in the organization.

### Departmental Executives

The executive heads of the functional departments are responsible for the preparation of the estimates of their departments at the time and in the manner prescribed by the adopted procedure.    They are also responsible in some cases for the periodic reports showing the performance for the period.    Some of the periodic reports are obtained from the accounting department, while some are obtained from the operating departments.    Usually the operating departments will submit reports more quickly than the accounting department, and promptness is necessary in order to use the reports effectively.    Any recommendations which a departmental executive desires to make with reference to changes in budgetary procedure will be transmitted in writing to the staff assistant to the president, who in turn will transmit it to the budget committee for consideration.

There is a difference of opinion among executives with reference to the extent to which the departmental head should delegate the duty of preparing the estimates of his department.    As explained in Chapter III, it is the opinion of the author that the preparation of the original estimate should be delegated as far as possible to the one who will be responsible for the carrying out of the estimate after it has been adopted.

### Board of Directors

In many businesses the budgetary program after it has been formulated and approved is submitted to the board of directors.    In case the program involves a radical change in policy or the acquirement of a large amount of capital, they may deem it necessary to modify it. The staff assistant to the president should have available data which will serve to show the modifications which are possible and their effect on the program as a whole.

If modifications are necessary, the board of directors may instruct the chief executive to prepare a budget giving effect to the changes which they desire. In this case all the departments may be required to submit new estimates, or the changes may be such that they can be made by the budget committee. In any case the changes as made must be transmitted to the departmental heads by the staff assistant to the president.

Although it is well and proper to have the budgets submitted to the board of directors for consideration and approval, they should be transmitted to it only after they have been put into completed form. It is obvious that the directors are not interested in the details of preparation, and therefore the budget committee should have completed its work before the budgets are sent to the directors. Undoubtedly the tendency for the board of directors to give consideration to the budgetary program will be increased in the years to come.

# CHAPTER V

## THE SALES BUDGET

### Importance of Sales Information

In the preceding chapters the fact has been emphasized that all of the functional departments of a business are closely related and that the activities of each department are dependent to a considerable extent upon the activities of all the other departments. In fact it is because of this inter-relation and interdependence of departmental activities that budgetary control is necessary. It is difficult to consider the activities of any one department without considering to some extent their effect on the activities of all the other departments, and vice versa. In the formulation of the plans of any one department for the ensuing budget period, it is necessary to consider at every stage of their development their effect upon the plans of every other department. Modifications and revisions are often necessary in order to effect coordination.

It will be necessary in the present chapter and in those which are to follow to discuss the functional departments separately, but it is deemed wise to emphasize again the interdependence of the activities of these departments, so that the reader will keep this characteristic of business organization constantly in mind.

The initial step in the budgetary program is usually made by the sales department. The reason for this is easily seen. The object of the operations of a business is to make a profit, and sales conclude the process which results in the making of a profit. Until the sales take place, consequently no profit is realized. Whenever the sales are profitable, the executives of a business desire to increase their sales, and they try to coordinate all the activities of the business to accomplish this end. It follows that the activities of the sales department exercise a very important influence over the activities of all the other departments. This influence is of primary importance in both a mercantile and a manufacturing business.

It is customary, therefore, for the sales department to prepare a sales estimate which sets forth the sales which are desired and deemed possible during the next budget period. This estimate must then be studied in comparison with the future possibilities of the other departments as set forth in their estimates, in order to arrive at a properly coordinated budget for the entire business. The revised sales estimate or the "sales budget" then becomes the working program of the sales department.

### Need and Importance of the Sales Estimate

The owners or officers of either a trading or a manufacturing industry of necessity must estimate the probable sales of their business for each season or fiscal period. These estimates may be made very unscientifically and be recorded quite informally, or they may be made as the result of a very careful analysis of all the factors involved and presented by means of a formal report. But, in any case, an estimate of sales must be prepared as a basis of planning for the future.

In a trading business, the nature and amount of goods to be purchased depends upon the plans of the sales department. In a manufacturing business, the volume and nature of production is dependent on the sales estimated. If a sales estimate is not made by the sales department, the probable sales must be estimated by the purchasing department or the production department; otherwise these de-

partments have no basis for their plans. It is the purpose
of the present discussion to emphasize the point that it is
properly the function of the sales department to prepare
this estimate, and to explain the method by which it is prepared.

It is evident that in a mercantile store goods must be
bought and placed on the shelves or in the warerooms before
they can be sold. It will later be explained how in a manufacturing business goods may sometimes be sold before they
are produced, but such is not the case in the typical mercantile business. Consequently, in this type of business, before
the buyers can make contracts and select the qualities and
kinds of goods that are to be offered for sale, the management must make estimates, however scientific or unscientific, as to the volume and character of sales expected for
any given period.

The small retailer whose business is restricted to one
particular specialized commodity, say a dealer in rare
oriental rugs, may say that he will buy what he can and
plan for the sale of the merchandise after he has it in his possession. But a large retail business, such as a department
store, that sells many thousands of different items of merchandise, must set up a program of what sales are expected
to be, if purchases are to be made intelligently in source
markets all over the world and deliveries to the shelves of
the store completed before the customers of the store come
to buy. Even in the case of the dealer of oriental rugs it is
probable that he will learn by experience that certain kinds
or types of rugs sell more readily than others. When he
makes his purchases, he will be guided by that experience
and will seek the popular kinds of rugs for his anticipated sales. In so far as he does this, he is estimating his
future sales. In other words, he is making an informal
sales estimate.

**Anticipated Sales the Basis for Action for All Departments**

Not only does the volume and nature of the sales anticipated, as reflected in the sales estimate, affect the buyers in their selection of goods, but it also vitally affects the operations and plans of the various functional managers of the business. The officers of the store who are responsible for providing proper space for counter stocks, for reserve stocks, and for wareroom stocks, must have before them some tangible data as to when such stocks will be purchased, when sold, and what volume of sales will be made. In department stores and mail-order houses, where large stocks are carried, this is especially important.

The operating managers above mentioned must work with an estimate of sales in mind, so that they may secure the proper sales persons and then train them to meet the needs of the organization. Similarly the operating officials must anticipate the volume and character of sales to a fairly accurate degree, if they are to employ an economical number of packers, wrappers, telephone operators, delivery men, and the like, and if they are to train these employees into an efficient working force animated with the service ideals of the store, and thoroughly familiar with the operations, processes, procedures, and schedules in retail selling and order buying.

The treasurer or other officer charged with the responsibility of financing the purchases and expenses of the store must have very definitely in mind the volume of revenue from sales that the store may reasonably expect to receive from week to week, and even from day to day. The owners themselves, or the president or general manager as their agent, must carefully study expected sales in investing capital in new divisions or departments of the store, in making additions or extensions of physical plant, or in making decisions concerning new forms of customers' credits.

### Place of Sales Estimate in a Wholesale or Retail Store

In short, the owners and officers of a wholesale or retail store of appreciable size must set up a sales program for each season or fiscal period in order that the customer may receive service resulting from coordinated purchasing, operating, financing, and plant maintenance and extension. For instance, in a department store, if the various departmental buyers who are purchasing goods in different markets are to work as a unit, they must know not only what volume of sales in their own particular lines they are anticipating by their contracts, but they must also know something of the character and volume of sales expected in all the other lines of the store, so that they may select and purchase qualities and quantities complementary and supplementary to the other lines of goods handled by the store.

But the departmental buyers must not only work in harmony with each other; they must work in harmony with the traffic manager, the superintendent of warehouses, and the superintendent of delivery service. The one vital point of contact between the selector of merchandise and the operating man who handles the order for the customer, is that they both promise their work on the same expectancy or estimate as to volume and character of business. It can be readily seen, therefore, that comprehensive and accurate information with reference to sales anticipated is of utmost importance in the internal control and management of a modern wholesale or retail store.

### The Sales Estimate in a Manufacturing Business

In a manufacturing business the sales estimate is as necessary for coordination of departmental activities as in the case of a mercantile establishment. The production manager must base his production program on the anticipated sales; otherwise excess stocks will accumulate or orders will go unfilled. The plant engineer must plan his building and equipment program to meet the production program demanded by the sales estimate. The employment or personnel department must consider the increased or decreased demand for employees which will result from the program of the next budget period. The purchasing agent must make contracts for raw materials and supplies and schedule deliveries in order to meet the demands of the production budget. The shipping department must adjust its capacity to meet the demands of the sales program. The treasurer must know the estimated revenue from sales as well as the probable disbursements arising from the financing of the sales program and the consequent production program, in order to provide for the necessary funds. Thus each department of the business is affected by the volume of business and the volume of business is determined by the amount of the sales. Consequently a knowledge of the amount of the sales anticipated is necessary in order to plan the operations of the business in such a manner as to secure coordination, and without coordination efficient administration is impossible.

### The Revised Estimate, or "Budget," the Result of Cooperation

It may be well to state again that it is not intended to imply by the emphasis placed on the importance of the sales estimate that the sales department should determine the policies of the business as a whole. The following discussion will show that though the sales estimate is usually prepared originally by the sales department, the sales department in its preparation should take into consideration the plans and possibilities of the other departments. In any case, the revised estimate, or "budget," which serves as the basis for future operations, is the result of the cooperative efforts of all the functional departments of the business.

It is revised and modified by the functional officers and the budget committee before it is adopted in its final form.

The purpose of the preceding discussion is to emphasize the need and importance of the sales estimate. It is now necessary to discuss its preparation and the method by which it is used.

## Threefold Basis of the Sales Estimate

The sales estimate is a report which gives in a summarized but comprehensive form the sales which the sales department desires and deems possible during the next budget period. In the preparation of this estimate, information of various kinds must be considered, which information may be classified under the following general headings:

1. *Knowledge of general plans and policies of the business.* Such information is obtained from the decisions of the executive officers and the board of directors.
2. *Knowledge of trade conditions.* Such information is obtained as a result of market analysis.
3. *Knowledge of the amount and nature of previous sales*, as shown by the accounting records. Such information involves sales analysis and comparisons.

It is necessary to discuss each of these briefly.

## 1. The General Plan and Policies of the Business

In most businesses, plans are made from time to time which affect the sales policies and the volume of sales of the business. A few examples will suffice to make clear the importance of considering such plans in making the sales estimate.

In many businesses there is a special department called by various names, such as sales engineering, sales promotion, sales development, or sales research department, whose function it is to study sales possibilities and to recommend changes in sales policies and methods.   As a result of such recommendations new lines may be added; old lines may be dropped; new territories may be entered; new agencies or branches established; new methods of distribution put into effect; changes in prices or terms of sale made; additional advertising carried on; more salesmen added; and numerous other changes made.

Whether or not a separate department is maintained to carry on work of the sort mentioned, such changes are made from time to time by all progressive firms, and the effect of such changes must be given careful consideration in the preparation of the sales estimate.   In some cases such changes are decided upon by the chief executive of the sales department, but since they affect to some extent the activities of all the other departments, it is customary for them to be considered by all the functional executives before they are adopted.   In the case of some sales policies which will vitally affect the business, it may be necessary for the board of directors to judge if so radical a change as that suggested by the program is desirable for the business.   In a business where proper methods of management are followed, the effect of new policies will be considered before they are adopted.   Therefore it is not difficult to give effect to these policies in the sales estimate.   The importance of giving careful consideration to their effect cannot be overestimated.

## 2. Market Analysis

Although the questions concerning market analysis are primarily problems of the larger one of sales management, they are nevertheless inseparably interwoven with a consideration of budget-making and control.   In fact, neither market analysis nor sales analysis can be intelligently considered apart from the other.   Each serves as a check upon the other.   Market analysis and statistical records show to what extent the potential demand has been satisfied and whether or not it is profitable to try to satisfy it. As has been pointed out before, the purpose of making sales is to gain a profit. But not every demand for goods is one which can be satisfied on a profitable basis. It is the function of accounting and statistics to assist in the determination of the results of past sales and thus to indicate the probable results of anticipated sales.

To mention all the factors which must be considered in making an analysis of the market in the case of a retail, wholesale, or manufacturing business is of course impossible. The buying power of the community, as reflected in its savings bank deposits; the industrial growth of the community, as reflected in its pay-rolls; the condition of crops and the profits of the farmer and stock-raiser in the surrounding agricultural region; transportation conditions in their relation to the delivery of goods; climatic changes and their effect on seasonable lines; these and many other general and local trade factors will each have a bearing on the sales to be expected for a retail store. Then the store will have to consider many local factors of importance to itself, such as new buildings and street improvements near the store; fire hazards; relationship of management to state officials with reference to state laws of employment, etc.; new forms of taxes adopted or proposed; character of store management; and the like.

In a wholesale or manufacturing business many of the factors above mentioned will have to be taken into account, and in addition others of a more general nature. For instance, general industrial and agricultural conditions throughout the territory reached by the retailers or jobbers to whom the company sells must be considered, and in deciding on methods of selling and advertising, and in estimating results, the density and character of the population in both old and potential territory must be taken into account. It will be understood that the "business cycle" must be given careful consideration in the determination of the sales possibilities of both a mercantile and a manufacturing firm.

In some businesses it is the function of the sales engineering department, or some other department performing the same function, to make the market analysis and present the data which serve as a basis for the sales estimate. In any case these data must be available if accurate forecasts are to be made. It is beyond the scope of this discussion to treat of all the problems involved in sales administration and management. The purpose of the present discussion is to emphasize the necessity for the careful and scientific consideration by the sales department of all the factors which may influence future sales, if the sales department is to prepare a sales estimate which will serve as a proper basis for coordination of departmental activities.

### 3. Sales Analysis

Having in mind that only a few of the usual factors in sales management have been mentioned, it seems at first thought as if it were impossible to use accounting records and reports to any advantage in estimating what the volume and character of sales are likely to be. The outstanding fact is that a sales program must be made, and in fact is made in the conduct of all businesses. Even if the president only "hopes to do slightly better this period than the preceding one," the sales program is the result of taking the revenue accounts of the last period with an additional margin of possibly 5 per cent. The directors who ask their officers to "hold your own despite the decline in the market or other conditions," are setting up a very definite standard of performance and accountability. The estimate of sales is based on the actual sales of the preceding period, or periods, plus or minus certain amounts or percentages. This modification is due to a more or less careful consideration of various general trade factors and various trade conditions peculiar to the business itself.

In some businesses it is the custom to take past sales and apply a more or less arbitrary percentage in order to arrive at the estimated sales of the following period. This method is unscientific and is usually inaccurate, for it does not take into account trade conditions or changes in market policies on the part of the business, and such changes occur almost continuously in most businesses. It is highly important that past sales be considered very carefully in making the sales program, but it is not wise to follow such statistics slavishly.

The sales accounts of a business tell the owner what past sales have been. If the total sales are credited to one account only, there is still the very valuable analysis by days, weeks, and months, of cash and accounts receivable gained by the store through creating sales, although this information may not be classified in a convenient form, and so may be difficult to obtain. If a proper analysis of sales is maintained by means of accounting or statistical records, there will be available information not only of value in making the sales estimate, but also of service to the various departmental managers. Although it is not safe to assume without investigation that the same ratio between various classes of sales will continue year after year, if the past tendency is known a fair estimate of the future ratio can be made. For instance, if the sales analysis shows that for the past five years the cash sales have averaged 25 per cent of the total, and the sales on account 75 per cent, the treasurer can usually assume that approximately the same ratio will hold good during the next year unless there are conditions which it is known will change the ratio.

## Various Kinds of Sales Information Desired

After the probable ratios between the various classes of sales are known, the departmental executives can use them in estimating the effect of the proposed program on their activities. To understand the analysis which should be made, it is necessary to consider briefly the nature of the information which may be desired.

If the problem is to estimate the sales for a retail store for the three months beginning June 1, the first question asked of the accountant is likely to be: What were the sales of last summer by days and weeks? The representative, or representatives, of the sales department who are responsible for the preparation of the sales estimate asks this in order to be able to make an estimate for the current period. The sales department, in turn, must answer the question of the amount of sales anticipated for this summer. In the preparation of the sales estimate, this information must be obtained and made available. The merchandise manager asks the question of the sales department in order that he may be equipped to fix delivery dates in his contracts with manufacturers and wholesalers. The operating superintendent asks it because he must estimate the number of employees required through the normal vacation period. The treasurer asks it because he must finance the purchase invoices, the store pay-rolls, etc. Even the finance committee of the board of directors may ask it if they are planning certain changes in the financial plans of the company.

In addition to this information, each officer may ask for data on last year's sales from the viewpoint of his particular responsibility. The operating superintendent asks, "What percentage of sales last summer were counter sales? What percentage of sales were over the telephone?" The treasurer asks for data as to cash sales, sales on monthly accounts, and instalment sales. The traffic manager asks for the

5

amount of sales to out-of-town customers by express and
by freight. These and many other questions of a similar
nature will be asked of the accounting department, and, in
order to be able to answer them, a proper analysis and classification of sales data is necessary.

### Classification of Sales Data

No arbitrary classification of sales data can be given, for
the analysis and classification made is determined by the
information desired by the various functional managers.
But it is safe to say that in planning for the future the officers and managers will desire sales to be classified in some or
all of the following ways:

1. By commodity or department
2. By terms of sales
3. By method of sale
4. By method of delivery
5. By territory of customers
6. By salesmen
7. By volume of sales to individual customers
8. By nature of customers
9. By rush vs. normal deliveries

The purpose of each of these classifications should be evident to the reader.

In a manufacturing business a shorter classification may
be required. This is due to the fact that it handles and sells
its commodities more directly than a trading company.
Where goods are sold in large quantities, as is usually the
case in the disposition of products by a manufacturing business, the problems of selling are less complicated. In such
a business sales may be classified as follows:

1. By commodities or groups
2. By territories
3. By salesmen
4. By customers

In a manufacturing business the terms of sale, method of sale, and method of delivery are usually uniform for all classes sold. Where this is true, no classification to indicate these is necessary.

The classifications of sales stated above are intended to be suggestive rather than all-inclusive. They are indicative of what may be done in the classifying of sales in order to make available information for the preparation of the sales estimate and for the use of the departmental managers in making their plans.

### Terms in Which Estimate Is Made

The terms in which the estimate should be made are dependent on the nature of the business and the purpose for which the estimate is to be used. In the past, estimates of sales and purchases and expenses have been made by some businesses for the purpose of financial control only. As a consequence they have been made in terms of value. For the purposes of financial control all estimates must be stated in terms of value; but for the purpose of sales, production, and purchases control, estimates must be stated in terms of physical quantities and not in terms of value only. There are possibly a few cases where sales and purchasing control may be effected in terms of value, but these cases are rare.

In a manufacturing business it is essential that the sales estimate be made in terms of physical quantities, for production orders are issued for a certain *number* of each item of goods produced and not in terms of dollars and cents. It is not enough for the production department to know that the estimated sales for the budget period are $3,000,000. It must know how many hundred of each of the items which the company offers for sale will be sold during the period, so it will know how many must be produced to meet the sales requirements. It is necessary that the sales estimate not only state the sales to be made, in terms of physical quantities, but it is also necessary that it state separately the sales of each item of goods which is offered for sale. Some companies make estimates in terms of sales classes or groups. These are of little value from the viewpoint of coordinating sales and production.

## Planning Sales in Terms of Items

Sales orders are made in terms of particular items of commodities, and if these items are to be available, production must be planned in terms of these items. A factory may have a large inventory and yet be unable to fill sales orders if the particular items called for by these orders are not on hand. To make the sales estimate serve as a basis for the coordination of sales and production, it is essential that the planning of sales be in terms of items and not in terms of values or groups or classes.

In most cases the same principle holds true in the retail or wholesale store. A customer does not want *a* pair of shoes but *the* pair of shoes of his particular size and shape. In order that the merchant may know how many customers want each particular make, size, and style and that he may procure the goods in advance to meet these demands, it is necessary to have records which will give such information with reference to past sales, and will furnish a basis for making accurate estimates of future requirements. Thus it is in all lines of merchandise—the demands of the customers call for particular items, and the sales and purchase budgets must be made accordingly. It is of course true that, in the case of goods subject to wide changes in fashion, estimates by items cannot be made accurately. But even in this case past statistics will show a fair indication of the customers' demands for different styles and kinds.

The necessity for making the sales estimate in terms of

items makes the task of preparing the estimate much more complex in many cases. The different items of merchandise sold by some firms run into the thousands. To estimate sales and plan production in connection with each of these items is a very difficult problem. In some cases the number of items may be so great that this is well-nigh impossible.

Under such conditions some method must be devised which will obtain the necessary results without the incurrence of prohibitive labor. In most cases a study of the sales of a firm handling thousands of items will show that the bulk of its sales is composed of a comparatively few items and that the remainder are slow-moving items of which the number of sales are few. This may make it possible to select a list of "significant" items which will contain those which constitute the bulk of the sales. In a recent case on which the author was employed, it was found that of 20,000 items, 682 constituted approximately 75 per cent of the total sales.

### Use of "Key" Items in Sales Estimates

In some cases it is found that there are certain "key" items of which the fluctuations in sales govern the fluctuations in a number of similar items. For instance, there may be a group of items which are the same except for size, and there may be one particular size in the group for which there is the greatest demand. It may be found that the sales of the less popular sizes fluctuate year by year in proportion to the fluctuation in the sales of the most popular size; and if this condition can be shown to be approximately correct it is then necessary to have the sales department estimate only the sales of the "key" items, the statistical department estimating the sales of the remaining items. It is only in certain businesses handling certain lines of merchandise that there exists a probability of such a condition arising, but where it does arise it greatly facilitates the preparation of the sales estimate.

When it is possible to select significant or key items, the sales and production budgets may be made, in terms of items, for the items on the significant list. The remaining items can be grouped by classes and the budgets prepared on them in terms of classes. Although the budgets on the groups will be in most cases unsatisfactory from the viewpoint of coordination of sales and production, this is not of so great importance for these items, which have a low turnover and are slow-moving, inasmuch as it is not difficult to provide sufficient inventory to meet the sales. By a proper system of inventory control, excess quantities can be avoided. For the purpose of the financial budget, the group budget on the non-significant items will usually serve satisfactorily.

It is not intended to imply by the foregoing discussion that budgets prepared in terms of classes or groups of items are desirable. It is intended only to suggest that this is one method of procedure when the items sold by a company are exceedingly numerous. If such a plan is followed, it will usually be found expedient to add gradually more and more items to the significant list as the work proceeds. If such a study is begun, it will usually result in the elimination of many of the "non-significant" items which it will be found are unprofitable and unnecessary. In the end this process will result in the proper budgeting of all items.

# CHAPTER VI

## THE SALES BUDGET (Continued)

### Responsibility for Preparing the Sales Estimate

As stated in the preceding chapter, the sales estimate is prepared by the sales department. As to which particular unit of the sales organization should be responsible for its preparation, an arbitrary rule cannot be formulated. In each case the organization of the company and its selling methods must be taken into consideration.

In a department store the departmental managers are usually held responsible for the preparation of the departmental estimates, and these are combined by the merchandise manager to make the estimate for the entire business. The departmental manager of course will consult with his assistants in the preparation of his estimate.

In a wholesale or manufacturing business which employs traveling salesmen, each salesman may be asked to make an estimate of the sales in his territory for the budget period. Such estimates will of course have to be checked very closely and revised by the central sales office in the light of the data which it should have available.

In a business which sells its products through branches, each branch may be requested to make an estimate of its sales. These estimates, like those of the salesmen, should be carefully checked by the central sales office.

When either salesmen or branches are requested to make an estimate of their sales, they should be provided with a record of their sales for one or more past periods, in order to be able to use these data in making an estimate of future sales.

Those who favor the making of estimates by salesmen and branches contend that those in closest touch with the customers are best able to judge future demands. There are some companies, however, who will not rely at all upon the estimates of the sales force. Instead, they favor the collection of data by the central sales office and the employment of special investigators who make a survey of the sales territory and report on possibilities. Using the data with reference to population, industrial conditions, etc., and the reports of the special investigators, in connection with past sales, they formulate the sales estimate. In some cases, after the estimate is prepared by the central office, it is sent to the branches or to the salesmen for criticism.

### Relation of Inventory Requirements to Sales Estimate

If a business has branches which carry an inventory of merchandise, a further complication arises in connection with estimating their requirements, since the amount desired by them from the parent company is dependent not only upon their anticipated sales, but also upon the condition of their stocks. Their inventories may be below normal on some items and show an excess on others. This condition is especially apt to exist at the time a system of budgetary control is installed. After the system becomes effective, material excesses or shortages in inventories should be eliminated, except in rare cases.

Each branch must of necessity report the condition of its inventories for each budget period, whether or not it is held responsible for initiating the sales estimate. Since the sales estimate must be submitted previous to the beginning of the budget period in order that the production budget or purchase budget may be prepared for use by the beginning of the period, it is necessary for each branch or selling unit which carries an inventory to estimate its inventory at both

## FACTORY REQUIREMENTS

First Quarter of 192___

| ITEMS | Sales Past Periods | Estimated Sales Jan. 1 to Mar. 31 | Estimated Inventory Mar. 31 | Estimated Inventory Jan. 1 | Amount Required for Stock | Direct Shipments | Total Required from Factory |
|-------|-------------------|-----------------------------------|-----------------------------|-----------------------------|---------------------------|------------------|------------------------------|
| (1) | (2) | (3) | (4) | (5) | (6) | (7) | (8) |

Figure 2. Form Showing Factory Requirements for Use in Preparing Sales Estimate

the beginning and the end of the budget period. This of course adds another difficulty to the making of an accurate estimate. To illustrate more clearly the nature of the information which the branch or selling unit must submit, a typical illustration may be taken.

The X Manufacturing Company distributes the major part of its product through its branches, but sells some goods to jobbers. The branches make the principal part of their sales from stock which they carry, but take some orders which are shipped direct from the factory. The general sales office submits to the branches a form ruled as shown in Figure 2.

The first column will be filled in by the general office. If the detailed sales records are kept at the general office, it also will fill in the second column. If, however, these records are kept at the branch, the branch will fill in this column. The remaining columns are filled in by the branch. Column (6) equals the sum of columns (3) and (4) minus column (5). Column (8) equals the sum of columns (6) and (7). In filling in column (4), it is necessary for the branch to have in mind some such terms as a "thirty-day" stock or a "sixty-day" stock. After the estimated sales for the period are determined, it is only a mathematical process to obtain the estimated inventory at the end. The foregoing illustration is given in order to indicate some of the problems which may arise in the making of an accurate sales estimate.

### Revision of Sales Estimate According to Production

After the sales estimate is submitted by the unit of the sales department which is held responsible for its preparation, it should be studied by the staff officers and revised in the light of their information and judgment. In the case of a manufacturing industry, it must be revised in the light of production capacity. It is useless to formulate a sales program which is beyond the capacity of the production department to satisfy. Consequently, data must be obtained which will show production capacity. In order for this to be accurate and comprehensive, it is necessary to obtain data which will show machine capacity. This necessitates the preparation of a card for each machine used in the process of manufacturing, showing the operations performed on the machine and its capacity in the performance of these operations. It is then possible to determine whether the quantities called for by the sales estimate can be produced. If not, it is necessary to determine which items should be reduced or eliminated.

### Revision of Sales Estimate in Terms of Profit

Another important factor in deciding the desirability of the sales program proposed by the sales department is the estimated profit. It is desirable that the profit to be obtained by the sale of each item called for by the sales estimate be determined, if possible. It is undesirable to produce and sell an article which does not yield a satisfactory profit if it can be prevented. Sometimes, however, because of competitive conditions it is necessary to sell certain items in order to meet sales demands for a complete line of articles. For instance, in the sale of valves, dealers find it necessary to carry several sizes in order to meet the demands of their customers. Some manufacturers produce all these sizes so that other manufacturers, in order to meet the demands of the dealers, may be required to carry a complete line for fear the dealer will place his order with the manufacturer from whom he can obtain a complete line. That a complete line may be maintained, it may be necessary for the manufacturer to produce certain sizes which he is unable to produce and sell at competitive prices without incurring a loss.

In the revision of the sales estimate in terms of profit, it is necessary to give careful consideration to the problem of providing complete lines, so that items may not be eliminated which will result in decreased sales of other items. On the other hand, the sales department has a tendency to overemphasize the necessity for complete lines, and care must be exercised to prevent the carrying of too many unprofitable items. There is considerable agitation at the present time for standardization. It is to be hoped that this movement will develop and will result in the elimination of many specialties, especially in the case of goods which are adapted to standardization. Such standardization will greatly simplify the problem of budgetary control.

## Consideration of Maximum Gross Profit

In revising the sales estimate in terms of profit it is necessary to consider not only the profit which has resulted from past operations, but also the probable profit which will result from the anticipated operations. Changes in method or volume of production, as well as changes in method or volume of sales, may affect materially the profit obtained. In order to estimate more accurately the effect of these changes in production or sales it is desirable to consider the cost of production and selling and administrative expense and the effect of the new program on these items. It is imperative that careful consideration be given to these factors in the revision of the sales estimate.

The sales program must provide for the maximum profit that trade conditions will permit consistent with the permanency of the business. Here is one of the vital points in making over the sales estimate of volume into a sales program. The management must decide not only what increase in business is desired, but also what volume of business can be had at a maximum gross profit of selling price to the customer over the purchase price or cost of production. Consequently the estimated volume of each line, even of each class and kind of goods, must be re-estimated at the volume that will produce the greatest amount of gross profit. Obviously it is better, from the standpoint of gross profits, to plan to sell $120,000 of merchandise at 30 per cent gross profit, than it is to sell $140,000 at 25 per cent.

### Revision of Sales Estimate in Terms of Selling Administrative Expense

It is to be kept in mind that gross profit is not the only consideration. Handling cost may more than offset gross profit. There is more net profit in selling $100,000 of merchandise over the counter for cash at a gross profit of 15 per cent and an operating and overhead expense of 11 per cent, than there is in selling $200,000 by the instalment plan at a gross profit of 27.5 per cent and an operating and overhead expense of 26.2 per cent. It follows that the re-estimated sales must be gone over again from the standpoint of expense. Sometimes it is difficult to obtain accurate information with reference to the expense of selling different lines or items. When possible, such statistical analysis should be maintained as will provide this information. In some cases the cost of obtaining such statistics is prohibitive. It is then necessary to resort to tests and estimates. From time to time studies can be made, and these may serve as the basis for drawing up fairly accurate estimates. These estimates, in turn, may be used to judge the profit possibilities of various lines or classes.

### Revision of Sales Estimate According to Financial Requirements

In the execution of sales and production, finances are required. An important factor, therefore, which must be given careful consideration in the formulation of the sales

program, is the financial requirements. There are two
ways in which the financial requirements may be considered.
After the sales estimate has been revised, taking into consideration production capacity, profits, and the like, the
amount of capital required to execute this program may be
estimated. If this amount is in excess of that which the
financial resources of the business will permit to be expended,
it is necessary to revise the sales program. In making this
revision the various factors previously discussed will be
taken into consideration.

Another method of considering financial requirements
is in connection with the revision of the original sales estimate. The amount of capital required to finance each
item of merchandise listed on the sales estimate may be
indicated and this factor considered in deciding which items
to reduce, in case reduction is necessary. In any case, after
an estimate has been made of the activities of all the departments of the business, it is necessary to prepare an estimate
of receipts and disbursements, based on the departmental
estimates, and to revise the departmental estimates if
necessary, to bring them into harmony with a workable
financial program. The process involved in the making
of the financial budget will be discussed in Chapters
XIX and XX.

### Formulation of the Sales Program

In the previous discussion the most important factors
which must be considered in the revision of the sales estimate have been explained. It should be realized, of course,
that no attempt has been made to treat of all the factors
which may need to be considered in particular cases. If
the sales estimate is considered and revised in the manner
suggested, the result will be the formulation of a sales program based on the following:

1. *Past sales* as reflected in the sales accounts of previous years.
2. *The general plans and policies* of the business as reflected by decisions of the executive officers.
3. *Trade conditions* as determined by the study and research of the sales department.
4. *The judgment of the sales unit* (or units), which makes the original estimate.
5. *The judgment of the central sales office*, which reviews the original estimates and makes such changes as it deems necessary.
6. *The production or purchasing capacity of the business* as reflected in the production and purchase estimate.
7. *The gross profit-earning capacity* of the different lines or items.
8. *The selling and administrative cost* involved in handling different lines or items.
9. *The financial requirements of the program contemplated.*
10. *The coordination of all the departmental estimates* into a well-rounded program for the business as a whole.
11. *The sales budget*, showing the volume of operations which the sales department is expected to perform, based on the budget of the business as a whole.

The process of making the sales program is not a simple one. Rather a sales program must be thought of as a combination of several estimates. It is a statement of past experience modified by future plans, which are in turn modified by trade conditions.

## Additional Factors in Determining Sales Program

Many factors have to be considered in determining the proper sales program. In the case of a new business the ideal sales program may be one that plans for all the sales that trade conditions will permit, the only restriction imposed by the owner being that no line may be handled at a net loss. Once a business is well established, however, it is not likely that this will be the sales program adopted. Experience will show that some lines can be handled with greater profit than others, because of the fact that the location attracts a certain class of customers whose general demands are for these profitable lines. Furthermore, certain of the personnel of the store will show greater aptitude in one or more lines. The obvious correction in this case is to strengthen the personnel, although that may be a matter of years of development. Thus, in many ways the established business may come to have a personality, a policy, a class of trade, a place of its own that can be deflected only by degrees, and this has an important bearing on its sales program.

Since so many factors have to be considered in the formulation of the sales program, it is possible for it to forecast only approximately the operations of the sales department. Consequently the sales program must not be regarded as an arbitrary rule or regulation, or as an unchangeable order to do certain definite things. A real sales program is a statement of profits that seem possible under conditions so far as conditions can be foreseen. The form of the statement is in the tangible and understandable terms of estimated sales, but the purpose and meaning of the program is to arrive at net profit results. If conditions change after the sales program is set up, then the sales program will be changed just so far as the contracts and decisions made under the program can be changed. In order to effect these changes, a proper system of reports which will serve as a basis for control of the sales budget is necessary.

### Control over the Sales Budget

As suggested in the preceding paragraph, the sales budget is a preliminary statement of the anticipated operations of the sales department. Other departments, by means of their budgets, attempt to coordinate their activities with those of the sales department, as shown by the sales budget. As the budget period proceeds, it is necessary to take into consideration the variation of the actual operations of the sales department from its estimated operations. It is necessary that a comparison be made at frequent intervals in order to determine the amount of this variation, so that revisions may be made in the sales budget for the remainder of the budget period, provided the comparison indicates that such a revision is necessary.

### Effect of Revision of Sales Budget on Other Budgets

After the sales budget is revised, it is necessary to revise the other budgets which are affected thereby. For instance, a sales budget may be made for the first three months of the year, and a production budget prepared to meet the sales program. At the end of January a comparison may show that sales made during the month are 50 per cent less than the estimated sales, and indications are that a like decrease will take place in February. The sales budget should then be revised and the production and financial budgets changed to correspond, if such changes are possible. In some cases commitments may have been made which make a complete revision of the other budgets impracticable. At least some revision, however, is usually possible. In the same manner comparisons should be made in connection with the other budgets, for if any of these changes are found necessary, they may make a revision of the sales budget necessary. For instance, if the production program had fallen down, it may be necessary to decrease the sales budget because of the inability to fill orders.

### Reports from Sales Units

In order to make a revision of the sales budget, it is necessary to have regular reports from the sales departments showing what the sales have been. Usually these reports are made monthly. If there are several units of the sales department making sales independently of the central sales office, it is necessary to have a separate report from each of these units. For instance, if a business has ten branches, each making sales from its own stock, it will be necessary to have reports from each of these branches showing the sales made, in order that the correctness of the original estimate can be judged and, if necessary, revisions made.

## Sales Orders vs. Shipments

In making a comparison between sales and estimated sales it is necessary to interpret "sales" to mean orders received rather than goods shipped. Otherwise there may be a wide variation between the sales made and the sales estimated, which is not due to the fact that the original estimate was incorrect. The goods may not have been shipped because of the failure of the purchasing department or the production department to supply the goods. If the sales department obtained the orders, it has fulfilled its function. In revising the sales budget it is also improper to consider shipments, since it is the orders received, and not the shipments made, which indicate the possibilities for the remainder of the period. In revising the production budget it will be necessary to consider the shipments in order to determine the shortage or the excess existing. In considering the orders received for the purpose of comparing sales with estimated sales it is necessary to exclude those received for future delivery.

## Method of Revising Sales Estimate

In case it is found necessary to revise the sales estimate because of a falling off of orders, it is possible to determine which items should be reduced, for the orders will be classified by items and the different items will be changed in proportion to the orders received for that item. In case the sales budget must be revised, because of a change in some other budget, such as the production budget or the financial budget, it is necessary to decide which items on the sales budget should be changed. Some firms list the items on the budget on a priority basis. In case some items must be reduced due to revisions in other budgets, the reduction is made on the last item on the list. If an increase seems desirable, the first item on the list is increased. The use of the priority list is of more significance in the case of some budgets than it is in connection with the sales budget. For instance, in the case of the plant and equipment budget it is a very practicable method of providing for a revision.

### Source of Information Used in Formulating and Controlling the Sales Budget

It is not always practicable or feasible to obtain from the formal accounting records all the information needed to serve as a basis for formulating or controlling the sales budget. A considerable part of such information may be obtained from statistical records kept in the various departments, or it may be obtained from a central statistical department. The majority of up-to-date sales departments are constantly gathering statistics which will serve as a basis for forecasting future sales. In many cases a special department is maintained for this purpose. These data are useful in making the sales estimate. The operating department may keep a record of the method of delivery; the advertising manager may have the sales tickets tabulated in his office to indicate sales by territories; other officials may record other data which they need.

In many businesses tabulating machines are used to collect the statistical data needed by the various departments. By means of cards which are punched to indicate various classifications of data and which are then sorted and assembled it is possible to obtain various kinds of data. In case considerable statistical information is necessary the tabulating machines are desirable. In any case the accounting records can provide quite useful analyses if these records are properly constructed and operated, the principal obstacle to this being the conception of bookkeeping as a science of formulas for the all important purpose of arriving at net profit or loss. Once a set of revenue accounts is rightly considered as a continuing analysis of transactions, no practical difficulty will be experienced in keeping as many co-equal sets of sales accounts as the making of the well-considered sales program demands.

### Difficult Problems in Preparing Sales Budget

The chief difficulties encountered in the preparation of the sales budget have been indicated in the preceding discussion. In order that these difficulties may not be disregarded or minimized, it is deemed desirable to summarize them here. They may be stated as follows:

1. *Market fluctuations*, which make it difficult to forecast future sales.
2. *Seasonal fluctuations*, which make it difficult to coordinate sales with production.
3. *Inadequate statistics with reference to past sales*, which make it difficult to estimate future sales.
4. *Lack of standardization*, which results in one firm handling hundreds of different items, with the consequent difficulty of estimating sales on each item.

Although it is impossible to eliminate these difficulties, it is possible to overcome them to a considerable extent.

By carrying on proper research work and by collecting proper statistics it is possible, to some extent, to estimate market fluctuation. Of course, in periods of violent readjustments following a panic or a war it is difficult to estimate the future trend of the market. The only resource, then, is to make the budget period as short as possible, keep the resources of the business in a liquid condition so that they will be adaptable to sudden changes, gather statistics at frequent intervals to make possible a revision of the budgets, and make such changes as are found necessary as quickly as possible.

Seasonal fluctuations may be provided for in some cases by having seasonal budgets so that the seasonal fluctuations can be provided for at each budget period. If it is impossible to do this, it is necessary to plan operations so as to meet these seasonal fluctuations and to make the budgets and budgetary reports correspond. The method of planning production to meet seasonal sales will be discussed in a later chapter (Chapter IX).

Inadequate statistics often present a very serious difficulty. The question sometimes arises as to the advisability of attempting budgetary control before more adequate statistics are obtained than are at hand. Although it may be impossible to make correct budgets on the basis of information available, there is a decided advantage in commencing the budgetary program and developing the statistical records as the work proceeds. By this means the statistics required can be clearly seen and the importance of obtaining them can be impressed upon all those responsible for their preparation. As the program proceeds it is possible to obtain statistics which will make possible such revisions as are found necessary. It is of course understood that if budgets are based on inadequate statistics, they must be used with much judgment.

It is usually necessary, for the purpose of coordinating sales and production, or sales and purchasing, to make the sales budget and the production or purchasing budget in terms of items. In a business handling many thousands of items this may be very difficult. It has been suggested previously that one method of attacking this problem is to select those items which represent the major part of the production and budget them. By gradually increasing the items selected for budgeting, an adequate system of budgetary control can be developed.

No method has ever been developed by which to forecast with exactness the future operations of a business. By careful study, plans can be made in most businesses which will correspond quite accurately with the results attained. Even in those businesses where it is possible to make plans which are only approximately correct, such plans are better than no plans at all.

It has been the purpose of this chapter and the chapter immediately preceding, to explain some of the most important considerations governing the preparation and use of the sales budget. In the following chapters the preparation of the budgets of the other functional departments and the coordination of the sales budget with these will be explained and illustrated.

# CHAPTER VII

## THE SELLING EXPENSE BUDGET

### Relation of Selling Expense to Sales

It must be evident to the reader that though it is necessary to formulate a sales program, in some such manner as explained in the two chapters immediately preceding, such a program is lifeless considered by itself. Making a formal statement of the volume of sales desired, or of the class of sales desired, does not produce the sales. There must be a sales "campaign" as well as a sales "program."

A political party does not win an election by merely nominating candidates and preparing a platform. In addition it must conduct a campaign to convince the public of the merits of its candidates and platform. In the same manner a business must conduct a sales campaign to convince the public of the merit of the product which according to its sales program it is offering for sale.

A sales campaign may be said to consist of two mutual parts:

1. A knowledge of the sales desired and deemed possible.
2. A plan for securing the results desired at the lowest possible cost.

The sales desired and deemed possible are determined by the sales program and are expressed in the sales estimate. But this program cannot be formulated without considering the cost which it involves in the way of selling expense. There are few firms which could not increase their sales if they desired to incur the necessary expense. Sales are desired only when profits will result. The probable profits should be determined before an attempt is made to secure the sales. In determining the probable profits, the selling

87

cost which the sales program will involve must be given careful consideration. It is obviously impossible for the budget committee or the board of directors to judge the desirability of the contemplated sales program as presented by the sales department unless they know the cost of this program.

## Need for Estimate of Selling Expense

The selling expense estimate is needed for the following purposes:

1. That the sales department may be able to judge the desirability of its contemplated sales program. Without a knowledge of its probable cost it is unable to prepare and present for executive consideration an acceptable program.
2. That the sales department may have a basis for planning its sales campaign. It must know the funds which are available before it can enter into contracts for services or engage personnel.
3. That the treasurer may know the probable disbursements required by the sales program and can plan to obtain the funds necessary to meet these disbursements.
4. That the budget committee may be able to see the financial requirements of the proposed sales and production programs at the time they are submitted to it for consideration. The selling expense in many cases constitutes one of the major items which appear on the disbursement side of the financial budget.

## Importance of Sales Expense Control

It is highly important that an effective control be exercised over sales expense if the greatest amount of profit is to be derived from the sales operations. Unless that is done, this type of expense is apt to increase unduly.

The services obtained from the expenditures of the sales department are in the main of an intangible nature and therefore difficult to appraise. For instance, it is usually difficult to determine accurately the benefit obtained from expenditures incurred for advertising, and the same is true to a considerable degree of expenditures for the services of salesmen.   There are some direct results which can be traced, but in many cases the major results are so indirect that they cannot be connected directly with the expenditure.

If a purchase of materials is made for the production department, it is possible to connect directly the materials received with the funds expended.   It is possible to judge the wisdom of the expenditure by determining the value of the materials.   But if space for advertising is purchased, it is usually not possible to determine the number of orders which result from the expenditure.   It is also difficult to determine for how long benefit may be derived from the advertising.   Orders may be received as a result of the advertising some time after the expenditure for it is incurred.   Again, a salesman may build up good-will for his company which will result in orders after his services are ended.   Because of this indefinite relation between cause and effect, executives are apt to think that the sales expense is necessary and should be incurred even though direct results cannot be seen, and therefore they may not scrutinize closely the amount and nature of this expense.

Moreover, hardly any satisfactory standards exist by which to judge selling expense.   It is possible to determine the amount of material necessary to produce a certain article, and use this amount as a standard to judge the future consumption of materials in the production of that article. But there is no exact means of determining the amount of selling expense which is necessary to secure a dollar of sales, and it is therefore more difficult to formulate a standard by which to judge the quantity of selling expense.

Because of these reasons it is especially necessary that formal and exact control of selling expense be exercised. This control involves three steps:

1. Determination of what is included in selling expense and the setting up of a proper classification thereof.
2. Determination of standards by which to judge the amount of selling expense, and the use of these standards in the formulation of a selling expense budget.
3. Determination of methods of enforcing the standards set, and the execution of these methods.

### Definition of Selling Expense

There is a considerable difference of opinion among both accountants and business men as to what should be considered as selling expense. This is probably due to several causes.

There are many items of expense which contribute more or less indirectly to the making of sales. Inasmuch as sales consummate the process which results in the securing of a profit, it is not difficult to reason that the purpose of many of the operations of the business is to secure sales and that the expense incurred in those operations should be treated as a selling expense.

The classification of expenses is discussed at some length in Chapter XVIII of this book in connection with the consideration of the expense budgets, and it is not desired to enter into this subject here. Suffice it to say that from the viewpoint of administrative control it is desirable that expenses should be classified so as to indicate the responsibility for their incurrence. Executive control can be exercised only in terms of organization, and members of an organization can rightly be held responsible only for that over which they exercise control.

If responsibility is taken as the controlling factor in an expense classification, selling expense will include all expenses which are under the control of the sales manager or executive head of the sales department, and in addition such miscellaneous items as are directly connected with sales and the amount of which is fixed or at least beyond the direct control of any officer.

An illustration of the former case is found in the salaries of employees in the sales department, who are under the direct control of the sales manager, while an illustration of the latter case is found in depreciation on delivery equipment, the estimated amount of which is usually determined by others than the sales manager. The depreciation may properly be treated as a sales expense, for it is connected directly with the sales function. Its amount, moreover, could not be affected by the action of the sales manager even if the determination of it were in his power, since it is assumed that the correct amount is to be stated.

These illustrations should be sufficient to enable the reader to determine the proper treatment of other items about which there may be a question. There are some few items the classification of which is dependent on a decision as to the purpose for which they are incurred, and in many instances there is no unanimity of opinion with reference to this purpose. These items will be discussed in Chapter XVIII on expense budgets.

## Classification of Selling Expense

It is customary to charge as a part of the cost of goods sold, all expenditures incurred in connection with the product up to the time when it is ready to be offered for sale. This is based on the theory that the sales department does not have jurisdiction of the merchandise prior to this time and is not responsible for the expenditures incurred in connection with it. The first expense incurred by the sales department is in the securing of sales orders. This expense will include the expenses of the sales office which directs the sales effort, the salaries of salesmen, and the expenses of salesmen. It may also include the cost of advertising. After the goods are

sold they must be prepared for delivery to the customer—
which involves packing or wrapping, and finally they must
be delivered to the customer, or to a transportation company which will effect the delivery.    On the basis of the
foregoing discussion it is possible to set up the following
classification of sales expense:

    1. Sales office expense
    2. Salesmen's salaries and expenses
    3. Packing and shipping
    4. Advertising

The first three of these items will be discussed in the
present chapter.   The control of advertising expense is
thought of sufficient importance to merit separate treatment
and its discussion will be postponed until the next chapter.

### Sales Office Expense

Sales must always be subject to some executive supervision and this supervision results in expense.   The nature
of the supervision exercised over sales will depend upon the
size and organization of each particular business.   In most
businesses there is a sales manager who is the executive head
of the sales department, and frequently he is assisted by a
staff.   In many cases there are district offices each under
the control of a manager who is subordinate to the general
sales manager.   Each district manager may have a staff
of assistants.   If a company has a sufficient volume of
foreign sales, it may have an "export" sales office in the
charge of a manager with the appropriate assistants.   In a
company distributing its product through branches, there
is a sales staff at each branch.

As the sales organization grows, care must be exercised
to avoid incurring unnecessary expense.   It is but natural
that each subordinate office will desire to enlarge its activities as much as possible and because of this tendency there

may be a duplication of work. There are many activities which can be performed better by the central sales office for the benefit of all the subordinate offices than by each office for itself. Every professional man who has done work on administrative control can recall instances of duplication of work in branch offices which existed because it had not been called to the attention of the general officers responsible for the control of branch expense.

The preparation of estimates of sales expense will do much to prevent incurring unnecessary expense by units of sales organization. These estimates will serve, in the first place, to call the attention of all the executives of the company to the expenses of each unit and to require them to consider these expenses *before* they are incurred, and in the second place, to provide comparison between different units. It should be apparent, if the estimate of selling expenses of the X unit calls for expenditures which are equal to 10 per cent of estimated sales, and the estimate of the Y unit calls for expenditures which are equal to 20 per cent of estimated sales, that the budget committee will call for an explanation. In fact the sales manager should have asked for an explanation before he transmitted the estimates to the executive in charge of the budget committee, and the latter should call the attention of the budget committee to the fact and to the explanation of the sales manager which it is assumed he attaches to the estimates when he transmits them.

### Salesmen's Salaries and Expense

There is usually little difficulty in deciding as to the items which should be included under this heading or as to the proper method of recording and reporting them. The chief problem is the controlling of such expenses, for they have a tendency to become unduly large unless an effective check is exercised. One of the chief sources of difficulty is the determination of the proper method of compensating the salesmen for their services.

If definite salaries are paid salesmen, it is often difficult to determine the equitableness of the amount paid. In an attempt to lessen the difficulty, salesmen may be paid in whole or in part on a commission basis. Some sales executives think that a salary plus a commission is the most desirable method on the theory that the work of a salesman cannot be judged entirely by the sales which are directly attributable to him. He may have a certain advertising value to the business which is not adequately measured in terms of the sales orders which he turns in. A salary, which is not directly dependent on the volume of sales, remunerates him for the work which he does towards building up the good-will of the firm; whereas the commission which he receives, based on the volume of sales secured or on the excess of sales over a certain amount, rewards efficiency and penalizes inefficiency. Those who are exponents of the payment of a commission only contend that the salesman is remunerated for the work he does in building up good-will by the additional orders which he will receive later on. If all orders received from the salesman's territory are credited to him, there is merit in this contention.

The method to be employed in remunerating the salesmen is a problem of the sales department, but as it has an important bearing on the preparation of the estimate of selling expense, it is of interest to the student of budgetary control. It may be added that, if a proper control is to be exercised over these expenses, it is necessary to have records and reports which will provide an analysis of sales and selling expense showing:

1. Whether the salesman or the territory is responsible for the sales.
2. Whether the sales which are being made are of the goods which the company most desires to sell. The latter, at least, can be

determined by obtaining the profit realized on sales made by each salesman and judging his efficiency in terms of profit rather than by volume of sales.

The nature of the reports used in exercising control of salesmen's expenses will be discussed later in this chapter.

## Packing and Shipping

The amount of the expenses incurred in packing and shipping merchandise depends upon the nature of the product sold and to a considerable degree upon whether a firm is doing a retail, wholesale, or manufacturing business. In a retail business the merchandise in most cases is wrapped by the salesmen, or by clerks who are located in each department for that purpose. It may be delivered to the customer by the sales clerk at the time of sale or by the regular delivery service of the business. In a wholesale and manufacturing business there is usually a separate shipping department which is responsible for the packing of the merchandise and its delivery to the transportation company. In a few companies freight is paid on all goods shipped, in which case we have the item of "freight out."

The shipping department is not always under the control of the sales department. In a manufacturing business it may be under the control of the production department. In a department store it may be under the control of the operating superintendent. If the shipping department is not under the control of the sales department, the latter cannot be held responsible for the shipping expense. But the estimate of shipping expense must be considered with the sales program, since it varies with the volume of sales.

## Some Packing Cost a Manufacturing Expense

Not all the expenses of packing, or at least of placing merchandise in containers, are to be treated as selling expense.  If the packing is that which goes directly on goods and is necessary to preserve them and to keep them in a condition to be sold, the charge is against the cost of the goods. Examples of such cases are the jars which hold fruit, the boxes containing cigars, the paper wrappers on chocolate bars, etc.  Such containers or wrappers are an integral part of manufacturing costs and should be so treated in the accounts and the reports.  If the wrappers contain advertising matter, some part of their cost may be charged to advertising expense.

### Allocation of "Drayage" Expense

The expense of packing goods for shipment may ordinarily be treated as a selling expense, as may also the expense of carrying the goods to transportation agencies for shipment.  Sometimes the same employees are used in connection with the unpacking of goods when received and in packing them for shipment after they are sold.  In such cases the expenses incurred in connection with both operations are usually charged to one account and then allocated as between cost of goods and selling expense.  In many cases the same transportation equipment, such as trucks or horses and wagons, are used to transport incoming and outgoing goods.  In such cases the total expense is usually charged to a "drayage" account and later allocated on some equitable basis, such as the ratio of cost of purchases to cost of goods sold.  In some cases the tonnage transported to and from the station may be available and can be used as the basis of allocation.

### Treatment of Freight Out

There is some difference of opinion as to the treatment of the expense incurred in shipping goods to customers if the transportation charges are paid by the vendor.  It is sometimes argued that such expenses, which are usually termed "freight out," should be deducted from gross sales, since "freight in" is added to purchases in determining the cost of goods sold.   Such a procedure seems logical and if transportation charges are paid by the vendor on all the goods sold, or on the major part of them there is little objection to this treatment since it must be assumed that the matter was considered in setting the sales price and a sufficient amount added to cover the anticipated cost of shipment.   If, as is usually true, the vendor pays these charges only in exceptional cases to obtain special orders, it would seem more proper to treat them as selling expense.   In these cases the granting of such concessions is under the control of the sales department and allowed only when this department thinks it is advantageous to do so in carrying out its sales program. Unless the sales department is charged with these expenses, it is apt to be too lenient in granting such concessions, and moreover the comparison of selling expense with sales, period by period, will not show exact results.

### Analysis of Shipping Expenses

As a matter of control it is often advisable to subdivide packing and shipping expenses.  A geographical analysis will often prove useful.  When uniform prices are quoted regardless of territory, an analysis of packing and shipping expense on a territorial basis will often show that some goods are being sold at a very small profit or even at a loss, because of the additional expenses incurred in connection with their preparation for shipment and delivery.   This is apt to be true particularly when a manufacturer of bulky articles has a national market.   One writer even goes so far as to say: "I have never seen such a division made by a national manufacturer, selling from coast to coast, which did not show that in some sections he was selling merely to help

7

his pride and not his profit; in distant markets, the extra packing and the high freight outward will commonly be found to absorb the entire normal profits."

## Use of Warehouses and Branch Depots

Whenever possible, sales should be made f.o.b. the place of manufacture. If because of the custom of the trade the freight must be paid by the vendor, then a business may find it profitable to establish branch depots or warehouses to which goods may be shipped in bulk and then distributed. Many national manufacturers have such warehouses. Some department stores in large cities establish warehouses in different parts of the city, from which they deliver goods to customers. Where warehouses exist it is necessary to give careful consideration to their cost in preparing the expense estimates.

## Treatment of Breakage

Another item of considerable importance in some cases is the loss arising as a result of breakage or damage occurring in the process of shipping. If there is a regular, unavoidable breakage it can properly be treated as sales expense. If there is a breakage in connection with one line which is not common to all lines handled, it is better to raise the sales price of this commodity sufficiently to cover the breakage and not attempt to allocate it over all goods sold.

## Importance of Proper Handling of Packing and Shipping Expenses

The matter of packing and shipping expense has here been given considerable space, for it has been the author's experience that in many cases definite responsibility is not fixed for the administration of the shipping department and consequently effective control of shipping expense is not exercised. The preparation and enforcement of careful estimates will aid in remedying this condition.

## Method of Estimating Selling Expense

One of the most useful devices a manager can have is that of expense standards. If he knows what is current practice in various fields of expenditure, he has a sort of norm against which to measure his own performances and with which to check his own figures in the preparation of budgets. Such standards are needed in controlling the operations of all the functional departments, but are particularly needed by the sales manager because of the nature of sales expense and its indefinite relation to results.

Unfortunately, not much has been done towards developing standard rates for selling expenses. Some few agencies, like the Bureau of Business Research of Harvard University, have gathered data which show the prevailing rates in certain lines of industry. These statistics are useful in enabling the executive to see how his business compares with others in the matter of selling cost. Certain trade associations, moreover, have gathered data with reference to the expenses of their members and made it available for the use of other members. In the past many firms have hesitated to give their competitors data with reference to expenses and costs. This attitude is changing to a considerable degree and we can expect that more and more there will be available useful data of this nature.

Even though data are obtainable which show the selling expenses of other firms, there is no assurance that the rates thus shown are desirable. Each firm must of necessity develop its own rates and determine the standards which are applicable to its conditions. If periodical estimates, based on scientific research, are carefully made and these estimates are controlled by accurate reports, a firm will gradually develop standards which will be very useful in making plans and judging results. Until such standards are available it must use the best data obtainable in preparing its estimates.

In preparing the estimate of selling expense it is necessary to consider each class of expense separately.  If the
sales office expense has been satisfactory in the past, the
amount shown by the past records may be used as a basis
for the current estimate, of course considering separately
each item of expense.  Consideration must be given to
salaries of the sales manager and his staff, salaries of clerical
assistants and stenographers, cost of supplies, etc.  In case
of district or branch offices it will be necessary to make a
separate estimate for each item of expense to be incurred in
these offices.  It should be evident that in no case should
the sales office expense be estimated on a percentage basis.
As sales increase, the ratio of "overhead" expenses to
sales should decrease.  If the sales office expenses are 3
per cent of sales when the yearly sales are $100,000, they
should be expected to be something less than 3 per cent
when sales become $500,000.

If salesmen are paid a commission they usually pay their
own expenses, and it is consequently very easy to estimate
the cost of salesmen's expenses and salaries.  The rate of
commission is applied to the estimate of sales, and the result
is the estimate of salesmen's salaries and expenses.  If the
salesmen are paid a salary and the company pays their expenses, it is necessary to consider each salesman individu-
ally.  After a list of all salesmen is made, there will be
placed after the name of each his present salary and the
normal amount of his expenses.  This list will be gone over
by the sales manager and his assistants.  If advances of
salesmen's salaries are contemplated, these will be shown.
Each salesman's expenses will be examined and revisions
made when it is thought that conditions warrant.  Gradually standard expense rates should be developed for each
territory and the salesmen's expenses based on these standards.  If the rates are fairly determined, each salesman can

be required to limit his expenses so that they will not exceed the standard.

If possible, standards showing the cost per unit for packing and shipping should be developed. If this is not feasible because of the variety of units sold, it is then necessary to develop a standard rate expressed in terms of a percentage of sales. In either case it should be kept in mind that as the volume of sales increases, the ratio of packing and shipping expense should decrease. Under normal conditions such a result is to be expected because there are certain items of overhead which will not increase in proportion to volume of goods handled.

After standard rates for packing and shipping expense are developed, it is only necessary to apply these rates to the sales volume as shown by the sales estimate to obtain the amount of the estimated packing and shipping expense. If there are conditions which indicate a deviation from the standard rates, these must be given consideration.

## Preparation of Selling Expense Budget

The sales office expense estimate will be prepared by the staff of the executive head of the office. If there be but one sales office, the estimate will be prepared by the staff of the sales manager. If there are branch or division offices, the staff of each office will prepare an estimate of that office, and after it is approved by the manager it will be forwarded to the sales manager at the general office.

The salesmen's salaries and expense estimate should be prepared by the immediate superior of the salesmen for whom the estimate is made. If there are branch and division offices, each of these will prepare an estimate for the salesmen belonging to that office, and after it is approved by the manager it will be forwarded to the sales manager at the general office.

The packing and shipping expense budget will be prepared by the head of the shipping department and forwarded by him to the sales manager.

The sales manager will make such revisions as he thinks necessary in the estimates of his subordinates and forward them to the executive in charge of the budget procedure, with such recommendations as he may desire to offer. The executive in charge of the budget procedure will forward these to the budget committee, which will make any revisions which it may think necessary and return the estimate with its approval to the executive in charge of the budget procedure. The latter will return them to the sales manager, who in turn will transmit to each subordinate his budget as approved.

In form the estimate of selling expense may be made as shown in Figure 3. The purpose of each of the columns shown on this form should be apparent to the reader.

In some businesses the controller prepares all expense estimates, including those for sales expense. Although the controller may very properly be given the authority to prescribe the form of the estimates and the reports to be used in their control, it is the author's opinion that he should not be responsible for their preparation. The reasons for this belief have been explained in Chapter III and need not be repeated here. As a member of the budget committee the controller will have an opportunity to pass upon all budgets submitted and should be able to offer constructive criticism of them. In some cases it may be desirable to refer the estimates to his office for review before they are considered by the budget committee.

## Control of the Selling Expense Budget

To exercise control of the selling expense budget, it is necessary to have a proper system of reports which will make

## SELLING EXPENSE BUDGET

Month_____                                    Season_____

| ITEMS | Original Appropriation | % of Original Sales Expectancies | Additions | Deductions | Present Appropriation | % of Present Sales Expectancies | Original Sales Expectancies | Additions | Deductions | Present Sales Expectancies |
|---|---|---|---|---|---|---|---|---|---|---|
| (1) | (2) | (3) | (4) | (5) | (6) | (7) | (8) | (9) | (10) | (11) |

Figure 3.   Selling Expense Budget

## REPORT ON SELLING EXPENSE BUDGET

| ITEMS | Original Appropriations | Additions | Deductions | Final Appropriations | Cash Disbursments | Credit Disbursments (Accounts Payable) | Undisbursed Balance | Contracts Outstanding for Salaries and Wages | Balance Available for Future Contracts or for Transfer |
|---|---|---|---|---|---|---|---|---|---|
| (1) | (2) | (3) | (4) | (5) | (6) | (7) | (8) | (9) | (10) |

Figure 4.   Report on Selling Expense Budget

possible a proper check of its operation.　These reports may
be divided broadly into two classes:

    1. Those which are used by the sales department in the enforcement
       of its budget.

    2. Those used by the executives and the budget committee to judge
       how well the sales department has succeeded in the enforce-
       ment of its budget.

The first class of reports may be well illustrated by those
required in enforcing the salesmen's expense budget.　The
reports used for this purpose may in turn be divided broadly
into two classes:

    (a) Those which are used primarily by the general sales office.

    (b) Those which are used primarily as reports to salesmen.

For the use of the general office it is useful to make a
report showing for each salesman the following comparisons:

    (a) Actual sales and estimated sales

    (b) Expense and sales

    (c) Actual expense and standard

    (d) Expense with average of territory

If in addition to the amounts these comparisons are expressed in percentages, the report is much more useful.　If
this report shows wide variations between the standard
and the actual, supplementary reports should be prepared
explaining the variations.

Reports may be sent to the salesmen monthly, or even
weekly if desired, showing a comparison between the estimated expense and the actual and also the profit earned by
their sales.　In some cases the gross profits by lines may be
shown on these reports, so as to indicate to the salesmen the
lines of merchandise which they should push.

For the use of the general executives and the budget
committee a report may be made in the form of Figure 4.

The purpose and value of each of the columns shown on this report should be apparent to the reader. In case this report shows wide variations between the actual and the estimated, supplementary reports should be submitted explaining the variations.

# CHAPTER VIII

## THE ADVERTISING BUDGET

### Relation of Advertising to Selling Expense

There has long been an argument among the executives in the marketing field as to the relation of advertising and selling—principally as to the proper relation between the advertising manager and the sales manager. Some have contended that the advertising manager should be the executive head of an independent department, while others have insisted that he should be subordinate to the sales manager. There is no intention of entering into this discussion here, but it is desired to emphasize that regardless of the organization by which the advertising is carried on, the advertising program must be considered as a part of the sales program as a whole and the advertising expense must be considered as a part of selling expense.

It should not be difficult for the reader to see why this is true. The purpose of the advertising and of the sales force is the same—to secure the maximum of profitable sales with a minimum of cost. There are some services in the marketing of a product which commonly can be performed more effectively by advertising than by the sales force, and the opposite is equally true. The advertising campaign must be planned with reference to the specific work which it is expected to perform in relation to the other sales work of the company. Consequently, neither the amount of the advertising expense nor the amount of the other items of selling expense can be determined independently. The advertising budget must be presented as a part of the larger selling expense budget.

## The Advertising Appropriation

It has long been the practice of many firms to make an annual "appropriation" for advertising expense. It may seem strange that a firm will make an advertising appropriation but will not make an appropriation for any other purpose. We rarely hear of an accounting appropriation, a manufacturing appropriation, a traffic appropriation, etc. It may at first be thought, since definite appropriations are made for advertising expense, that this class of expense is more effectively and scientifically controlled than are the expenses of the various other departments. Further study will lead one to doubt if this be true. Rather one is apt to find that the practice of establishing definite appropriations for advertising expense is based upon two reasons:

1. Outside counsel, in the form of advertising agencies, have often been employed to direct the advertising and it was necessary to have a definite agreement with them with reference to the amount which they were permitted to spend.

2. Business executives have not regarded advertising expense as they have the other expenses of the business, but rather as an additional expense which while it might be beneficial was not necessary for survival. As they knew no definite way of determining the amount of the advertising expense, they guessed at a lump sum which they thought they could afford, and took a chance on obtaining results from it. In many cases it was a policy of cast your bread on the waters and trust it to return.

The professional advertising agency has rendered a service by teaching business executives the necessity for formulating an advertising program and coordinating this program with the sales program. It is but natural, however, for these specialists to be enthusiasts for advertising and it is open to question whether they have always given as much attention to scientific methods of calculating the amount of the advertising appropriation as they have to the attempt to make it as large as possible. In many cases this proved a short-sighted policy because it produced a reaction when the management failed to see adequate returns for the money expended. This remark is not intended as a criticism of advertising agencies, for many of them have rendered very useful service in advising executives with reference to the amount of the advertising which they should do, as well as the kind of advertising which would be most effective. Their errors have probably not been greater or more numerous than those of the professional accountant or the engineer.

### Methods of Calculating Advertising Cost

In recent years both advertising experts and business executives have come to realize, first, that advertising expense is a necessary expense of operation, no less than the expense incurred in carrying on any of the other functional activities of the business; second, that the advertising program is closely related to the program of the business as a whole and that therefore the amount of the advertising expense should be based on contemplated plans of the business as a whole. As a result considerable attention has been given to the proper method of calculating advertising expense. The following methods are those in most current use:

1. The advertising expense of the current period may be based on the expense of the previous period, adding or subtracting a certain percentage depending on the opinion of the executives with reference to the success of the advertising program of the preceding period. The general manager may say to the advertising manager, "Last year we spent $110,000 for advertising expenses; this year you may spend 5 per cent more." Such a budget refers the advertising manager to the expense accounts of the preceding year for his working program.

2. The advertising expense of the current period may

be based on the estimated sales of the current period, determining the amount by taking a certain percentage of the total volume of sales. For instance, the general manager may say to the advertising manager, "Last year we spent 5 per cent of sales for advertising expense. Here is our sales expectancy for this year. We expect you to secure the sales at an advertising cost of 5 per cent or less." This method is more scientific than that suggested in (1) for it requires the advertising manager to connect cause with effect—advertising expense with sales to be secured. It should be apparent that the advertising expense should not be based on past sales. The advertising of the current period can have no effect on, or no relation to, the sales of past periods. It is to make possible the attainment of the current sales program that the advertising program is intended, and the amount to be expended under the advertising program can only be determined properly by considering the current sales program.

3. The advertising expense of the current period may be based on the estimated sales of the current period, determining the amount by allowing for advertising so much per unit of the product which it is planned to sell. For instance, it may be agreed that so many cents will be spent for advertising for each crate, ton, dozen—or other unit used in the estimate—which is expected to be sold.

Readers interested in other methods of calculating advertising cost may well read articles by John A. Murphy, in December 9, 1920 and December 16, 1920 issues of *Printers' Ink*.

## Advantages and Disadvantages

Opinion differs with reference to the merits of these different methods. No definite rule can be laid down to govern the policy to be followed by all businesses. In the opinion of the author the first method is the one least to be desired. It is apt to result in careless planning of advertising cost, since it is so very easy to add or subtract a certain percentage of past expenses and not to consider the question further. It is also apt to result in basing present expenses on past expenses without giving proper consideration to the contemplated changes in the sales program. At least it fails to compel a consideration of present plans. The ideal in the designing of methods of administrative control is to secure those which will compel coordination and at the same time promote progress.

To base the advertising appropriation on a percentage of the volume of sales tends to simplicity, and in a business where the fluctuation in sales is not great may give satisfactory results. This condition is more apt to prevail in a business handling a staple and well-established line than in a business handling specialties. In a business having many and varied lines it may be the only feasible method, since calculation of the unit cost of advertising for each item of goods sold may not be practicable. This method has the disadvantage of fluctuating unduly in some cases because of the fluctuation in the price of purchases of materials, supplies, and labor, and consequent fluctuation of the selling price. In a period of depression as many units of commodity may be sold as before the depression, but at a price which will greatly decrease the total sales in terms of dollars and cents. In this case if the advertising appropriation is based on the sales volume expressed in terms of dollars and cents, it will be greatly decreased, whereas it may be desirable to keep up the advertising campaign in order to maintain the sales volume in spite of the adverse conditions. There is something to be said for the possibility that if the sales price of the commodities sold has decreased, the cost of advertising will decrease also.

If advertising is calculated as so much per unit of product

sold, it tends to concentrate attention on the purpose for which the advertising is incurred and incidentally to call attention to the unit cost and unit profit realized on the articles sold. This method is also apt to cause the advertising appropriation to fluctuate less, since the units sold are apt to vary less than the returns from sales. There may be some argument for having the advertising fluctuate as the sales fluctuate. At least there are occasions when this is true. There are also other occasions where the advertising may fluctuate in reverse order to the fluctuations in sales. A financially strong enterprise may increase its advertising during a period of depression in order to reduce the decrease in sales to a minimum and to establish itself in the market so as to take advantage of the contemplated period of prosperity.

It would seem, regardless of whether the unit costs or the percentage method is used, that revisions will have to be made in case of changing conditions which affect the general plans made at the time the advertising appropriation is determined. The advertising appropriation should be regarded as only an estimate and subject to revision no less than the other estimates. Of course, in making such revisions outstanding commitments must be considered.

There is reason to believe that advertising managers have placed great emphasis on the basis of determining the amount of the advertising appropriation, because it has been difficult to get appropriations approved and consequently it was desirable to get a definite basis established which would give them the maximum amount under all circumstances.

Regardless of the basis adopted for calculating the advertising appropriation, each individual business must make constant study of its advertising program with the object of revising it as soon as the necessity is indicated.

## Determining the Amount of the Advertising Appropriation

After the basis on which the advertising appropriation is to be calculated is decided, it is necessary to determine the desired amount in dollars and cents. Theoretically the rate may be determined without consideration of the total, but it is doubtful if this is ever done. A firm may decide that it can well afford to spend one cent per article sold for advertising, but if the total thus determined runs beyond the amount necessary to pay for the advertising plans contemplated, the rate per unit will be reduced. If a percentage of sales is used as the basis the same procedure will be followed. After the total is determined the rate will be revised, if necessary, to make the total somewhat near the amount which the executives think desirable.

In determining the amount of the appropriation two important factors must be given consideration:

1. What is the purpose of the advertising—what is to be accomplished by it?
2. How is the advertising appropriation to be expended—how is the purpose of the advertising to be accomplished?

## Purpose of Advertising

If we assume that a business has previously done no advertising, the selling price of its commodity will be composed of the following items: manufacturing or purchase cost, selling expense, administrative expense, and profit. Expressed in the form of an equation we have:

$$\text{Cost of goods sold} + \text{selling expense} + \text{administrative expense} + \text{profit} = \text{selling price}$$

Obviously, if it is determined to incur expenditures for advertising, some of the members of this equation will be changed. Either the left-hand members must be decreased, or the right-hand member must be increased.

The competitive condition of the market may be such that by the advertising a sufficient demand can be created for the product to make possible an increase in the selling price. If this be true, the cost of the advertising may be consumed by the increase in selling price and the other members of the equation left undisturbed. This condition is not apt to exist in many cases under present competitive conditions. In fact, only in the case of a monopoly can such a result be expected to be obtained permanently.

If the purpose of the advertising is to maintain the present volume of sales during a period of bitter competition, the expense may be met out of profits. The company may desire to maintain its position in the trade even though smaller profits are to be secured at the present time. It may be thought that the lessened profits at this time will be more than compensated for by increased profits in the future. Similarly a company may incur advertising in order to ward off hostile public opinion and to prevent undesirable legislation. Public utilities have done considerable advertising of this nature during past years. More recently some of the packing companies have followed the same practice. Advertising of this nature may well be met out of profits because it is thought that it will prevent lessened profits in the future. Again, a firm may incur expenditures for advertising which will lessen current profits but build up good-will which in turn will result in larger future profits.

In some cases advertising is incurred because it is thought that it will increase the volume of sales and thus result in a decrease of the cost of goods sold, the selling expense, or the administrative expense.

In a manufacturing business, an increase in the volume of sales, with the consequent increase in the volume of production, will usually decrease the cost of production because of the decrease in the unit cost of overhead. It may also

8

make possible a more economical use of labor and materials. For instance, the production may become of sufficient volume to make possible the use of scrap in the production of a by-product.   In a mercantile business the increased volume of sales may make possible more economical purchasing with a lower unit cost for goods purchased, but the savings in this connection are rarely comparable with the decrease in the unit cost of goods manufactured when the volume of production is increased.

The increased volume of sales may reduce the unit selling cost.   If the advertising enables each salesman to sell more with the same amount of effort and expense, the unit selling cost will be decreased accordingly.   In addition to the cost of salesmen, the overhead expense incurred in maintaining the sales manager and his staff is usually an appreciable amount, and an increase of sales will not usually cause this expense to increase in proportion.

Finally, an increase in volume of sales should have a desirable result on the administrative expense.   There is every reason why the ratio of administrative expense to sales should decrease as the volume of sales increases.

### Importance of Defining Purpose in Advance

The foregoing discussion shows that there may be several reasons why advertising should be undertaken.   The primary purpose of pointing out these various purposes is to emphasize that the results which it is expected to obtain as a result of the advertising should be clearly in mind before the advertising is begun.   So far as possible, data should be prepared to show the possible results of the advertising. The most difficult problem is that of determining the effect of the advertising on the volume of sales.   If this can be forecast it is usually possible to estimate the approximate effect of the advertising on the manufacturing cost, selling expense, administrative expense, and net profit.

Unfortunately, some firms make advertising appropriations expecting to obtain a large increase in volume of sales, without stopping to determine whether the increase in volume which is anticipated would produce satisfactory results —that is, whether the savings resulting from the increase will be equal to the cost of the advertising. Only recently a manufacturing firm entered into a large contract for advertising and the president showed the author the estimated increase in sales which he expected to obtain as a result of this advertising. A few moments' calculation showed that if the anticipated volume of sales was obtained the factories of the company would not be able to produce goods to satisfy 75 per cent of the sales orders. In this case, regardless of whether the advertising failed or succeeded so far as producing the contemplated volume of sales, the firm was bound to lose as a result of the contract. This is but another instance of lack of coordination, which a proper program of budgetary control would rectify.

All of which is to say that advertising is merely a means and not an end in itself. It is a potent force in modern management but it produces satisfactory results only when it is used with judgment and is coordinated with the other functional activities of a business.

## Method of Accomplishing Desired Purpose

After deciding that it is desirable to use advertising for some particular purpose, it is necessary to determine the most effective way of accomplishing this purpose. It is not enough to decide that there are many people who need and can afford the product which you sell and that you can profitably spend a certain amount in order to get them to purchase a certain volume. It is also necessary to decide in what way they can be reached so as to persuade them to purchase.   In other words, it is necessary to decide upon the medium of advertising to be used.

There is a multiplicity of ways in which advertising may be accomplished.   To the layman the various possibilities present a confusing complexity.   Because of this very complexity it is necessary that very careful consideration be given to the contemplated program.   Although the advertising department should be given considerable freedom of judgment, this freedom should be manifested in the main before, instead of after, the advertising appropriation is approved.   It does not seem desirable that the department be given a lump sum without any conditions being attached to its use.   In addition, it is impossible to judge the amount to be appropriated until the method in which it is to be spent has been determined.   It is only by balancing the two factors—the purpose to be accomplished by the advertising and the method of accomplishing this purpose—that it is possible to work out a well-balanced advertising program.

### Preparation of the Advertising Budget

The preliminary estimate of advertising expenses should be prepared by the advertising manager.   He should have before him the contemplated sales plans of the business, and also be familiar with the general plans and policies of the business as a whole.   If the advertising manager is subordinate to the sales manager, he will submit his estimate to the latter for approval.   In any case he must work in cooperation with the sales manager in formulating the advertising program, as the advertising program is but one part of the sales program.   The sales manager, or the advertising manager, depending on whether the latter is subordinate to the former, will transmit the advertising program to the executive in charge of the budgetary procedure, who

## ADVERTISING APPROPRIATION REPORT

Month_____ Season_____

| ITEMS | Original Appropriation | % of Original Sales Expectancies | Additions | Deductions | Present Appropriation | % of Present Sales Expectancies | Original Sales Expectancies | Additions | Deductions | Present Sales Expectancies |
|---|---|---|---|---|---|---|---|---|---|---|
| (1) | (2) | (3) | (4) | (5) | (6) | (7) | (8) | (9) | (10) | (11) |
| | | | | | | | | | | |

Figure 5.   Advertising Appropriation Report

will in turn submit it to the budget committee which will make such changes as it thinks necessary before approving it. As will be shown in the manual on budgetary procedure discussed in Chapter XXIII the budget committee will have before it all the proposed budgets at one time so that it can consider them as a whole. If the committee thinks that important changes in the estimate are necessary, it will call the advertising manager before it and give him an opportunity to defend his requests.

After the estimate has been approved by the budget committee it may be submitted to the board of directors for consideration and approval. When it has been finally approved, it then becomes the advertising *budget* for the current budget period. It will be transmitted by the executive in charge of the budgetary procedure to the advertising manager and will constitute his working program for the period.

### Form of the Advertising Budget

The advertising estimate should be made in such form as to show:

1. The lines of goods which are to be advertised and the amount to be spent on each of them.
2. The methods by which the appropriation is to be spent and the amount to be spent by each method.

The budget as approved will show the same information as the estimate and this makes possible the exercise of a proper control of advertising expenditures (1) by purposes and (2) by methods of expenditure.

The executive in charge of the budgetary procedure is responsible for seeing that supplementary data are prepared and submitted to the budget committee with the advertising budget which will enable it to judge the possible results of the proposed advertising program, It is expected that a considerable portion of these data will be prepared by the advertising manager in support of his request. He should at least present data to show the anticipated effect of the proposed program on the volume of sales. The executive in charge of the budgetary procedure will usually have to supply the data showing the effect of the increased volume of sales on the manufacturing, selling, and administrative cost. In preparing this he may be assisted by the controller and his staff.

### Control of the Advertising Budget

After the advertising budget is adopted it is necessary to take measures to secure its enforcement. The advertising budget may be thought of as a fixed amount of money voted to the advertising manager by the budget committee or board of directors. So it is—the advertising budget is at once an estimate and a limitation of authority to spend. We have seen, however, that the sales program is based on trade conditions and must be currently modified and amended as trade conditions change. Similarly, the advertising budget is based on the sales program to a considerable degree and may need to be modified and amended when the sales program is changed. In order that the relation between the advertising program and the sales program may be clearly seen, it is desirable that there be prepared at the end of each month a report similar in form to Figure 5.

Mr. W. A. McDermid, in *Administration* for July, 1921, suggests the following method of controlling the advertising appropriation:

> The physical control of the appropriations—the forms by means of which the advertising executive knows where he stands day by day—are relatively simple. They have been modified in many details for different concerns, but a majority are based on the following:

1. The budget sheet:

   Regardless of the method by which the appropriation has been determined, there is laid out an estimate, roughly distributed month by month, with subtotals at convenient intervals.

2. Detail sheet:

   (a) For space. These sheets show, with as much detail as may seem advisable, the publications, dates of insertion, size of space, and cost. The advertising agency usually works this out in compact form both for its guidance and approval.

   (b) For sundry costs. These sheets are usually more of a guess than the space sheets, but they cover estimates for literature, printing, engraving, and innumerable incidental costs. They should be binding only as to outside limits.

3. Budget control sheet (see Figure 6):

   With this before him and his general budget approved, the manager knows where he stands all the time. If the appropriation or scale of expenditure warrants, this could be made weekly or even daily.

The advertising budget presents a plan under which the advertising manager may engage expert labor, make newspaper contracts, etc. As such contracts are made and obligations incurred, the advertising budget comes by degrees to a stage where amendments are difficult. For example, after a contract has been made for printing a shoe catalogue, it is of little use to decide that the money involved can be expended to better purpose in street-car advertising. A report is needed, therefore, which will show the amounts under each appropriation item still available for contract or for transfer to other purposes. Such a report may be made in the form of Figure 7.

A little consideration of this report should make apparent the value and purpose of each of the columnar headings. Columns (1) to (4) inclusive show original plans and the

## ADVERTISING APPROPRIATION REPORT
### (Monthly Cumulative)

Month _____ Season _____

| DISTRIBUTION | THIS MONTH | | | | | SEASON TO DATE | | | |
|---|---|---|---|---|---|---|---|---|---|
| | Gross Expenditure | Credits | Net Expenditure | Budget | "Over" or "Under" | Net Expenditure | Budget | "Over" or "Under" | Balance For Season |
| Magazine * | | | | | | | | | |
| Newspaper * | | | | | | | | | |
| Farm Paper * | | | | | | | | | |
| Trade Paper * | | | | | | | | | |
| Miscellaneous | | | | | | | | | |
| Total Space | | | | | | | | | |
| Periodical | | | | | | | | | |
| Newspaper | | | | | | | | | |
| Miscellaneous | | | | | | | | | |
| Total Art Work | | | | | | | | | |
| Periodical | | | | | | | | | |
| Newspaper | | | | | | | | | |
| Miscellaneous | | | | | | | | | |
| Total Engraving | | | | | | | | | |
| Catalogues | | | | | | | | | |
| Folders | | | | | | | | | |
| Total Literature | | | | | | | | | |
| Dealers Cuts | | | | | | | | | |
| Photographs | | | | | | | | | |
| Dealers Helps | | | | | | | | | |
| Miscellaneous Printing | | | | | | | | | |
| Delivery Charges | | | | | | | | | |
| Miscellaneous | | | | | | | | | |
| Total Sundry | | | | | | | | | |
| Space * | | | | | | | | | |
| Literature | | | | | | | | | |
| Miscellaneous | | | | | | | | | |
| Total Export | | | | | | | | | |
| Grand Total | | | | | | | | | |

* See Detail Sheets

Figure 6. Advertising Appropriation Report (monthly cumulative)

REPORT ON ADVERTISING EXPENDITURES

| ITEMS | Original Appropriations | Additions | Deductions | Final Appropriations | Cash Disbursements Against each Appropriation | Credit Disbursements Accounts Payable | Undisbursed Balance | Contracts Outstanding for Salaries and Wages | Formal Contracts for Printing Etc. Outstanding | Open Market Orders Outstanding | Balances Available for Future Contracts or Transfer |
|---|---|---|---|---|---|---|---|---|---|---|---|
| (1) | (2) | (3) | (4) | (5) | (6) | (7) | (8) | (9) | (10) | (11) | (12) |

Figure 7. Advertising Expenditures Report

changes made in these plans, with the present status of the appropriation as a result of these changes. Column (5) shows the cash disbursements which have been made. Columns (6) and (7) show the amounts which must yet be financed. Columns (8) to (10) inclusive show commitments which may or may not be subject to adjustment. Column (11) shows the amount available for new contracts or for transfer to other appropriations if this is found advisable.

The reports used in exercising control of the advertising, like all reports used in budgetary control, must be made promptly and accurately if they are to be of service. This necessitates that the accounting department must render reports immediately after the end of the month or other period used as a basis for control, and it must maintain accounts which will provide a proper distribution of the expenditures incurred under the advertising budget.

# CHAPTER IX

## THE PRODUCTION BUDGET

### Relation of Production Budget to Sales Budget

The sales program, as shown by the sales budget, contemplates the delivery of certain commodities or services to customers. To execute this program it is necessary that these commodities or services be produced by the firm which offers them for sale or that they be purchased from other firms. But these commodities or services must not be merely delivered; they must be delivered at the time and in the quantity demanded by customers. This necessitates the making of plans which schedule deliveries from the factory or the vendors in such a manner that sales demands may be met.

The execution of these plans requires the preparation of a production or purchasing budget, and the formulation of a production or purchasing program. The general principles involved in the control of the quantity of production and of purchases are very similar, but their application in the two cases are sufficiently different to make a separate treatment of the two problems desirable. It is the purpose of the present chapter to discuss the production budget. A later chapter will deal with the purchasing budget.

### Relation of Production Control to Production Policies

From the viewpoint of budgetary control, manufacturing industries may be divided broadly into two general classes:

> 1. Those which manufacture a standard commodity or commodities, and produce and place them in stock in anticipation of sales demands.

2. Those which produce goods in accordance with the customers' specifications, and hence cannot manufacture for stock but only in response to orders.

In the first case, it is necessary to plan production so as to have available the goods required when the sales order is received. In the second case, it is necessary to plan production so as to be able to produce the goods as quickly as possible after the order is secured. The preparation of a production budget for a manufacturing industry producing for stock, will be first explained. Such modifications as are necessary for a business producing on special order will then be stated.

## Adjusting Sales Plans with Production Capacity

It has been explained in the discussion of the preparation of the sales budget that the sales estimate, as submitted by the sales units, should be revised by the production department with reference to production possibilities. In making these revisions the production department should not only consider the possibility of producing the volume called for by the sales estimate, but also the possibility of producing this volume at an economical cost. The sales estimate may call for the production of some items in such small quantities that they cannot be produced economically, or it may call for such a volume of production of some items that it would be necessary to incur so great an amount of extra expense to produce the amount required that it would be unprofitable to do so.

It may also be that the sales estimate is such that it does not provide for a well-balanced production program. It may call for so many of some items and so few of others that the result would be the overloading of some departments or some machines, and a lack of work for other departments or other machines. The production department should have available data on production capacity which will indicate all this, so that it can suggest the necessary revisions in the sales estimate.

To be able to make these revisions it is necessary for the production department to have data of two kinds:

1. It must have an analysis of each of the products offered for sale which shows the manufacturing operations necessary in its production.
2. It must have a record of each of the machines operated by the company, showing the operations the machine performs and the number of operations it can perform in a specified time.

If these data are available it is possible to determine the volume of the operations required to produce the goods called for by the sales estimate and to balance this against the machine capacity of the plant.   Three situations may arise:

1. The sales budget may approximately equal the production capacity.   This is the desirable result.
2. The sales budget may exceed the production capacity, in which case one of three things must be done:
   (a) The sales budget may be reduced.
   (b) Additional equipment may be secured.
   (c) Some goods may be purchased from outside sources.
3. The sales budget may be less than the production capacity, in which case it may be desirable to attempt to increase the sales program so as to provide for a more desirable production program.   In some cases this may be impossible.   Under these conditions some machinery may be left idle until an increase in sales can be secured.   If it is evident that the decrease in sales is permanent, the production capacity may be reduced by the sale of the unnecessary equipment.

It is not an easy matter to coordinate sales possibilities with production capacity.   In fact it is one of the most difficult of administrative problems.   The need for this coordination is so great, however, that it is worth while to spend any amount of effort in order to secure it. The first step in the solution of the problem is the preparation of data to show what the possible sales are and what the available production capacity is.

In so far as possible, a manufacturing business should select its machinery and equipment so that it will be well-balanced and flexible, as this makes it possible to adapt production to variations in sales demands. There is a limit, however, to the extent to which machinery can be adapted to different uses, and there should be an attempt to harmonize the sales program with the factory possibilities. Often it is possible to shift the emphasis of the sales program by means of extra efforts on the part of the salesmen and by the nature of the advertising, and to increase the sales of the items which the factory is best adapted to produce.

### Determination of Production Requirements

If the production department makes a careful revision of the sales estimate, and if its recommendations are given proper consideration, the sales budget will represent factory requirements which are both possible and profitable. After the sales budget is adopted, the production department has an estimate of the requirements of the sales units during the next budget period. Presumably these requirements state the number of each item of goods manufactured by the company which must be provided to the selling units during the period. In order to translate these requirements of the sales units into an estimate of production for the period, it is necessary for the production department to take into consideration the inventory of finished goods at the beginning of the period and the estimated inventory of finished goods at the end of the period.

To illustrate: The ten sales units of the X Manufacturing Company estimate their requirements from the factory

for article Y for the next budget period to be 120. The
records of the factory show that the inventory of article Y
at the beginning of the budget period is 30, and it is estimated that an inventory of 20 at the end of the period will
be sufficient. The estimate of production on article Y for
the period will be $120+20-30=110$. Each item on the
sales budget must be considered in the same manner in order
to determine the estimate of production for the period.

### Relation of Inventory of Finished Goods to Estimate of Production

But the problem of the production department is not
merely to produce the quantity of goods that are to be sold
during the budget period. It must do more than that; it
must produce the goods in anticipation of sales orders and
place them in the finished storeroom so that customers may
be served promptly and according to the delivery dates
given in the sales contracts. An easy solution of this problem would be to manufacture before the beginning of the
budget period, or shortly thereafter, all the goods that are
to be sold during the period. For example, if the owners or
officers of an automobile factory estimate that they will sell
200 automobiles during the budget period, the production
manager may manufacture and place in the storeroom these
200 automobiles on or before the first day of the period.
Such a procedure is clearly impracticable except in rare
cases.

In the first place, the production manager must distribute his manufacturing processes throughout the year, so far
as this is practicable, in order that he may make the fullest
possible use of floor space in his factory and of machinery
and equipment, and, more important still, in order that he
may give employment continuously through the year to all
of his skilled employees and to as many of his unskilled em-

ployees as possible. From every standpoint it is clearly undesirable for the production manager to make up all the product in advance of the selling period and then shut down the factory for several weeks or months. To a less degree, it is undesirable for the production manager to operate his factory at 100 per cent capacity for eight months of the year and at 50 per cent capacity during the other four months. Under any system of finished stock control, there will be varying production requirements at different seasons of the year, but two very important considerations from the standpoint of the factory superintendent are: (a) that a sufficient amount of finished stock shall be on hand to meet sales orders, and (b) that this stock shall be constantly replenished from goods in process in the factory.

In the second place, it is clearly undesirable to manufacture goods in complete anticipation of the demands of the selling period, because of the large amount of capital required. If automobiles to the value of $500,000 are expected to be sold during the year 1922, it is clearly undesirable to have all these automobiles on the floor of the wareroom on December 31, 1921. The $500,000 invested should be at productive use, and it is an economic loss to maintain stocks of finished goods on hand for any longer period than is absolutely necessary to make reasonably sure of prompt shipment to customers.

From the foregoing discussion it can be seen that it is not enough to know the total amount to be produced during the budget period. It is necessary, in addition, to schedule production so that a sufficient amount of goods will be on hand at all times to meet sales demands and yet prevent an excess of inventory and the consequent loss on the capital invested. In order to accomplish this, it is necessary to set up a schedule for the inventory of finished goods and to set up a schedule of production which will maintain the in-

9

ventory schedule.   The ideal schedule would be one which delivered to stock each day the exact amount of goods which would be sold during the day.   If such a schedule could be maintained during 300 sales days of the year, the stock of goods in the finished goods storeroom would be turned over 300 times.   In such an ideal situation, $40,000 of stock might be delivered into the stockroom daily and be sold 300 times.   As will be seen readily, such a $40,000 stock so operated would satisfy the requirements of a sales volume of $12,000,000.

Unfortunately the daily sales are not uniform in amount and production is not sufficiently standardized to insure a uniform daily delivery to stock; consequently, for both these reasons it is impossible to deliver into stock each day the same amount of goods that is to be shipped to customers on that day.   It is, therefore, necessary to carry an inventory to provide for the lack of coordination of sales and production.   A most important problem of production control is to determine the desirable amount for this inventory and to plan production so as to maintain it at this amount.

The inventory of finished goods is not a fixed or uniform amount.   Since its purpose is to take up the slack between production and sales, this should be evident.   It is a constantly varying amount.   Because of its constant fluctuations, it is necessary that an effective control be exercised over it.   This control involves the following:

1.  The establishment of maximum and minimum limits, to serve as a check on its size.
2.  The establishment of adequate records and an adequate procedure to enforce these limits.

### "Maximum" and "Minimum" Limits as a Basis of Inventory Control

"Maximum" and "minimum" limits should be established for each item of finished goods carried in stock.   The "maximum" states the amount above which the inventory should never be permitted to go except by special permission of the executive officers; the "minimum" states the amount to which the stock of any item can be depleted before the placing of a production order to replenish it. When the sales orders reduce the stock to or below the minimum, a production order should be issued for the amount decided upon as the "quantity to order."

The production department should establish minima, quantities to order, and maxima, in accordance with the following principles:

1. There should be at all times sufficient stock on hand to satisfy customers' demands, if such demands are consistent with the capacity of the factory.
2. There should not be larger stocks on hand than can be turned over in a period necessary for the production of a similar quantity, unless such quantities do not constitute an economical run.
3. Goods should be produced in quantities large enough to insure economical production.

The following factors should be considered in establishing minima, quantities to order, and maxima:

1. Production period
2. Probable sales
3. Margin of safety
4. Economical run

## Production Period

The production period is the time required from the placing of an order until the finished goods are delivered to the storehouse. Obviously this period cannot be established exactly and will vary according to the quantity ordered, since it will take longer to produce 10,000 items than to produce 1,000 items. Sufficient data can be collected, however, to estimate the approximate length of this period for different quantities of production. In the absence of better statistics it may be necessary to use the average production period, as shown by the records of past production. Obviously investigation and study should be made to determine the desirability of this *average* period and changes made in the light of this investigation.

### Probable Sales

The probable sales for the budget period are stated in the sales estimate. By using the ratio of the average production period to the budget period, the probable sales for the production period can be determined. To illustrate, if the production period is thirty days and the quarterly sales estimate is 600 units of item Y, the probable sales for the production period are 200.

### Margin of Safety

Neither probable sales nor the length of the production period can be forecast with exactness. Consequently, if the minimum is established as the probable sales for the production period and a production order is issued when the minimum is reached, it will be only in rare cases that stocks on hand will be exactly depleted when the newly manufactured product arrives at the storehouse. Probable sales may be oversold; strikes, breakdowns, and delays in deliveries of raw material may interfere with the normal course of production. It becomes necessary, therefore, to have a quantity of finished goods on hand in excess of the probable sales for the production period at the time the production order is issued. This excess may be termed the "margin of safety."

The margin of safety is usually estimated at from 10 to 25 per cent of the probable sales for the production period. Its amount will vary in different businesses and may well vary with reference to different items in the same business. Whenever the inventory of any item falls below the margin of safety the production manager should be notified. He may find it necessary to resort to emergency measures to replenish the stock if there are indications that the margin of safety is not sufficient to supply the sales demand until additional stock is received from the factory. If a well-organized planning system is maintained, it will be possible to determine the length of time before additional goods will be received. It is, of course, not necessary to resort to emergency production or purchasing each time the inventory falls below the margin of safety. In fact, its purpose is to provide for just such cases. It is desirable, however, to call the attention of the production executive to the fact that the margin of safety is reached so that he may take action if he deems it necessary. Used in this manner, the limit set by the margin of safety serves as a danger signal.

## Economical Run

In determining the "economical run" it is necessary to determine the time necessary for "tearing down" and "setting up" the machines used in making each item. This involves the collection of data showing machine operations, so that the machines required in the production of each item can be determined and the cost involved in "setting up" these machines for the production of each item estimated. It is impossible to set an arbitrary standard for, or to determine with exactness just what constitutes, an economical run, but certain limits can be set up. The problem of determining what constitutes an economical run usually arises only in connection with slow-moving items, of which only a limited amount is sold during the production period. In the consideration of such items, it is necessary to offset the high unit cost of producing them in small quantities against the capital cost of carrying a large inventory.   Considerable judgment must be used and considerable research should be carried on in determining the most profitable procedure.   Such a study may often result in the elimination of some items from the manufacturing program.   It may be determined that it is cheaper to purchase the small amount needed from other manufacturers, or it may be decided to eliminate them from the sales program.   Whether they can be eliminated from the sales program will depend, of course, upon the effect of this elimination on the sale of other items.

### Method of Calculating "Maximum" and "Minimum"

As previously explained, the probable sales for the production period are the quantity expected to be turned over during that period.   The margin of safety is the amount which it is thought necessary to carry in addition to insure against contingencies.   Therefore, the quantity to which stocks can be depleted before a production order is started is the sum of the probable sales for the production period and the margin of safety.   This is the minimum.   Whenever stocks are depleted to this quantity, a production order is started.   The product specified on the order goes through the production process and arrives at the storeroom, ideally, when stocks have been reduced to the margin of safety.

Quantities to order must be established under two sets of conditions.   Each condition of facts will influence the quantity which is to be ordered.   These conditions and the procedure in each case are as follows:

1. Where the probable sales for the production period is less than the amount of the economical run, the latter amount becomes the quantity to order.
2. Where the amount of probable sales for the production period is equal to or greater than the amount of the economical run, the former amount becomes the quantity to order.

The maximum is the sum of the minimum and the quantity to order. It is the danger mark which must not be exceeded. In the case of many products the maxima will never be reached, since, during the time that goods are being produced, stocks on hand are being depleted by shipments on orders. From the foregoing it can be seen that the maximum is established by adding to the minimum the "normal" quantity to order, that is, the quantity to order in case the production order is issued when the stock on hand exactly equals the minimum. As a matter of practice, the production order is usually issued when the inventory is slightly below the minimum, since the sales order which reduces the inventory to the minimum will probably reduce it somewhat below. In some cases it is better for the production order to be made out for the difference between the actual inventory and the maximum, than to be made out for the difference between the minimum and the maximum. The reasons for this are apparent.

### Finished Goods Records

To enforce the requirements with reference to maxima, quantity to order, and minima, as outlined in the preceding paragraphs, it is necessary to maintain a finished goods record which provides a perpetual inventory of finished goods. The maximum, quantity to order, and minimum, as established for each item of finished stock, will be shown on the finished goods record. Usually this record is kept in what is termed a "balance of stores" form which is especially adapted for exercising effective inventory control. The form of a balance of stores record is illustrated in Chapter X.

It should be understood that it is not intended to lay down an arbitrary procedure in the foregoing discussion. The method of establishing maxima, minima, and quantities to order has been discussed somewhat in detail, and a definite procedure has been explained in order to indicate the problem involved in enforcing a production budget based on a sales budget.  Although the procedure outlined is typical of that which must be employed by any factory which produces for stock and which attempts to execute a production program in a systematic manner, variations of considerable consequence will of necessity be made in adapting this procedure to particular cases.

### Relation of Production Planning to the Production Budget

A balance of stores record properly operated results in the issuance of production orders with sufficient frequency to provide for the replenishment of stock in accordance with the finished goods schedule prepared under the production program.  But in order that these production orders may result in deliveries according to schedule, it is necessary that there exist an effective production control.  Such control usually necessitates the establishment of a systematic organization to carry on production planning.  This organization is usually called the planning department.  It is not possible or desirable to discuss here the organization and operation of a planning department.  This is a matter of production management.  It is important to keep in mind, however, that the planning function must be performed either by a separate organized department or by different individuals in different departments, if the production budget is to be translated into an effective production program.

### Relation of Production Costs to the Production Budget

The preceding discussion has treated primarily of the problem of producing the volume of finished goods called for by the production budget.  What constitutes finished stock in a particular business depends upon the character of the product offered for sale to customers of the business. The finished stock of the X Foundry Company becomes the raw material of the Modern School Desk Manufacturing Company. The lumber, as it comes from the mill of a lumber company, may be finished stock if the lumber company offers the green lumber for sale to its customers. Or sawed lumber may be seasoned and planed, and so made into finished lumber of the higher grades. Materials are either (a) raw materials; (b) goods in process; or (c) finished stock, depending upon the stage of their utility to the customers of the selling company.

For census purposes we may classify certain materials as "raw materials," or basic materials, but that classification does not hold in the reports of any particular company where the only test must be that finished stock is stock in the form demanded by customers.

The finished stock of a company may be produced in the factory of the company from raw materials; or it may be assembled and altered from parts in the alteration room of the company; or it may be purchased as finished stock. The present discussion is confined to a consideration of the finished stock of a manufacturing company which is produced in its factory. All such stock is produced by the employment of labor and equipment in the performance of certain operations upon raw materials by which they are transformed into the finished product.

Although it is not the function of the budgetary program to prescribe the method by which production is carried on, since this is the province of the planning department, it is necessary for effective production control that a budget be prepared for each of the elements of production cost—materials, labor, and overhead—to the end:

1. That the necessary amount of materials and labor will be available and excess amounts will be prevented.
2. That the cost of materials, labor, and overhead shall be under effective control.
3. That the cost of financing the production program may be determined for the purpose of the financial budget.

The preparation of the materials, labor, and manufacturing expense budgets will be discussed in the chapters immediately following the present one.

### Control of Production on Special Orders

Many manufacturing businesses receive some special orders for goods which they do not carry in stock but which they produce in response to the requests of customers. There are a few businesses which produce all their goods in accordance with the customers' specifications, and therefore produce only on special orders. A foundry is a good illustration of the latter class. In either case, the problem of production control is not greatly different from that of the business which manufactures for stock on standard orders.

In the case of a business which manufactures on both standard and special orders, it is necessary to determine what proportion of the orders received will be special orders. In making the sales estimate the special orders should be estimated separately, so that the production department can estimate the goods to be produced for stock and those to be produced to order. To make an accurate estimate of the probable special orders to be received, it is necessary to make a careful analysis of past sales to learn the trend of special orders by years and by territories. The effect of market conditions on the number of special orders received may also be useful. The policy to be followed in handling special orders—whether they are to be given the right of way or are only to take up unused time—will have a considerable bearing on the planning for their control.

Whether a business manufactures on standard or special orders, the first step in the planning of production control is the preparation of the estimate of production. The next step is to provide for the performance of this estimate. This involves the preparation of three supplementary estimates: the estimate of labor, the estimate of manufacturing expense, and the estimate of materials. When goods are produced for stock it is necessary to take into consideration the finished goods inventory requirement in determining the production requirements, while in the case of special orders the question of finished goods does not enter. It is necessary, however, to estimate carefully the quantity of production, so that the necessary labor and materials may be secured. It is usually urgent to produce the goods called for by special orders as quickly as possible, which makes it the more imperative that plans be made carefully, so that delays will not result from a lack of materials or labor.

It can be seen, therefore, that the preceding discussion, with the exception of that dealing with the control of finished stock, applies equally well to a manufacturing business producing for stock and to one producing on special orders.

## Preparation of Production Budget

As shown by the foregoing discussion, the production budget is the result of a coordination of the sales possibilities and the production capacity. Its preparation involves a procedure similar to the following:

I. PREPARATION OF SALES BUDGET:
1. Sales estimates are prepared by sales units.
2. These are revised by the general sales office.
3. They are then forwarded to the production department where a comparison is made between the requirements of sales estimates and the production capacity. If the production department thinks revisions are necessary these are shown on the sales estimates.

4. Estimates as approved by the production department are forwarded to the budget committee for final revision and approval. This committee will decide any differences which may exist between the programs of the sales and the production department.

II. PREPARATION OF FINISHED GOODS BUDGET:
   1. Estimate of finished goods requirements prepared from the sales budget by the production department.
   2. This estimate is forwarded to the budget committee for its consideration and approval.
   3. After the estimate of finished goods is approved by the budget committee, it is enforced by the production department by means of the balance of stores records operated under maximum and minimum standards.

It will be noticed that the "production budget" really resolves itself into a "finished goods" budget. In order to carry out this budget it is necessary to prepare supplementary budgets for materials, labor, and manufacturing expense.

It is usually necessary to have the production budget prepared in the office of the production manager. It is desirable to have the records of machine capacity centralized and these are often kept in the central office. In some cases these records are kept by the planning department, which may then perform the detail work involved in the preparation of the production budget, whereupon the budget will be carefully revised by the production manager before it is submitted to the budget committee.

## Control over Production Budget

To exercise control over the production budget and to make revisions when necessary, monthly reports are required which show a comparison between the estimated and the actual performance. These reports will vary somewhat, depending on the one for whose use the report is

## MONTHLY REPORT ON FINISHED STOCK BUDGET

| ITEMS | Estimated Sales for Month | Production Quota for Month | Actual Sales for Month | Revised Production Quota | Delivered to Stock during the Month | Balance in Quota Not Delivered or Excess of Amount Delivered over Quota | Orders Outstanding under Quota Not Delivered | Balance in Quota Not ordered or Excess or Ordered over Quota |
|---|---|---|---|---|---|---|---|---|
| (1) | (2) | (3) | (4) | (5) | (6) | (7) | (8) | (9) |
| | | | | | | | | |
| | | | | | | | | |

Figure 8. Monthly Finished Stock Budget Report

intended.   The balance of stores records are intended to
enforce automatically the production budget; but no
matter how carefully these records are operated, errors will
occur which will make them fail to accomplish this purpose
perfectly.   When these errors occur, they ought to be
detected as quickly as possible and measures taken to
remedy them.

For the use of the general officers a finished stock
budget report made in the form shown in Figure 8 is very
serviceable.

This report serves to show to what extent coordination
between sales and production is being achieved.   If the
commodities sold by the company are not too numerous,
each commodity should be shown on this report.   Where
the commodities are very numerous, it will be necessary to
show them on this report by groups or classes.   In this case
judgment must be used in interpreting the report, for it is
obvious that there might be very close coordination between the sales and production of a group and yet there
might be items in the group on which large inventories
existed and other items for which unfilled orders were on
hand.

The amount shown in column (2) in Figure 8 is taken
from the last revision of the sales estimate.   Column (3)
shows the estimated quota for finished goods based on the
estimated sales shown in column (2).   Column (4) shows
the actual sales for the month, and column (5) shows the
revised finished goods quota, the revision being based on the
actual sales as shown in column (4).   Column (6) shows
the actual deliveries to stock of finished goods.   Columns
(2) and (4) provide a comparison of estimated and actual
production for the month.   Columns (5) and (6) provide a
comparison between the actual production and the revised
production quota.   A comparison of columns (3), (5), and

(6) will show two things: (a) by how much the original estimate of production was incorrect; and (b) how much the actual production varied from the estimated. The information shown in column (4) is taken from the sales records for the month, and the information shown in column (6) is taken from the balance of stores records. Column (7) shows the difference between columns (5) and (6). Column (8) shows the manufacturing orders outstanding in the factory at the end of the month. These orders should be shown by the records of the planning department and also on the balance of stores records. Column (9) shows the amount to which the production budget for the next month should be revised.

If a monthly quota system is maintained on stock deliveries, the unfilled orders at the end of the month as shown by this report furnish valuable data for use in production control. It is possible that a large amount of unfilled orders represents poor production management. In some cases these unfilled orders may be due to traffic mismanagement, to poor warehouse control and operation, to general trade depression, or to strikes and similar causes. In each case the data given in the report as to outstanding unfilled orders presents material for executive judgment, executive orders, and executive discipline and control. Such a budget and reporting system makes use of sales, inventory, and production accounts as a basis for future plans. The reports under such a system offer comparisons between estimated sales and estimated production, and actual sales and actual production. Such reporting makes constant use of accounts, and the requirements of the reports to be made determine what grouping of sales accounts should be followed. Similarly, reporting requirements indicate the analysis to be followed in classifying inventory accounts and cost sheets.

### Significance of Finished Stock Budget Report

Every functional officer of a factory has his own particular interest in the showing made in the monthly report of
delivered and undelivered orders under the monthly quota.
The officer in charge of the employment of labor studies the
outstanding orders and quota balances with reference to
labor that may be needed in meeting rush deliveries into
stock. The traffic manager is vitally interested in outstanding orders, since the amount for a given item may or
may not indicate the necessity for action as to terminal
facilities, warehousing, reloading, and the like. The advertising manager notes with concern the balances in quotas
for which orders have not been placed, since such balances
may indicate a departure from advertised promises of service. Or the monthly report may show production in
excess of quotas and may indicate to the sales manager
the necessity for extra efforts to move the surplus inventory. Of course, the treasurer is interested in the amount
of outstanding orders and the problem of financing their
production.

The monthly report discussed in the foregoing paragraphs
furnishes the basis for immediate management decisions.
It also provides a progressive month-by-month commentary
on the accuracy of the estimating and planning in the business. Such monthly reports reveal errors in business judgment and make for better estimating for the next budget
period.

# CHAPTER X

## THE MATERIALS BUDGET

### Need for Estimate of Materials

After the finished goods which are to be produced during the budget period are determined by means of the production budget, it is necessary to estimate the materials which are necessary to produce these goods. This estimate is necessary:

1. That the purchasing department may make plans by which to secure the necessary materials by the time they are needed in production.
2. That the treasurer may know the probable disbursements required by the purchasing program and can plan to obtain the funds necessary to meet these disbursements.
3. That the budget committee may be able to see the financial requirements of the proposed sales and production programs at the time they are submitted to it for consideration. It will be shown in a later chapter that all the departmental budgets are used as a basis for the preparation of a financial budget, which the budget committee uses as a means of judging the desirability of the proposed budgets. The materials budget usually gives rise to one of the largest of the disbursement items on the financial budget. Its use is therefore essential to the preparation of the financial budget.
4. The materials budget is also necessary for the preparation of the estimated balance sheet and estimated statement of profit and loss, which are discussed in Chapters XXI and XXII.

### Determination of Material Requirements—By Commodities

In the same manner in which the production department maintains an analysis of each of its products to show the manufacturing operations required in its production, it should maintain an analysis which will show the materials required in the production of each commodity.  By the use of this analysis it is possible to estimate, on the basis of the production budget, the materials which will be required to produce the goods called for by the production program. The preferable way of making this estimate is to take each item on the finished goods or production budget, and to determine the amount of each kind of material which will be required to produce it.  To illustrate, the production budget calls for the manufacture of 1,000 cast iron valves of X size. The product analysis shows that it takes 4 pounds of pig iron to produce this valve.  Consequently it will be necessary to purchase 4,000 pounds of pig iron to make possible the production of the 1,000 valves.  If each item on the production budget which requires the use of pig iron is considered in this manner, the total purchases of pig iron can be determined.  In the same manner each item on the production budget will be considered to determine the amount of materials of each kind that is necessary for its production.

It is easy to see that this method of determining the material requirements may in some circumstances be quite difficult.  In the first place, there may be so many commodities produced and so many different kinds of materials may enter into each that it may require an immense amount of clerical work to determine the material requirements for each commodity.  Again, there may be a considerable variation between the quantity of raw material required in the production of a commodity and the quantity of material which is in the finished product.  This is due to shrinkage and waste, which are usually unavoidable.  If this shrinkage and waste are fairly uniform, as they should be under normal conditions, it is possible to estimate them fairly accurately, but in some cases it is difficult to estimate their amount with any accuracy.

## By Ratios of Former Periods

In some cases, instead of estimating the material requirements for each commodity produced, it is expedient, in order to obtain the probable material requirements for the period, to find the ratio between the production volume for several periods and the volume of materials of each kind required for this production, and apply these ratios to the production budget of the current period.   These estimates will be more accurate if separate ratios are determined for different classes of product manufactured.   The reason for this is apparent, for different quantities of raw material will be required for different classes of finished product and the ratio between the different classes is apt not to remain the same during different periods.

To take a simple illustration, the M Manufacturing Company produces 10,000 different articles which can be grouped into three principal classes, known as Class A, Class B, and Class C.   The articles in each class are composed of the same materials but vary as to size and design. The three principal raw materials used in the manufacture of the three classes are the commodities X, Y, and Z.   Each of these commodities is used in the manufacture of each class, but in varying degrees.   Commodity X is used principally in the production of Class A, commodity Y principally in the production of Class B, and commodity Z principally in the production of Class C.   It may be assumed that in terms of pounds the ratios are as follows:

      Class A—Commodity X 60%, Y 20%, Z 10%
      Class B—Commodity X 10%, Y 60%, Z 20%
      Class C—Commodity X 20%, Y 10%, Z 60%

The remaining 10 per cent in each case is composed of miscellaneous materials.

If the ratio between the tonnage of the three classes

fluctuates from period to period, it can be readily seen that the quantity of X, Y, and Z required in production would fluctuate accordingly.   For instance, if it is determined that it is desirable to increase the production of A 20 per cent and to decrease the production of C a like amount, the effect on the requirements for each of the commodities X, Y, and Z is apparent.   There are few businesses producing several different articles in which the ratio between the volume of these articles produced each year does not vary materially. The foregoing illustration serves to show that if such variations exist, inaccuracies will result from estimating the material requirements by the use of the ratio of materials to total production.

### Standard Material Rates as an Aid

During recent years accountants and industrial engineers have given much attention to the development of standards by which to judge production.   The principal emphasis has been placed on standard rates for manufacturing expenses, but there has been some consideration given to the development of standard rates of material and labor.   There seems to be no good reason why standard material rates should not be developed.   If these are set up they will serve at least three useful purposes:

1. They can be used in the estimating of costs and the establishment of prices on contracts.
2. They will serve as a means of judging the efficiency of the manufacturing operations and will assist in the elimination of waste due to errors or improper use of material.   By comparing the material used with the standard, it will be possible to locate the excessive use of material.
3. They will be of important service in estimating material requirements and in preparing a purchasing program.

Where standard rates of material to be used in the manufacture of each product are established, the task of preparing the materials budget is greatly lessened. It is only necessary to multiply the standard rate of material set on each commodity by the number of units of that commodity which is to be produced, to determine the material requirements.

### Relation of Materials Requirements to Materials Inventory

By means of one of the methods explained in the foregoing discussion it is possible to estimate the materials required to satisfy the production program. To translate the requirements of the production program into an estimate of materials which will serve as a basis for the materials budget, it is necessary to take into consideration the inventory of materials at the beginning of the period and the estimated inventory of materials at the end of the period.

To illustrate: The production budget calls for the manufacture of 1,000 articles X, and it is estimated that it will take 4,000 pounds of commodity Y to produce these. The records of the factory show that the inventory of commodity Y at the beginning of the budget period is 1,300 pounds, and it is estimated that an inventory of 1,200 pounds at the end of the period will be sufficient. The estimate of materials on commodity Y for the period will be 4,000 lbs. + 1,200 lbs. − 1,300 lbs. = 3,900 lbs. Each commodity which is to appear on the materials budget must be treated in this manner if an accurate estimate is to be prepared.

But the problem of the purchasing department is not merely to purchase the quantity of materials that are to be used in production during the budget period. It must do more than that; it must purchase the materials in anticipation of factory requisitions and place them in the storeroom so that the needs of the factory may be served promptly. An easy solution of this problem would be to purchase before the beginning of the budget period, or shortly thereafter, all the materials required during the period. For example, if the officers of a foundry estimate that 100 tons of pig iron will be required during the budget period, the purchasing agent may purchase and have on hand the 100 tons on or before the first day of the period. Such a procedure is clearly impracticable except in rare cases.

In the first place, it is clearly undesirable to purchase materials in complete anticipation of production requirements because of the large amount of capital required. If this procedure is followed, a large part of the capital invested in the materials is tied up for a considerable period of time before the materials are needed. It usually is desirable not to maintain stocks of materials on hand for any longer period of time than is necessary to make reasonably sure of the prompt satisfaction of factory requisitions. There are of course circumstances which make another procedure desirable, and these are discussed later in this chapter.

In the second place, it is usually not profitable to maintain storehouses of sufficient capacity to provide space for an inventory of raw materials in excess of that needed to meet the current demands of the production program. The space required for such storerooms is usually costly and the labor required to care for them is an additional expense. Again, if the material is subject to deterioration or obsolescence, it may decrease in value during the time it is left in the storeroom. Insurance and taxes may also be increased because of its possession.

From the foregoing it can be seen that it is the problem of the purchasing department to schedule deliveries of materials so that a sufficient amount of materials will be on hand at all times to meet the production needs and yet not be excessive with the consequent loss arising from such excess. To accomplish this it is necessary to set up a schedule for the inventory of materials to be maintained and one for deliveries which will maintain the inventory schedule. The ideal schedule would be one which delivered to stock each day the exact amount of goods which would be sold during the day. If such a schedule could be maintained during 300 production days of a year, the materials stock would be turned over 300 times.

Unfortunately the daily factory requisitions are not uniform in amount, and purchase deliveries cannot be enforced with sufficient exactness to insure a uniform daily delivery to stock; consequently it is impossible to deliver into stock each day the amount of materials that is to be requisitioned by the factory on that day. It is necessary, therefore, to carry an inventory to provide for the lack of coordination of purchase deliveries and production requirements. It is the problem of the purchasing department, acting in cooperation with the production department, to determine the desirable amount for this inventory and to plan a purchasing program that will maintain it at this amount.

The inventory of materials is not a fixed or uniform amount. Since its purpose is to take up the slack between purchase deliveries and production requirements, it should be evident that it is a constantly varying amount. Because of its constant fluctuations, it is necessary that an effective control be exercised over it. This control involves the following:

1. The establishment of maximum and minimum limits, to serve as a check on its size.
2. The establishment of adequate records and an adequate procedure to enforce these limits.

## Maximum and Minimum Limits as a Basis of Inventory Control

Maximum, minimum, and quantities to order are used in the same manner in the control of raw materials as they are used in the control of finished goods.  The factors which must be considered in the establishment of these quantities for materials are somewhat different in terminology from those which determine the same quantities for finished goods, but they are very similar in nature.  Instead of considering the production period, it is necessary to consider the purchasing period, or the length of time between the sending of the purchase order and the receipt of the goods. Instead of considering probable sales, it is necessary to consider the probable factory requisitions for materials.  Instead of considering the economical run, it is necessary to consider the economical quantity to purchase with reference to terms, price, and deliveries.

The method by which these facts must be considered in establishing control of raw materials should be apparent after the rather extensive explanation of the control of finished goods which has been given in the preceding chapter.

### Record of Materials

To enforce the requirements with reference to maximum, quantity to order, and minimum, it is necessary to maintain a materials record which provides a perpetual inventory of raw materials.  The maximum, quantity to order, and minimum, as established for each item of materials, will be shown on the materials record.  Usually this record is kept on what is termed a "balance of stores form," which is especially adapted for exercising effective inventory control.

There are many variations in the form of the balance of stores record.  A typical form is shown in Figure 9.

To illustrate the use of this type of balance of stores, the entries appearing thereon will be explained.  Suppose that on the day the balance of stores record is opened, April 1, a physical inventory shows that there are 12,500 pieces in the stockhouse bin.  This quantity is entered in the balance

## BALANCE OF STORES SHEET

| ORDERED Date | ORDERED Quantity | ORDERED Ord. No. | RECEIVED Quantity | RECEIVED Price | ISSUED Quantity | ISSUED Ord. No. | Date | Balance | APPLIED Quantity | APPLIED Ord. No. | Available or Shortage |
|---|---|---|---|---|---|---|---|---|---|---|---|
| 4–1 | | | | | | | | | | | |
| 4–1 | 10,000 | 672 | | | | | 4–5 | 12,500 | | | 12,500 |
| | | | | | 4,000 | E 6784 | 4–10 | 8,500 | 4,000 | E 6784 | 8,500 |
| | | | | | | | 4–15 | | 1,000 | W 8270 | 7,500 |
| | | | | | | | 4–20 | | 4,000 | N 9274 | 3,500 |
| | | | | | 1,000 | W 8270 | 4–25 | 7,500 | | | |
| | | | | | 4,000 | N 9274 | 4–28 | 3,500 | | | |
| | | | | | | | 4–30 | | 1,000 | S 4620 | 2,500 |
| 5–2 | 10,000 | 672 1004 | 10,000 | | 1,000 | S 4620 | 5–1 | 13,500 | 1,000 | S 4620 | 12,500 |
| | | | | | | | 5–2 | 12,500 | | | |
| | | Car. Fwd. | | | | | | | | | |

| MIN. STOCK 12,500 | MAX. STOCK 22,500 | QUAN. TO ORDER 10,000 | UNIT WT. 5 | No. OF PIECES SOLD 1920, 125,000 / 1921, 130,000 / 1922, 12,000 |
|---|---|---|---|---|
| | ITEM 1 INCH CAST IRON ELBOW, BEADED | | | GROUP 101 |
| | | | | COMMODITY NO. 101006 |

Figure 9. Balance of Stores Sheet

column. This column shows at all times the amount on hand. After looking through the files of factory requisitions it is found that all requisitions for this particular commodity have been filled so that the quantity of 12,500 is available for use. This quantity would be entered, therefore, in the Available or Shortage column. An examination of the purchase order files shows that there is outstanding a purchase order for 10,000 pieces of this commodity, this amount being the Quantity to Order. The 10,000 on order is entered in the ordered column. The record is now ready for the receipt of the current entries.

On April 5 a factory requisition, No. E 6784, is received for 4,000 pieces. The number 4,000 is entered in the Applied column and substracted from the amount in the Available or Shortage column, thereby reducing the balance in this column to 8,500. On April 10 the quantity specified on requisition E 6784 is delivered to the factory and an entry is made in the Issued column, reducing the Balance column to 8,500. The other entries for requisitions received, balance on hand, and quantities delivered to factory, are similar to the ones described above. On May 1, 10,000 pieces of stock are received from the vendors to whom purchase orders have previously been issued. This quantity is entered in the Received column and added to the quantity in the Balance column and the Available or Shortage column.

The value of the Applied column lies in the fact that it makes possible the reserving of materials for use on an order though it may not be desirable to requisition them from stock at once. In a factory operated under a proper planning system, a "bill of materials" showing the materials required for the entire order is prepared for each production order issued. On the basis of this bill of materials entries are made on the materials balance of stores reserving the materials needed for the order. Some of these materials may not be taken out of stock for several days, but it is desirable that they be reserved so that there will be no danger that the order may be delayed because of the lack of materials. If this method is not followed, materials may be on hand when the order is issued but before the materials are requisitioned from stock they may have been used on another order.

### Relation of Purchasing Policies to Materials Budget

In the preceding discussion it has been assumed that the materials budget is based on the production requirements and that the purchases will be scheduled to correspond with the production schedule. The only deviation from this assumption which has been recognized in the foregoing discussion, is that in establishing quantities to order care must be taken to see that the quantities stated are sufficient to constitute economical purchases. In determining what constitutes an economical purchase it is necessary to consider (1) the possibility of getting lower prices or better terms by making larger purchases, and (2) the possibility of saving in freight costs by purchasing in large lots instead of small ones. In each case it is necessary to balance the savings which may be made by purchasing in large quantities against (1) the loss incurred by tying up capital in excess inventories, (2) the possible loss due to deterioration or decrease in price of the inventory, and (3) the possible financial embarrassment which may result from having capital invested in inventory which cannot be quickly realized.

There are many factors which may affect the purchasing policy of a firm, and there are some of these which are opposed to the control of purchases by budget. For instance, some firms think it is a function of the purchasing department to speculate on market changes and tendencies. In these firms, during periods of rising prices, large quantities of materials will be purchased and deliveries scheduled far in excess of production demands. It is undoubtedly true that under these circumstances a firm may make large savings by placing large orders while the prices are increasing. It obtains materials for future use at a lower price than it could obtain them if it waited to purchase them when needed. It is also more assured of their delivery than if it waited until their purchase is indicated by the materials budget.

This policy is apt to prove a dangerous one if careful control is not exercised. If the purchasing department is once given the opportunity to purchase in large quantities, unrestrained by the limitations of present requirements as shown by the materials budget, it is apt to make the most of its opportunity and continue the policy of quantity buying as long as prices continue to rise. When the turn in prices comes, the firm is apt to find itself burdened with an inventory far beyond its needs, with large deliveries scheduled to be made for several months, all of which has been purchased at the peak of prices. In many cases, even if the firm escapes serious financial embarrassment it loses more on its high-priced inventories than it gained from the quantity buying during the period of rising prices.

A falling price level often has the opposite effect on the purchasing policy of many firms. The possibility of buying materials in the near future at reduced prices and the ease with which goods can be procured tend toward "hand-to-mouth" buying. It is very desirable to exercise caution during a period of declining prices, but the purchasing policy may be so conservative that it will result in a decided loss. Parsimonious buying may result in unbalanced inventories and make it impossible to give proper service to customers, with the consequent loss of trade. Small purchases may also result in higher prices and freight rates.

It is the author's opinion that the purchasing department is not equipped to speculate and that it is not its function to attempt to do so. We have not yet developed methods of forecasting with sufficient accuracy to make it possible to speculate on market trends without the incurring of great risk. As Mr. Arthur E. Swanson very well says in the November, 1921 *Administration:* "The difficulty which even very experienced and well-trained business men encounter in predicting even approximately the trend of price levels and business activity, has caused many to follow a sort of straddling policy in reference to economic trends. They do not buy very far in advance when the level appears to be on a long upward swing, or very close when the level appears to be on a downward swing. They are satisfied with an average buy."

Whatever may be the purchasing policy of a firm, it is the function of the materials budget to show the materials required by the production program, and to show a schedule of deliveries which will meet the needs of this program. If the management desires to disregard the purchasing program shown by the budget in order to carry into effect purchasing policies which it has adopted, that is its privilege. It is the opinion of the author that it is only in exceptional cases that it is wise for it to do so.

### The "Stores" Budget

The purchasing department purchases not only the materials which become a part of the manufactured product, but also numerous "supplies" which are used in carrying on the manufacturing operations. It also purchases the supplies used by all the operating departments. Under a well-developed system of inventory control it is customary to term as "stores" all the materials purchased for all purposes and to place them in a storeroom from whence they are requisitioned for use. When the requisitions are issued it is indicated whether the stores for which they call are to be charged as "materials" or as "supplies."

Because of this method of handling materials and supplies, it is the practice of some firms to prepare a *stores* budget which takes the place of the materials budget. The stores budget includes the estimated purchases for both materials and supplies. It is claimed that it is easier for the purchasing agent to make a stores budget than it is to estimate separately the materials and supplies. It is also claimed that it is easier to compare the estimated with the actual performance if the materials and supplies are shown in one budget. This contention is based on the fact that both the materials and supplies are charged to a Stores account when purchased and are not distributed as between materials, manufacturing expense (manufacturing supplies are charged to manufacturing expense when consumed) and departmental expenses, until they are requisitioned from the storeroom for use. Consequently the stores accounts give a ready means of checking the estimate of purchases, while the materials and manufacturing expense accounts do not, since purchases do not correspond with consumption during any specific period.

There is considerable merit in these contentions, and the author has found it advisable in some cases to prepare two budgets, the first based on purchases and the second on consumption. The consumption budget is essential if standard costs are to be established for material, labor, and manufacturing expense, and it is the belief of the author that such standards are essential for effective production control.

### Preparation of Materials Budget

After the production budget is prepared, the production department can prepare an estimate of the materials required to produce the goods called for by this budget. If a well-developed planning department is in operation, it will have available data which will make it possible to prepare this estimate without difficulty. In such cases it is customary to delegate the preparation of the materials estimate to the planning department. After its preparation, the materials estimate is carefully examined by the production manager and his staff. If there is not a planning department in operation, the estimate of materials requirements will be prepared by the staff of the production manager. After the estimate of materials has been approved by the production manager it will be transmitted to the purchasing department, which will make an estimate of the purchases which must be made to meet the estimate of materials.

The foregoing procedure is not always followed. In some businesses the production budget is sent to the purchasing department, and it is required to estimate both the materials required and the purchases which are necessary to meet these requirements. It is the author's opinion that the estimate of materials can best be made by the production department, since it usually has available the information which is necessary for its preparation, or if it does not, it can obtain the information easily. It should be evident that if the production department, through the planning department or otherwise, prepares bills of material for production orders, it must have available data from which it can estimate material requirements. If the purchasing department collects the data necessary to make this estimate, it will usually lead to a duplication of data, the same information being collected and recorded by both the production and the purchasing departments.

In other businesses the production department prepares both the estimate of materials and the estimate of purchases. This procedure leads to equally undesirable results.

The purchasing department must have available for its own use the data necessary for the preparation of the estimate of purchases; and if this task is undertaken by the production department, it will be necessary for it to collect duplicate data which it is not as well qualified to interpret and use as is the purchasing department. Furthermore, the purchasing department may rightly resent what it regards as an undue usurpation of its functions. One of its primary functions is to collect data and formulate a purchasing program which will meet the needs of all the departments and result in the most profit to the company. If the production department prepares the estimate of materials which usually constitutes the major part of the purchases made, it is depriving the purchasing department of its initiative and judgment.

### Materials Budget Form

As in the case of all other forms used in budgetary control, it is not feasible to prescribe a form for the materials budget which will satisfy all conditions. The author has found the form shown in Figure 10 serviceable in most cases. The illustration is designed for use when the budget period is three months in length. If the period is for a longer period of time, further columns may be added.

In most cases the materials budget will need to be prepared prior to the beginning of the budget period; therefore, all the information shown on the budget report, including the beginning inventory, must be estimated. The estimated beginning inventory can be obtained from the budget report of the previous period, since the ending inventory of one period will be the beginning inventory of the next period. The estimated purchases will be based on the estimate of materials submitted by the production department, with such modifications as the purchasing department may think

| ITEMS | FIRST MONTH | | | | | SECOND MONTH | | | | | THIRD MONTH | | | | |
|---|---|---|---|---|---|---|---|---|---|---|---|---|---|---|---|
| | Inventory Beginning | Estimated Purchases | Estimated Inventory at End | Estimated Disbursements for Purchases of Previous Month | Estimated Disbursements for Purchases of Current Month | Inventory Beginning | Estimated Purchases | Estimated Inventory at End | Estimated Disbursements for Purchases of Previous Month | Estimated Disbursements for Purchases of Current Month | Inventory Beginning | Estimated Purchases | Estimated Inventory at End | Estimated Disbursements for Purchases of Previous Month | Estimated Disbursements for Purchases of Current Month |
| | | | | | | | | | | | | | | | |

Figure 10. Materials Budget

PERIODIC REPORT ON MATERIALS BUDGET

| ITEMS | Estimated Purchases | Actual Purchases | Per Cent of Increase or Decrease | Estimated Inventory | Actual Inventory | Per Cent of Increase or Decrease | COMMENTS |
|---|---|---|---|---|---|---|---|
| | | | | | | | |

Figure 11. Periodic Materials Budget Report

11

necessary. For instance, the purchasing department may purchase more during the month than called for by the materials estimate because the latter amount may not constitute an economical purchase. The estimated inventory at the end of the month is obtained by adding the estimated purchases to the beginning inventory, and substracting the estimated consumption of materials as shown by the estimate of materials submitted by the production department. If the quantity of purchases and the quantity of materials consumed are the same, the beginning and ending inventories will be the same. A comparison of the beginning and ending inventories is of significance to the budget committee, since in case of an increase in inventory the purchasing department may be asked to explain the cause.

The estimated disbursements for purchases of previous months can be obtained from the unpaid invoice file. The accounts payable section of the accounting department may be asked to supply this information, since this section maintains the unpaid invoice file. The estimated disbursement for purchases of the current month will be determined by estimating the time of delivery of the purchases and allowing for the usual discount period. It can be readily seen that the information shown in this column can be only approximately correct, but this does not destroy its usefulness, since the purpose of showing the estimated disbursements on the materials budget is only to indicate, in a convenient form for the use of the treasurer and the budget committee, the probable financial requirements of the contemplated purchasing program. As will be explained in the discussion of the financial budget, these estimates will be checked and revised, if necessary, by the executive in charge of the budgetary procedure and the treasurer in the preparation of the monthly estimates of cash receipts and disbursements.

After the estimate of material purchases is prepared by the purchasing department, it is forwarded to the executive in charge of the budget procedure and is transferred by him to the budget committee, together with the other departmental estimates and the estimates of cash receipts and disbursements which are prepared from the departmental estimates. After the estimate of materials is approved by the budget committee, it is transferred by the executive in charge of the budget committee to the purchasing department, whose working program it constitutes for the budget period, subject, however, to monthly revisions which may be made by the budget committee.

## Control of Materials Budget

The materials budget, like all other budgets, must be checked up at frequent intervals in order that errors in the original budget may be detected and corrections made as quickly as possible. To make this possible it is necessary to have a monthly report which will provide comparisons between the estimated and the actual purchases. The report illustrated in Figure 11 will serve this purpose.

The purpose and value of the information shown in each column of this report should be evident. The executives should study this report in the light of the production for the month compared with the estimated production. They should also give consideration to the comments shown in column (8), since there may be special considerations which have brought about a deviation from the materials budget. Such deviations should be made as a general rule, however, only in response to executive direction or permission. This report will be submitted to the executive in charge of the budget procedure, and will be transferred by him to the budget committee with such recommendations as he may think desirable. By a study of this report the budget committee will be able to make such revisions as are necessary in the materials budget for the remainder of the budget period.   These revisions will be communicated to the purchasing department by the executive in charge of the budget procedure.

It is evident that the budget committee and the treasurer will want, in addition to the report shown in Figure 11, a report which will show the disbursements for material purchases during the month compared with the estimated disbursements for the month.

# CHAPTER XI

## THE LABOR BUDGET

### Need for Estimate of Labor

After the finished goods which are to be produced during the budget period are determined by means of the production budget, it is necessary to estimate the labor required to produce these goods. This estimate is necessary in order:

1. That the personnel department may make plans to have available the necessary workmen at the time they are needed in production.
2. That the treasurer may know the probable disbursements required by the labor program and can make plans to obtain funds for these disbursements.
3. That the budget committee may be able to see the financial requirements of the proposed sales and production programs at the time they are submitted to it for consideration. The labor budget must be combined with the selling expense budget, the materials budget, and the other budgets requiring disbursement of funds, in order to show the total disbursements of the budget period, before the budget committee or the board of directors can judge the advisability of undertaking the financial obligations imposed by the proposed budget program.
4. The estimate of labor is also required in preparing the "general budget" or estimated balance sheet and statement of profit and loss.

It is particularly important that the personnel department have information with reference to the labor requirements considerably in advance of the time when it is necessary for these requirements to be satisfied. To obtain an efficient working force is not an easy task, and capable workmen cannot be secured by issuing a purchasing order as can materials. If skilled laborers are required, the task of supplying them is usually not an easy one. In many cases they must be trained before their services can be used effectively. A well-organized personnel department will gather information of its own accord, which will afford it an approximate estimate of the labor requirements, but it does not have an approved program on which to work until it receives the labor budget.

### Determining Labor Requirements by Analysis of Each Product

In the same manner in which the production department maintains an analysis of each of its products to show the manufacturing operations and materials required in its production, it should maintain an analysis which will show the labor required in the production of each commodity. If a planning department is in operation this analysis will probably be maintained by this department, for the analysis is necessary for its use in preparing time tickets for distribution to the different departments when production orders are being scheduled. If this information is not available in the planning department, it may be available in the estimating department, the pay-roll department, or the personnel department. If none of these departments have such records, it is necessary that the records be prepared by the staff of the production manager.

By the use of this analysis it is possible to estimate, on the basis of the production budget, the labor which will be required to produce the goods called for by the production program. The preferable way of making this estimate is to take each item on the finished goods or production budget and determine the amount of labor of each kind which will be required to produce it. To illustrate: The production budget calls for the manufacture of 1,000 units of articles X of Y size. The product analysis shows that article X passes through four processes. Process A requires four hours of labor, process B two hours, process C three hours, and process D five hours. It takes, therefore, a total of fourteen hours to produce one unit of article X. If 1,000 are to be produced it will take a total of 14,000 hours. It is, of course, probable that the labor used in the different processes will not be of the same grade, in which case the total labor required for each process will need to be estimated separately. If each item on the production budget is considered in this manner, it will be possible to determine the total labor requirements of the production program.

## Other Methods of Estimating Labor Requirements

It is easy to see that this method of determining the labor requirements may in some circumstances be quite difficult. There may be so many commodities produced and so many different kinds of labor may enter into each, that it may require an immense amount of clerical work to determine the labor requirements of each commodity.

In some cases it is thought expedient to use the budget of machine capacity, discussed in connection with the production budget, as a basis for estimating labor requirements. The number of "machine hours" required by the production budget having been obtained, an estimate is then made of the workmen who will be required to operate these machines. In other cases it has been found expedient to obtain the ratio between the production volume for several periods and the volume of labor of each kind required for this production, and apply these ratios to the production budget of the current period to obtain the probable labor requirements. These estimates will be more accurate if separate ratios are determined for the different classes of product manufactured. The reason for this is apparent, for different quantities of labor will be required for different classes of finished product, and the ratio between the different classes is apt to vary from period to period.

The illustration given on page 161 in connection with the discussion of the method of estimating material requirements is equally applicable to the determination of labor requirements.

In some businesses the estimate of labor requirements is made by determining the labor cost per unit of production for several periods, and then applying this unit cost to the estimate of production for the current period. For instance, it may be determined that the average labor cost as shown by the records for several periods is $30 a ton. The estimate of production calls for the manufacture of 1,000 tons; therefore the estimate of labor is $30,000. If the unit cost is determined carefully and is calculated separately on each product, an estimate made in this manner may serve satisfactorily for purposes of financial control; but it does not provide satisfactory information for the use of the personnel department. In a business where the volume of production is fairly uniform and the working force stable, it is not so important that the personnel department receive a report showing labor in terms of hours. It must always be remembered that the cost of obtaining information must be balanced against its value. Budgetary control is no exception to the general rule that profit and loss is the ultimate test of the merit of any method of administrative control.

## Use of Standard Labor Rates

Some of the most valuable work of industrial engineers has been in the establishment of standards by which to judge labor. The first work performed by the exponents of "scientific management" was the establishment of standard time limits for the performance of tasks. These rates were first established in connection with factory labor and were used to speed up production. There seems to be no good reason why such standard rates with proper modifications might not be applied to all departments of a business and used very extensively in the enforcement of administrative control. It is interesting to note that a large manufacturing firm in the East is now scheduling very definitely its salesmen and making a careful study of how each employs his time with the intention of developing standards by which to judge salesmen's activities.

Standard labor rates serve three useful purposes:

1. They can be used in the estimating of costs and in the establishment of prices on special orders and contracts.
2. They serve as a means of judging the efficiency of workmen. If the rates are fair and equitable, a workman's efficiency can be judged by his ability to reach the standard. In many cases his wages are based on the standard, so that he has an incentive to reach or exceed the standard if possible.
3. They give important service in estimating labor requirements and in formulating a labor program.

Where standard rates of labor to be used in the manufacture of each product are established, the task of preparing the labor budget is greatly lessened. It must be remembered, however, that varying conditions may make the actual labor cost more or less than the standard, and it is the actual as near as it can be estimated which is necessary for budgetary control purposes.

### Relation of Labor Requirements to Production and Labor Policies

The preceding discussion has explained the method of determining the amount of labor required to produce the amount of goods called for by a production program based on a sales program. It might seem from the discussion that it is the intention to advocate that the production program always fluctuate in harmony with the sales program and that the labor supply be made to fluctuate with the production program. If this could be done, the determination of the labor requirements, once the sales requirements were obtained, would be merely a mathematical process. But the formulation of a labor program, which is a prerequisite to the maintenance of an effective working force, is not so simple as this. In the establishment of a labor program it is necessary to consider not only the immediate but also the long-time labor requirements of a firm. This leads to a consideration of both the production and labor policies of the firm in question. One or two simple illustrations will assist to make this more apparent.

Previous mention has been made of the fact that the production program may not be varied in all cases to correspond with the fluctuations in the sales program. It may be impossible to control the fluctuations in the sales, although some businesses, notably department stores, have done much towards accomplishing this end. But the volume of production is under the control of the firm, and within the limits of its resources can be varied to suit its needs. It may be found more profitable to maintain a uniform production, building up during the dull season an inventory to meet the excess demands of the rush season, than to cause the production program to fluctuate in harmony with the sales program. This procedure may provide for a better use of equipment and make possible the maintenance of a more stable and better trained working force. If this policy is to be followed it must be kept in mind when the personnel department is formulating its labor program. It is apparent that the labor program must be based on a "long look ahead" rather than on a "flash-light glimpse" of the present condition.

Some business firms provide homes for the use of their workers, charging in many cases a nominal rent for their use. In some cases the business is located in a village and most of the inhabitants work for the firm; and in case workmen are laid off during dull seasons, it is necessary that they journey to another village to obtain work. If they remain in the village it is necessary for them to continue to live on the property of the firm unless they suffer considerable hardship. In many cases the workmen regard the houses in which they live as their permanent homes. In fact one of the reasons for their being willing to work for the small wages they usually receive in these cases is because they expect to have a permanent home. In such cases a firm may attempt to provide some work for all its employees during each month of the year if possible. If necessary, it will reduce wages or work the laborers in shifts, so that each may work part time, but it will attempt to retain the full personnel on the pay-roll, so long as it expects to need them for future use. In carrying out this policy, it may pile up inventory during dull seasons which will be used during the rush seasons.

In addition, in the formulation of its labor program each firm must consider its relations to labor unions, the state labor laws, and similar agencies. More than all, it must consider its attitude towards its workmen, its welfare program, and the long-run policy it desires to maintain in handling its labor force.

Like any other administrative device, a budget should not restrain the management from exercising its legitimate functions; it should only aid the management by providing information which will serve as the basis for judgments. This is particularly true of the labor budget.

### The Pay-Roll Budget

The personnel department contracts not only for the personnel which is necessary to perform the operations required in the manufacture of the product of the firm, but also the personnel which is necessary to perform the supplementary operations which are required in order that the manufacturing operations can be performed.   For instance, it employs janitors and repair men as well as machine operators.   In addition it employs personnel for all the other departments of the business as well as for the production department.

In consequence of this situation it is the practice of some firms to prepare a *pay-roll* budget which takes the place of the labor budget.   The pay-roll budget includes an estimate of the entire pay-roll of the company.   The pay-roll budget probably arose from the practice of having the labor budget prepared by the pay-roll department.   This department found it easier to make an estimate of its total pay-roll than to analyze it and present separate estimates.

### Reasons Against Employment of Pay-Roll Budget

It is the opinion of the author that usually this plan is not desirable for the following reasons:

1. It is very apt to lead to inaccurate estimates.   It is so very easy to add or substract a certain amount from the total and report the result as an estimate.   The method usually results in the employment of ratios between pay-roll and volume of business, and such comparisons are unsatisfactory because the pay-roll does not fluctuate in proportion to volume of business.

2. The pay-roll budget is apt to make difficult an accurate check on the estimates.   If it contains the cost of the entire pay-roll of the company, it is difficult to determine the cause of the variations between the actual and estimated, which are bound to occur.   Furthermore, the amounts shown on the budget will not correspond with the amounts shown in the records, since the pay-roll in the latter is classi-

fied by departments, and in the production department *direct* labor is recorded under labor, while *indirect* labor is recorded as manufacturing expense.

3. It is desirable to have each functional department prepare an estimate of its total expense, including its payroll. This procedure requires the head of each department to consider what his costs have been and what he plans they will be in the future. This is one of the important purposes of the budgetary program, and the budgetary procedure should be designed so as to obtain this result.

The present chapter is restricted to a consideration of the "direct" labor employed in production. "Indirect" labor will be considered in connection with the manufacturing expense budget, and the personnel cost of the functional departments will be considered in connection with the budgets of these departments.

### Preparation of Labor Budget—Approved Procedure

After the production budget is prepared, the production department can prepare an estimate of the labor required to produce the goods called for by this budget. If a well-developed planning department is in operation, it will have available data which will make it possible to prepare this estimate without difficulty. In such cases it is customary to delegate the preparation of the labor budget to the planning department. After it is prepared it is carefully examined by the production manager and his staff. If there is not a planning department in operation, the estimate of labor may be prepared by the staff of the production department, the pay-roll department, or the personnel department. In any case it must be approved by the production manager.

After the estimate of labor requirements is approved by the production department, it will be transmitted to the personnel department, which will make an estimate of the cost of the labor required. In some cases the personnel department makes an estimate of the labor requirements and then transmits the estimate to the pay-roll department, where the estimated cost is entered. Thereafter the estimate of labor requirements is returned to the personnel department for review.

### Less Satisfactory Methods of Preparing Labor Budget

The foregoing procedure is not always followed. In some businesses the production budget is sent to the personnel department, or to the pay-roll department, which must estimate both the labor required and the cost of securing it. It is the author's opinion that the estimate of labor required can best be made by the production department, since it usually has available the information necessary for its preparation.

If the personnel department collects the data necessary to make this estimate, it will usually lead to a duplication of data, since the same information will be collected and recorded by both the production and personnel departments. It is admitted that some of this information is useful and even necessary for the personnel department, but it is not necessary to have it in as great detail as is required for making the estimate of labor.

In other businesses the production department prepares both the estimate of labor requirements and the estimate of labor costs. This procedure leads to equally undesirable results. The personnel department must have available for its own use the data necessary for the preparation of the estimate of labor costs, and if this task is undertaken by the production department, it will be necessary for it to collect duplicate data which it is not as well qualified to interpret and use as is the personnel department. Furthermore, the personnel department may rightly resent what it regards

## LABOR BUDGET

| DEPARTMENT | Amount Last Period | Average Amount Last Four Periods | Estimated Amount for Present Period | Estimated Production for Period | Average Production for Last Four Periods | DISTRIBUTION | | |
|---|---|---|---|---|---|---|---|---|
| | | | | | | First Month | Second Month | Third Month |
| | | | | | | | | |

Figure 12. Labor Budget

## MONTHLY REPORT ON LABOR BUDGET

| DEPARTMENT | Estimated Production | Actual Production | Per Cent of Increase or Decrease | Estimated Labor Cost | Actual Labor Cost | Per Cent of Increase or Decrease | Ratio of Estimated Cost of Labor to Estimated Production | Ratio of Actual Cost of Labor to Actual Production | Ratio of Cost of Labor to Cost of Production During the Last 4 Periods |
|---|---|---|---|---|---|---|---|---|---|
| | | | | | | | | | |

Figure 13. Monthly Labor Budget Report

as an undue usurpation of its functions.   One of its primary
functions is to collect data on labor requirements and formulate a labor program which will meet the needs of all the
departments and result in the most profit to the company.
"Labor program" is here used in a broad sense, and does
not refer to estimating labor costs only.   If the production
department prepares the estimate of labor cost, it may be
such as to conflict with the general program of the personnel
department.

### Form of Labor Budget

The author has found the form shown in Figure 12 of
service in the presentation of the labor budget.   It can be
modified to suit the needs of each particular case.   This
form is intended for use in presenting the labor budget to
the budget committee.   The production and personnel departments will need more detailed reports in preparing the
estimate.   The illustration is designed for use when the
budget period is three months in length.   If the period is
for a longer period of time, additional columns can be added.

If the estimate is prepared in this form, it will be possible
for the budget committee to determine whether the current
estimates are in excess of past expenditures, and, if so, what
the cause of the increase is.   If this increase is deemed
unjustifiable, the estimate can be revised accordingly.
The value of the monthly distribution to the treasurer in the
preparation of his cash budget is quite evident.

It may be desirable to show an analysis of the labor costs
of each department.   At least the production and personnel
departments will employ such an analysis.

### Approval by Budget Committee

After the estimate of labor is approved by both the production and personnel departments, it will be forwarded to

the executive in charge of the budget procedure. He will transmit it, with such recommendations as he may think necessary, to the budget committee. The latter will consider it in connection with the other budgets submitted to it, and will make revisions if it thinks they are necessary. It will return the budget as approved to the executive in charge of the budget procedure, who will transmit a copy of it to the production and personnel departments.

## Control of Labor Budget

The labor budget, like all other budgets, must be kept under effective control, and this involves the preparation at frequent intervals of reports which provide a comparison between the actual and estimated performance. It is usually desirable to have a monthly report which shows these comparisons. A report in the form shown in Figure 13 will serve this purpose.

The purpose and value of the information shown in each column of this report should be evident. The executives should study this report, giving particular attention to the effect of any variations in the production program on the labor cost.

This report will be submitted to the executive in charge of the budget procedure, and will be transferred by him to the budget committee with such recommendations as he may think desirable. By a study of this report the budget committee will be able to make such revisions as are necessary in the labor budget for the remainder of the period. These revisions will be communicated to the personnel and production departments by the executive in charge of the budget procedure.

12

# CHAPTER XII

## THE WELFARE EXPENSE BUDGET

### Relation of Welfare Expense to Labor Cost

The preceding chapter has dealt with the method of estimating and controlling the cost of labor used in manufacturing operations, in so far as that cost is represented by the wages paid to workmen. But all firms incur some expense in the securing and maintenance of the labor force, in addition to the compensation paid to the members of this force. This expense for the purpose of budget making may be divided into two groups:

1. "Welfare" expense
2. Administrative expense of the personnel department

It is the purpose of the present chapter to treat of the first of these, while the second will be discussed in Chapter XVIII in the treatment of the expense budgets. It is not always easy to make a clear line of demarcation between these two classes of expenses, but the following discussion will serve to show certain distinguishing features between the two.

Practically all large industrial and mercantile firms now place considerable emphasis upon desirable working conditions for their employees as a basic factor in labor expense control. The welfare of the employee is studiously considered from the standpoint of his loyalty to the employer as well as from the standpoint of his efficiency as a productive workman. His health and personal habits have an important bearing also upon his availability for service now and in the future as a trained employee.

## Classification of Welfare Expense

The large corporations, under their welfare plans, incur various kinds of expense. Programs for better conditions of employment usually include at least medical inspection, first-aid medical services, and restrooms for women employees. These programs may include any or all of the following classes of expense:

1. Medical inspection
2. Medical attendance and hospital expense
3. Payment of wages while on sick leave
4. Dental inspection and dental work
5. Inspection of the eyes and fitting of glasses
6. Picnics, dances, and other entertainments
7. Night classes in English, civics, arithmetic, and other elementary subjects
8. Tuition in evening schools of commerce
9. Restrooms
10. Gymnasiums
11. Prizes for athletic and literary contests
12. Lunches free or at cost
13. Books and magazines
14. Contributions to savings fund
15. Contributions to pension and old-age retirement funds

The foregoing list is intended to be suggestive of the kinds of expenditures which may be incurred in improving the working conditions of the employee. It is not the function of this discussion to pass judgment on the nature of this work or the kind of expenditures which it should include. That problem lies in the field of personnel management. But granting that certain kinds of expenses exist, it is the province of the budgetary program to effect their control. It is also unnecessary to enter here into a discussion of the title by which these expenses should be known. There are some who object to the term "welfare expense" because it is thought that it has an improper connotation. From

the viewpoint of our problem the title of this expense is
immaterial.

### Relation of Welfare Expense to Functional Departments

The welfare expenses are largely impersonal. The basis
for welfare work must be democratic if it is to result in increased loyalty and self-improvement on the part of the
average employee. This requirement leads to the opening
of all the advantages to each employee alike, whether the
employee is an officer of the company or a machine helper.
It is sometimes necessary to make exceptions to this rule,
but they should be as few as possible. All employees alike
are required to submit to medical inspection, all employees
alike are given medical service, all are permitted to use the
gymnasium, and all share in the pension fund, although their
share may be affected by their previous earning power.

Because of this impersonal character of practically all
welfare expense, it is not possible to charge any particular
item of it as a part of the direct cost of a particular job or as
a direct charge to the expenses of a particular operating department of the business. It may be that more employees
of the production department avail themselves of the use of
the bowling alley than employees of the sales department,
but this does not warrant charging the major part of the
expenses of maintaining the bowling alley to production
expense. In most cases the clerical employees will make
greater use of the books and magazines than will the manual
laborers; but so long as the publications are available for the
use of all the departments, they cannot be treated as an
expense of any particular department.

The independent nature of the welfare expense of any of
the departments is seen also if the purpose of the expense
is considered. For example, a physical examination of each
employee may be required to prevent possible poor health

or breakdown of any necessary or trained employee. All this is general expense. We cannot say accurately that any part of this expense has been incurred for the benefit of a particular laborer or even for the benefit of a particular productive unit or operating department. All departments are benefited by the maintenance of an efficient working force.

Again a part of welfare expense is incurred with the idea of creating loyalty on the part of the employees towards the company. It is desired that they should be stimulated to a definite feeling of cooperative interest in their fellow employees. Thus, the bowling club prize, awarded by the president of the company to the winner of the individual high score in the contest open to all employees, is by no means to be charged directly to the department where the winner is employed.

The foregoing discussion and illustrations should be sufficient to show that welfare expense is general in nature and is seldom particular to any employee or department. The welfare expense budget is discussed in connection with the several budgets prepared for manufacturing operations, because it is in connection with manufacturing industries that the administration of personnel has been most difficult and the need for welfare work has been most felt; but it is not intended to imply that this expense is primarily for the benefit of the production department. In a manufacturing business the bulk of the personnel will usually be in the production department and the greatest fluctuations in the number of personnel will also occur here, so that in estimating the amount of the welfare expense it is necessary to give careful consideration to the production program.

### Estimating Welfare Expense—Per Capita Cost Method

Welfare expense will be incurred in the case of any particular concern to the extent that the concern finds it profitable to improve its conditions of employment so as (1) to compete with other concerns as a place of continuous employment, and (2) to improve the efficiency of its workmen. A business with a factory located in a country town will not find it necessary to incur certain expenses to so great an extent as will a business whose factory is located in a congested tenement district. The former will incur less for medical services and in the maintenance of sanitary conditions. On the other hand, it may find it worth while to maintain homes for its employees in order to attract a better class of workmen to live in the semi-rural locality, and thus incur an expense not common to industrial firms located in cities.

There is no means by which welfare expense can be determined exactly. It will vary with the number of employees, and will also vary from month to month and year to year, given the same number of employees. For instance, an epidemic may break out at any time which will require additional expense for medical inspection and service.

Perhaps the best method of estimating the amounts for a budget on welfare expense is to determine the per capita cost of each class of expense, and then to multiply the average per capita cost of past years by the estimated average number of employees for the coming period. If the per capita method is employed as a basis for estimating welfare expense, it is desirable to have a report showing the amount of each class of expense in past years. Then if statistics can be had as to the average number of employees in past years, the amount of money spent, say, for doctors and nurses in 1921, can be divided by the average number of employees for 1921 to obtain the per capita expense during this year. If it is thought that the same per capita cost should be maintained during the year 1922, the per capita cost of 1921 will be multiplied by the estimated average number of employees for 1922 to obtain the estimated total expense for 1922. It will be noticed that by this method it is assumed that the expense is for the benefit of all employees alike. It would seem that this is proper, since doctors and nurses are employed not for the benefit of any particular employees, but for the welfare of all as a productive group.

### Points to be Allowed for in Estimating Welfare Expense

It may be desirable to work out two per capita figures for the past year: first, a per capita cost of all employees; and second, a per capita cost based on the number of only those employees who have been directly benefited by the kind of welfare expense under consideration. Thus the per capita cost in 1921 for entertainments should be the per capita cost for all employees whether or not they have attended the entertainments. The per capita cost should be figured on the average number of employees, since entertainments are open to all employees. As a secondary figure, it may be useful to have the per capita cost of entertainment expense based on the actual number of employees who have attended the entertainments.

If the plant is subject to periodical shut-downs due to irregular volume of business, or to seasonal strikes resulting from adjustments of wage scales, or for other reasons, it will be necessary to distinguish between (1) per capita average for continuing expense, such as the salaries of the head surgeon, the head nurse, the librarian, etc., and (2) *per capita per diem* average for all expenses that are incurred only during the days of actual plant operation. For example, a per capita per diem limitation may be set on free lunches, gymnasium operating expenses, and similar expenses which are incurred day by day according to the fluctuating number of employees.

It is necessary to use the average number of employees in arriving at per capita cost. In any large industrial or mercantile business there will be a larger number of individual names that have appeared on the pay-rolls during the year than the average number continuously employed. Thus one man may be employed on a job from January to March inclusive, another man from March to August inclusive, and still another man from September to December inclusive. This gives three employees, if we are considering the total number of employees actually engaged during the year. From the standpoint of the average number of employees, these three men constitute only one employee, since taken together their services have equaled the services of one man employed continuously throughout the year.

If it is possible to do so, labor turnovers should be figured from two different standpoints. First, the turnover of labor on account of irregular volume of business should be determined. For example, a thousand men may be discharged in May simply because there is no work for them, and a thousand new men may be employed in September, because a new volume of work has been obtained. This labor turnover is due to irregularity of volume of sales and production, and should be distinguished from the labor turnover caused by dissatisfaction of employees.

In estimating the average number of employees for a particular year, consideration should first be given to the sales program of that year as an index to the labor program that will probably result from irregular volume of business. The result thus obtained must be modified by consideration of the labor turnover in the year in question, that may presumably result from normal dissatisfaction of individual employees or from strikes and other manifestations of labor unrest.

## WELFARE EXPENSE BUDGET

| ITEMS | Amount Last Period | Estimated Amount This Period | Average Number of Employees Last ____ Period | Estimated Average Number of Employees This Period | Per Capita Last Period | Per Capita This Period | Per Capita Last Period for Those Directly Benefiting |
|---|---|---|---|---|---|---|---|
| (1) | (2) | (3) | (4) | (5) | (6) | (7) | (8) |

Figure 14. Welfare Expense Budget

## MONTHLY REPORT ON WELFARE EXPENSE

| ITEMS | Amount Last Period | Estimated Amount This Period | Average Number of Employees Last ____ Periods | Estimated Average Number of Employees This Period | Per Capita Last Period | Per Capita This Period | Per Capita Last Period for those Directly Benefiting | Actual Number of Employees Reported | Actual Amount of Expense Reported | Actual Per Capita Cost |
|---|---|---|---|---|---|---|---|---|---|---|
| (1) | (2) | (3) | (4) | (5) | (6) | (7) | (8) | (9) | (10) | (11) |

Figure 15. Monthly Welfare Expense Report

### Preparation of Welfare Expense Budget

The control of welfare expense or the expense of conditions of employment, like the control of any other activity in the business, demands first of all that a budget, or estimate, or program, or quota, be set up, indicating the plans for welfare expense for the coming period.   This budget should show information for each distinctive class of welfare expense.   For instance, it may show the welfare expense classified under the fifteen headings given on page 179.   In form the welfare expense budget may be as shown in Figure 14.   The purpose of each of the column headings is apparent.

The welfare expense budget should be prepared by the personnel department.   It should be based on the general plans of the business as shown by its various departmental estimates, and should be in harmony with the general policies which have been adopted by the company.   The personnel manager should discuss with the budget committee prior to the preparation of the estimate of welfare expense, any new plans which he desires to inaugurate, so that he may have the benefit of the judgment of the principal executives of the company in its preparation.

The personnel manager will transmit the welfare budget with his approval to the executive in charge of the budget procedure.   The latter will transmit it to the budget committee with any comments he thinks necessary.   The budget committee will make any revisions which it may think are required and return the budget, with its approval, to the executive in charge of the budget procedure.   The latter will return it to the personnel manager.

### Control of Welfare Expense Budget

The budget on welfare expense is effective only if a monthly report is prepared, showing the information given in the seven columns of the welfare budget contrasted with actual number of employees reported, and actual amount of expense for each class of welfare expense, and actual per capita cost. This report may be made in the form shown in Figure 15.

It is quite likely that the actual per capita will vary to a considerable degree from the estimated per capita, but the budget report does furnish a basis for planning welfare expense and also offers the means whereby the management responsible for welfare expense can keep such expense within reasonable control.

The monthly report will be submitted by the executive in charge of the budget procedure to the budget committee, and the latter may, if it thinks this report shows the necessity, make revisions in the welfare expense budget. The executive in charge of the budget procedure will communicate these changes to the personnel manager.

# CHAPTER XIII

## THE MANUFACTURING EXPENSE BUDGET

### Need for Estimate of Manufacturing Expense

After the finished goods which are to be produced during the budget period are determined by means of the production budget, it is necessary to estimate the manufacturing expenses which are necessary to produce these goods. This estimate is necessary in order—

1. That the various departments which are responsible for securing the "services" which compose manufacturing expense, may make plans to have these services by the time they are needed in production. The nature of these services and the departments responsible for their procurement will be explained later in this chapter.
2. That the treasurer may know the probable disbursements required by the manufacturing expense program and can plan to obtain the funds needed for these disbursements.
3. That standard rates for manufacturing expense may be established more accurately. The method of establishing such rates is discussed later.
4. That the budget committee and the board of directors may be able to see the financial requirements of the proposed sales and production programs at the time they are submitted for consideration, and that they may see the effect of the manufacturing expense cost on the estimated financial statements. In addition they should be able to see the relation of the volume of production to the manufacturing expense. The significance of this relationship will be explained later in the chapter.

The reader will notice that the estimate of manufacturing expense combined with the estimate of labor and the estimate of materials constitutes the estimated cost of the manufactured product, since the elements of manufacturing cost are materials, labor, and manufacturing expense.

## Definition of Manufacturing Expense

The costs incurred in the production of the finished product are divided into two broad classes, "direct" costs and "indirect" costs.

Direct costs are payments or charges for labor and material expended upon a definitely determined unit or product. Small costs, however, are not charged directly to the product, even when the latter can be determined, unless the increased accuracy of the records justifies the clerical work entailed. It follows, therefore, that indirect costs are those which cannot be charged economically or directly to the product. An example of a direct cost is the cost of the raw material in a chair. Indirect costs arise from the following sources:

1. Indirect material—good examples of which are rags used to wipe off chairs and tools; or new tools used to replace those discarded.
2. Indirect labor—for instance, wages of foremen who supervise the employees in several departments where chairs are made.
3. Fixed charges—depreciation, taxes, insurance, etc.

Adherence to the above cost classification adds to the accuracy of the records for this reason: By charging items directly to the cost units (when economical), the remaining costs (indirect costs) are less than if certain items legitimately "direct" were treated as indirect costs. Indirect costs are distributed over the product in as accurate a manner as possible, but such charging is less accurate than direct charging. For instance, raw material can be accurately measured and charged directly against the chair. The depreciation of the equipment used in manufacturing the chair cannot be determined with any measuring device. It must be estimated. Consequently the total depreciation of equipment is distributed over all units of product (chairs) made. Any charging, therefore, which reduces the distributable costs, thereby increases automatically the accuracy of the cost records. The growing observance of the principle of direct—that is to say correct—charging has done much to improve the exactness of cost accounting.[1]

It is the purpose of the present chapter to treat under the heading of "manufacturing expenses" the items termed "indirect costs" in the foregoing quotation. "Indirect expenses," "burden," and "overhead" are other terms by which these expenses are known.

## Components of Manufacturing Expense

The items which compose manufacturing expense will vary in different businesses, depending on the nature of their operations. The following are those which appear in most cases:

| | |
|---|---|
| 1. Indirect material | 8. Maintenance |
| 2. Supplies | 9. Depreciation |
| 3. Indirect labor | 10. Power |
| 4. Supervision | 11. Heat and light |
| 5. Inspection | 12. Small tools |
| 6. Experimental work | 13. Taxes |
| 7. Repairs | 14. Insurance |

The foregoing items are sufficient to indicate the nature of those which generally compose manufacturing expense. The reader can probably supply other items of manufacturing expense from his experience. Some accountants would combine such items as "indirect labor," "supervision," and "inspection." From the viewpoint of estimating their amount, it is desirable to have them separate.

## Classification of Manufacturing Expense

It is usually desirable that manufacturing expense be classified by departments and that subclassifications be maintained for each department. Detailed departmental

---

[1] Jordan and Harris, Cost Accounting, page 23.

classifications are necessary as a basis for effective control. The departmental classification makes possible the fixing of responsibility, and the classification within the department makes possible the meeting of the responsibility. It also affords a more comprehensive basis for judging the success with which the responsibility has been met.

To illustrate concretely, the X Manufacturing Company has four departments and manufactures one commodity. In 1918 the unit cost of the commodity was $12, while in 1919 it was $15. In attempting to find the cause of the increase, the first analysis will be to determine how much of the total cost is material cost, how much is labor cost, and how much is manufacturing expense. This analysis shows that the manufacturing expense per unit was $3 in 1918, and $4 in 1919. An analysis of the cost of manufacturing expense by departments for the two years shows the following:

| Year | Dept. A | Dept. B | Dept. C | Dept. D |
|------|---------|---------|---------|---------|
| 1918 | $.80 | $.90 | $.60 | $.70 |
| 1919 | 1.20 | .95 | .65 | 1.20 |

This analysis shows that the principal increases in manufacturing expenses are in Departments A and D. The responsibility for the increase is fixed on specific departments, but it is now necessary to determine whether the increase is due to inefficiency of the departmental heads or to causes over which they had no control. To ascertain this, it is necessary to examine the analysis provided by the departmental accounts.

This examination shows that in Departments A and D a large amount of miscellaneous supplies and indirect labor is necessary. Owing to the increase in the price of supplies and labor during the year 1919, the manufacturing expense of these departments was increased. If it is shown that approximately the same *quantity* of supplies and labor was used as previously but its price had greatly increased, the departmental foreman cannot be held responsible. If, on the other hand, it is found that the increase in manufacturing expense in these departments was due to the use of an increased *quantity* of supplies and labor per unit of product, there is then circumstantial evidence of inefficiency on the part of the departmental foreman, and he should be required to show cause for the condition. This simple illustration serves to show the necessity for a detailed analysis of the expenses of each major group if responsibility is to be fixed and variations explained.

A proper classification of expenses is of importance both from the viewpoint of accounting records and budget reports.

### Determination of Manufacturing Expense Requirements

The estimate of manufacturing expense, like the estimate of materials and of labor, is based on the estimate of production. It is somewhat more difficult to correlate the manufacturing expenses with the production, than it is to correlate materials and labor with production. This is due to two reasons:

1. The various items which go to make up the manufacturing expenses are secured from various sources and their procurement is not centralized under one individual, like materials and labor. For instance, the indirect material is obtained by the purchasing agent, the indirect labor by the personnel department, the taxes are paid by the treasurer, the repairs made by the maintenance department, and so on. This lack of centralized responsibility makes it difficult to fix the duty for the preparation of the manufacturing expense budget on those who are responsible for the expenditures which result in the procurement of the "services" of which it is composed.

2. Manufacturing expenses do not vary as a rule in proportion to the variation in production. Usually they do not increase or decrease as rapidly as production. This is due to the fact that there are "fixed" charges which are affected little if at all by the volume of production. For instance, taxes and insurance on machinery will be the same whether the machine is run at full or half capacity. There are other charges such as depreciation and supervision which will be affected by the volume of production but not in proportion. If production is sufficient to employ ten men in a department, it is necessary to have a foreman, and the same foreman may be able to supervise properly twenty men when production increases to the point where they are needed. Because of this condition it is impossible to estimate manufacturing expenses in lump by means of the ratio between manufacturing expense and production, if the production varies from one budget period to another.

The cost accounting department is the one place where all the items of manufacturing expense are shown. Its records show what the manufacturing expenses of the past periods have been and it is possible for it to prepare on the basis of these records an estimate of what the manufacturing expenses will be. The estimate, of course, must take into consideration the production program for the period as shown by the estimate of production. To do this properly the cost department should classify the manufacturing expenses as "fixed" and "variable." These terms must be used with caution, for there are few if any expenses which may be literally termed as "fixed." If this classification is made, it will not be difficult to estimate the fixed charges, but very careful attention must be given to the effect of the production volume on the variable charges.

13

It tends to simplicity and economy to have the estimate of manufacturing expense prepared by the cost accounting department. The chief objection to this procedure is that this department is apt to place too much emphasis on the statistics of past performance and too little emphasis on the contemplated performance. One method of correcting this difficulty is to have the cost department classify its estimate so as to show the expenses to be incurred by each unit or department, and then have each unit or department approve that part of the estimate for which it is responsible. For instance, the purchasing department could approve the estimate on indirect materials, the personnel department the estimate on indirect labor, the treasurer the estimate on taxes and insurance, and so on.

It is, of course, possible to have each separate unit or department make an estimate of that part of the manufacturing expense for which it is responsible, and then have these combined to make up the complete estimate. The separate estimates may be checked against the accounting records to test their accuracy. This method requires a great amount of care in getting the necessary information needed by each department for making its estimate and in seeing to it that each prepares the estimate properly. When it is possible to do so, there are decided advantages in having the estimate of manufacturing expense prepared by the staff of the production department, since this department is responsible for its enforcement. The only disadvantage of this procedure is that this department often does not have the data to make possible the preparation of an accurate estimate.

## Distribution of Manufacturing Expenses

One of the most difficult problems with which engineers and accountants have had to deal in the attempt to ascertain costs of manufactured product, is the allocation of the manufacturing expenses to the various classes or units of product. This problem gives rise to two questions:

1. What expenses should be allocated to the product?
2. What method should be employed in allocating these expenses?

For many years accountants as a whole assumed that *all* manufacturing expenses should be allocated to the product and therefore gave their undivided attention to the answering of the second question.

A number of methods of allocating manufacturing expenses were developed. These ranged from the simple method of using a percentage on direct labor cost, to the complex method of using a machine rate plus the "supplementary" rate. The reader is doubtless familiar with these various methods since they have been well explained in many texts on cost accounting and articles in magazines.[2]

The purpose of all these methods as originally developed is to allocate as accurately as possible *all* the manufacturing expenses of a period to the goods produced during that period. During recent years engineers and accountants have come to realize that it may not be desirable to allocate all the manufacturing expenses to the product produced. No doubt they were first led to see this by the fact that if all expenses during a period of depression are charged to the product produced during that period, the cost of the product is exorbitant. It is easy to see that if a plant is running at 60 per cent capacity and all the fixed charges of the plant are allocated against the 60 per cent of normal production, the costs will be greatly increased. If these costs are used as a basis for establishing sales prices, the

---

[2] Those readers who may desire a discussion of the various methods of distributing overhead may well read one or more of the following: Jordan and Harris, Cost Accounting; Nicholson and Rohrbach, Cost Accounting; Scoville, Cost Accounting and Burden Application; Eggleston and Robinson, Business Costs; Church, Manufacturing Accounts and Costs.

competitors are very apt to get the business; and as sales fall off there will be a further decrease in production with a further increase in cost, with the consequent increase in sales price, which results in a decrease in sales, and so on around the circle.

Faced by this situation, accountants and engineers realized the necessity of developing some method of handling manufacturing expenses which would prevent the charging to product of expenses which were not the result of the production of this product.   To this end, predetermined or standard rates were established by which the product was charged only with the same amount of expenses which it would have been charged if the plant was running at its normal capacity.   In the establishment of normal capacity the production of past years when the plant was operating under what was thought to be normal conditions was taken as a basis.   The manufacturing expense not absorbed by the standard rates was charged direct to the profit and loss account.   Those who are interested in the historical development of the use of the standard rate will be interested in reading pages 397–399, "Cost Accounting," by Jordan and Harris.

### Relation of Standard Rates to Manufacturing Expense Budget

From the viewpoint of administration, the importance of the standard rates for manufacturing expense is obvious. These standard rates may also be of considerable significance from the viewpoint of budgetary control.   It has been pointed out in the discussion of materials and labor, that if standard rates have been set, it is only necessary to multiply these by the quantity of finished goods called for by the production budget to obtain the estimate of materials or estimate of labor.   If standard expense rates have been set, a similar procedure may be followed in preparing the estimate of manufacturing expense. The standard expense rate for each product may be multiplied by the quantity of this product called for in the production budget in order to obtain the estimated manufacturing expense. If the product passes through two or more departments, it will probably be necessary to use a different rate for each department. It is obvious that the actual expenses may be greater or less than the standard, and this variation must be given consideration in preparing the estimated statement of profit and loss and the financial budget.

One objection to this method from the viewpoint of administrative control, is that if the production varies in quantity, the standard rate should be made to vary also. In the establishment of standard costs it has been the practice of accountants to select one or more periods during which they think there has been normal production, and use the costs of these periods as standard costs, or at least to regard the production of these periods as standard production and determine the standard costs on the basis of the quantity of production. For the purpose of distributing the costs of production evenly over all periods and thereby determining a uniform cost, there is decided merit in this method. It would seem, however, from the viewpoint of administrative control, that it would be much more accurate to have the standard costs based on the anticipated production of the period under consideration.

The manufacturer does not care so much to know how his costs compare with what they should be if he produced the quantity which he produced during some previous period, as he desires to know:

   1. At the beginning of the period, what his costs will be if he manufactures what he plans to manufacture during the period.

2. During the period, how his actual costs compare with what he estimated they would be.

3. At the end of the period, why there is a variation between the estimated and the actual, if such a variation exists.

It is not intended to imply that the use of standard rates as a means of equalizing costs may not be desirable, but only to emphasize that standard costs based on past production may not give the manufacturer the information he most needs in judging the desirability of contemplated plans or of controlling these plans after they are put into operation.

### Relation of Budget Program to Standard Rates

If the manufacturing expenses are allocated by means of the "machine rate," the estimated activity of the plant can be given effect in the establishment of the standard machine rates. Mr. E. O. Sommer in *Industrial Management*, January, 1920, discusses one method by which this is done in the following quotation:

> The object in establishing a machine hour rate is to determine the cost of running a machine one hour. This can be done by:
>
> 1. Classifying and dividing the machines into units of like operation.
> 2. Estimating the percentage of activity at which the plant is expected to operate.
> 3. Determining the operating expenses of each unit for a given period.
>
> In classifying machines, the department may be taken as a unit if all the machines perform the same operation; should, however, the department include machines of unlike operation, we shall have to go a step further and subdivide the department into various machine groups, each machine in a group performing the same operation. This subdivision may lead us so far as to consider a single machine as a unit.
>
> Thus, having classified the processing machines of the plant into units, our concern is to collect all expenses which will be incurred

in the operation of these individual units during a given period. These expenses we may place into two main groups:

1. Comprising such items as can be directly charged against certain units, as labor, floor space, current repairs, etc., necessary for the operation of that unit.
2. Representing indirect expenses, which although they are largely direct charges against the department, still cannot be allocated to individual units, but are to be prorated on a suitable basis.

The percentage of activity, the third factor in the calculation of predetermined rates, must be estimated with utmost care.   If we could assume that the plant will be able to work at and maintain a 100 per cent activity, our task of calculating an hourly rate would be a simple one. We would obviously divide the total working hours of the week, or month, or year, into the total operating cost for that period and arrive at a cost per hour.

Since, however, an activity of 100 per cent can hardly be realized, a method must be found to ascertain the highest possible percentage of activity (budget activity) at which the management may expect to keep the plant working.

Should the statement reveal that the plant will not be kept operating at full capacity it will be the problem of the management to investigate the cause of this condition and to find a way to bring the activity to a normal level.   Overequipment, decrease in the demand for the product, or competition may account for reduced activity.

Many expenses, as rent, depreciation, etc., accrue as time goes on whether the machine be active or idle, and the cost per hour will naturally increase in the same proportion as the activity decreases. To illustrate this, let us assume that these fixed overhead expenses for a group of machines be $2,400 per year.   Taking the year at 50 weeks of 48 hours each, or 2,400 working hours, the overhead would be, at 100 per cent activity, $2,400 for 2,400 hours—$1 per hour; at 90 per cent activity, $2,400 for 2,160 hours—$1.11 per hour; at 85 per cent activity, $2,400 for 2,040 hours—$1.18 per hour.

Should the budget activity for the ensuing period be 90 per cent, it would be a serious error to distribute the operation cost on a basis of 100 per cent activity.

Assume for example that the budget rate has been based on a

90 per cent activity and assume further that the actual activity during a period be 90 per cent, all expenses then will be gradually charged to the process, and the debit and credit side of the operating account of this particular machine group will be in balance.

Should, however, the actual activity fall below the percentage used in the calculation of the machine rate (budget rate), there would remain in the operating account a balance of undistributed expenses. This balance, which is due to curtailed production, should not be debited to the production account either directly or by increasing the budget rate, but be charged to profits. Any increase over the budget activity would result in a credit balance on the operation account and be a credit to profit and loss.

If a comparison of the actual and budget figures of the individual cost factors should reveal that a fluctuation is due to change in prices, a revision of the budget will be necessary and a new rate must be determined.

A difference between the actual and budget activity would indicate either an increase or decrease in the production. Since a loss or gain due to fluctuations in the activity does not result from the manner of operating a unit, any difference due to this cause should be eliminated from the operation account.

This can be accomplished best by calculating an "idle time" and "overtime" rate, which will represent the hourly cost of all those charges which are incurred regardless of whether the machine group is active or idle. We shall credit the operation account at the "idle time" rate for the total idle hours in the budget period, and charge an account called "Idle and Overtime." Inversely, we shall debit the operation on account at the "overtime" rate for the total active hours in excess of the budget hours, and credit the "Idle and Overtime" account. A balance, left in this account at the end of the budget period, which will then either show a loss due to curtailed production or a gain due to increased activity, is closed into the sales account.

The author does not intend to endorse the general application of the particular method described in this quotation, but the general principle it illustrates, that standard rates should be related to the budget program, is worth emphasis.

## Relation of Standard Rates to Volume of Production

It should of course be understood that in the setting of standard rates based on estimated activity as explained in the foregoing quotation, only the expenses which are properly applicable to the estimated production should be included.

To accomplish this end the following procedure is necessary:

1. Determine the "normal" production of the plant. This of course cannot be established with exactness. Generally speaking, the normal production is that which would be accomplished if the plant was operating so that the equipment as a whole would be used at the greatest efficiency, at which it can *reasonably be expected* to be used. *Normal* production is usually less than the *maximum* production. In determining normal production, all parts of the equipment must be given careful consideration. The old adage that "a chain is no stronger than its weakest link" is approximately true of the equipment of a plant. For instance, the melting department of a foundry may be able to turn out sufficient melt to produce 100 tons of castings during a certain period, but if the moulding floor is only large enough to make possible the moulding of 75 tons, the normal capacity of foundry cannot exceed 75 tons.

2. Determine the manufacturing expenses which would be incurred if the factory operated at normal capacity.

3. Determine the estimated production under the budget program for the current period.

4. Determine the ratio of (3) to (1) and apply this ratio to (2), to obtain the manufacturing expenses applicable to the current period. Judgment will have to be used in doing this because of the changing price level and other factors which may necessitate modifications of this mathematical result.

5. On the basis of the result obtained in (4) and the estimated activity of the current period, establish standard machine rates. There is a difference of opinion as to what should be included in the establishment of machine rates. It is not worth while to enter into this discussion here.

### Modification of the Standard Machine Rate Plan

The author fully realizes that there are many businesses which will find it impracticable to follow the plan for establishing standard expense rates which has been outlined in the foregoing discussion. Many manufacturing firms do not find it expedient to establish machine rates at all. Nevertheless the general principles developed by the foregoing are applicable to all manufacturing firms, namely:

1. That the product of each period should be charged only with the manufacturing expenses which contribute to its production, and should not be burdened with the expenses arising from unused capacity or idle time.
2. That a standard rate for charging the expense to the product should be established and that the undistributed burden should be charged directly to profit and loss. In case of production above the normal, the excess should be credited to profit and loss.

These principles can be applied regardless of the method employed in the distribution of manufacturing expenses.

### The "Miscellaneous" Expense Budget

In the discussion of the materials budget it was explained that some businesses prepare a "stores" budget which includes both *direct* and *indirect* material, and in the discussion of the labor budget it has been explained that sometimes a "pay-roll" budget is prepared which includes both *direct* and *indirect* labor. When this procedure is followed, two of the large items of manufacturing expense are eliminated from the manufacturing expense budget. In this case there may be prepared a "miscellaneous" expense budget which will include all the expenses other than indirect labor and indirect material.

It is easier to prepare the miscellaneous expense budget and to have the indirect materials and labor included in the stores and pay-roll budget respectively. But it is doubtful if this method gives as effective control of manufacturing expenses. It is desirable that all manufacturing expense be shown as a total and that standards be set up by which to judge its amount. It is of course possible to set up these standards independent of the budgets, but it is much more effective if they are correlated so that each will check the other. It is emphasized throughout this book that the budgets should be prepared in terms of "units of responsibility." The production department is responsible for all the manufacturing expense and it is better that its total amount be shown in one budget—the manufacturing expense budget.

It is admitted that this procedure necessitates the purchasing agent to make up an estimate of purchases for the *indirect* materials included in the manufacturing expense budget. Obviously the purchases of these materials will not correspond with their consumption, and it is the latter which is shown on the manufacturing expense budget. In some cases the purchasing agent may find it necessary, in order to secure an economical purchase, to buy at one time sufficient to last for a considerable number of periods.

For the purpose of the financial budget it is the disbursements which are desired, but for the purpose of the estimated balance sheet and estimated statement of profit and loss the consumption is necessary. It is thought best, therefore, to have the composite budget for manufacturing expenses prepared, and to support this with the estimate of purchases with the consequent disbursements.

### Preparation of the Manufacturing Expense Budget

The method of preparing this budget has been indicated by the preceding discussion. If it is assumed that the original estimate of manufacturing expense is prepared by the cost accounting department, a copy of it will be sent by this department to each department responsible for incurring expenditures under it. Each of these departments will indicate any changes which it thinks necessary, and return the estimate with its approval to the cost department. The purchasing agent will attach to the estimate of the cost department an estimate of purchases of materials which are necessary to supply the indirect materials called for by the program.

The cost accounting department will prepare an estimate for submission to the executive in charge of budgetary procedure. On this estimate it will give effect to the revisions which have been made by the various departments. If it does not approve of these revisions, it will show both its estimates and the revisions, and make such comments as it thinks appropriate.

If the original estimate is prepared by the production department, it will follow the same procedure as outlined above for the cost department. As previously explained, it is desirable that the estimate be prepared by the production staff, but it is more frequently prepared by the cost department.

The executive in charge of budgetary procedure will transmit the estimate received from the cost accounting department or the production department to the budget committee. He may accompany it with such comments as he thinks appropriate. The budget committee will consider the estimate of manufacturing expense in connection with all the other estimates which it receives at the same time, and will make any revisions it deems necessary. It will transmit the estimate as approved to the executive in charge of the budget procedure, who will transfer a copy of it to each of the departments which are interested in its

## MANUFACTURING EXPENSE BUDGET

| ITEMS | Amount Last Period | Average Amount Last Four Periods | Estimated Amount for Present Period | Estimated Production for Period | Average Production for Last Four Periods | DISTRIBUTION | | |
|---|---|---|---|---|---|---|---|---|
| | | | | | | First Month | Second Month | Third Month |
| | | | | | | | | |

Figure 16.  Manufacturing Expense Budget

## MONTHLY REPORT ON MANUFACTURING EXPENSE

| ITEMS | Estimated Production | Actual Production | Per Cent of Increase or Decrease | Estimated Cost of Manufacturing Expense | Actual Cost of Manufacturing Expense | Per Cent of Increase or Decrease | Ratio Estimated Manufacturing Expense to Estimated Production | Ratio of Actual Cost of Manufacturing Expense to Actual Production | Ratio of Cost of Manufacturing Expense to Production during the Last Four Periods |
|---|---|---|---|---|---|---|---|---|---|
| | | | | | | | | | |

Figure 17.  Monthly Manufacturing Expense Report

enforcement. In form the manufacturing expense budget may be made as shown in Figure 16.

## Control of Manufacturing Expense Budget

The cost accounting department will prepare monthly reports showing a comparison between the actual and estimated manufacturing expense. This report may be in the form shown in Figure 17. The columnar headings on this report are self-explanatory.

This report will be submitted to the executive in charge of the budget procedure and will be transferred by him to the budget committee. The committee will study this report in connection with the other monthly reports, and will make any revisions in the manufacturing expense budget which it thinks are necessary as indicated by the reports. Any changes it makes will be transmitted to the departments concerned by the executive in charge of the budgetary procedure.

In addition to the general report on the budget as a whole, there should be prepared a separate report for each department in the factory, showing a comparison between the actual and standard performance. In case the general report shows a wide variation between the actual and the estimated expenditures, these detailed reports will provide information which the executive in charge of the budget procedure can use in explaining these variations to the budget committee.

## Review and Summary of Production Control

In Chapters IX to XIII, inclusive, an attempt has been made to outline the procedure necessary to effect a coordination of sales and production, and to prepare and execute a production program. Previously in Chapters V and VI the method by which the sales requirements are determined has been explained. In summary form the procedure discussed in these chapters may be outlined as follows:

I. PREPARATION OF SALES BUDGET
1. Estimates prepared by sales units.
2. Revised by general sales office.
3. Revised by the production department in the light of production possibilities and desirabilities.
4. Revised by the controller or other officer in the light of profit possibilities.
5. Forwarded to the budget committee for final revision and approval.

II. PREPARATION OF "PRODUCTION" BUDGETS
1. *Finished Goods Budget:*
   (a) Estimate of finished goods requirements prepared by the production department from the sales estimates.
   (b) Revision and approval of finished goods estimates by the budget committee.
   (c) Enforcement of this budget through the means of the balance of stores records operated under maximum and minimum standards.

2. *Materials Budget:*
   (a) Estimate of materials requirements prepared from the finished goods estimate by the production department (the duty of preparing this estimate is usually delegated by the head of the production department to the planning department).
   (b) Estimate of material requirements, after approval by the head of the production department, is transmitted to the purchasing department and this department prepares an estimate of the material purchases required and the disbursements resulting therefrom.
   (c) Estimate of materials and purchases revised and approved by the budget committee.
   (d) Enforcement of materials budget through the means of the materials balance of stores records operated under maximum and minimum standards.

3. *Labor Budget:*
   (a) Estimate of labor requirements prepared from the finished goods budget by the production department (the duty of preparing this estimate is usually delegated by the head of the production department to the planning department).
   (b) Estimate of labor requirements, after approval by the head of the production department, is transmitted to the personnel department and this department makes an estimate of the cost of supplying this labor.
   (c) Estimate of labor requirements and labor cost revised and approved by the budget committee.
   (d) Enforcement of the labor budget by the production department with the assistance of the personnel department, through the agency of a centralized production control system.

4. *Manufacturing Expense Budget:*
   (a) Estimate of manufacturing expense requirements made by cost accounting department or production department.
   (b) Estimate of manufacturing expense requirements approved by the production manager and the head of the various departments responsible for the incurrence of the expenditures for which it provides.
   (c) Estimate as approved in (b) transmitted to budget committee for revision and approval.
   (d) Enforcement of the estimate by the production department through the agency of a centralized control system.

III. MONTHLY REPORTS FOR CONTROL AND REVISION OF BUDGETS
   1. Report on finished stock budget as shown in Figure 8 (page 141).
   2. Report on materials budget as shown in Figure 11 (page 161).
   3. Report on labor budget as shown in Figure 13 (page 175).
   4. Report on manufacturing expense budget as shown in Figure 17 (page 205).

IV. MONTHLY REVISION OF BUDGETS
   1. Budget committee receives monthly reports on all departmental estimates, including those outlined under (III).

2. The committee considers these reports with reference to their relation to each other and makes such revisions as are deemed necessary.

3. Any revisions made in the budgets outlined in (II) will be communicated to the production department and the other departments concerned.

It should be understood that the procedure given in this outline is intended to be suggestive and not arbitrary. Each firm must adopt a procedure to fit its particular needs. It is thought that if the foregoing procedure is understood properly, it will not be difficult to make the adaptations required in any particular case.

14

# CHAPTER XIV

## THE PURCHASES BUDGET

### Relation of Purchases Budget to the Sales Budget

In the preceding chapters considerable attention has been given to the method by which the manufacturer plans a production program which will result in a proper coordination between production and sales. But the merchant has a similar problem of coordination, which he can solve only by formulating a purchasing program which will perform the same function for him as the production program performs for the manufacturer.

The amount of goods which is to be purchased by a merchant is determined primarily by his estimate of future sales. Goods are purchased only to be sold, and sales can be consummated only when goods are available for sale. The general manager of a mercantile store is charged with a double responsibility. He must maintain such stocks of goods as will enable the store to fill customers' orders, and at the same time he must avoid the accumulation of stock beyond the sales demands, as such excessive accumulation results in loss from tied up capital, and probably also from the obsolescence and deterioration of the merchandise.

The general manager can meet this responsibility only by anticipating sales demands and setting up as nearly as possible a schedule of deliveries to stock which will satisfy but not exceed these demands.

In merchandise planning, therefore, the first step is the determining of the amount of future sales; the second step is the determining of the purchases necessary to meet these sales; and the third step is the setting up of a purchasing program which will coordinate the deliveries of purchases with the sales deliveries required by the sales program. The first step has been previously discussed. The second and third will be dealt with in this chapter.

### Determination of Purchases Requirements

The ideal purchases program, from the viewpoint of the economical use of capital, would be one which provided for the delivery to stock each day of the exact amount of merchandise which will be sold that day. Such a program is not feasible for two reasons:

1. In a mercantile store, it is necessary to have some merchandise on hand for display purposes. The customer desires an assort-·ment from which to select his purchases. This necessitates the keeping on hand of a considerable quantity of merchandise. The amount which must be kept is dependent on the extent of the sizes, varieties, and grades of the merchandise which is kept for sale.

2. It is impossible to estimate sales demands or to plan purchases deliveries with sufficient accuracy to have the same amount delivered each day as is sold on that day. To provide against a failure to meet sales demands it is necessary to keep a certain amount of merchandise on hand, which is termed the merchandise inventory.

The principal problem in merchandise planning is to determine the size of the inventory which should be maintained, and to set up a purchases program which will schedule deliveries to stock in such quantities and at such times as to provide for its maintenance at this amount. The problem of purchases requirements resolves itself, therefore, into a problem of finished stock requirements.

The problem of setting up an estimate of finished stock requirements necessitates:

1. An estimate of the sales that will be made of each kind and class of goods. This estimate is provided by the sales program.
2. A statement of the inventory of finished goods that has proved sufficient in meeting the sales requirements of preceding periods.

This information is used as a basis for the preparation of an estimate of the finished goods inventory requirements throughout the coming selling period.

## Method of Determining Inventory

If inventory figures are to be available for prompt use in the preparation of the purchases budget, it is necessary that a definite method by which inventory is to be secured be determined and the appropriate procedure for the enforcement of this method be established.

There are three methods in current use by which inventories may be obtained. These will be discussed under the following headings:

1. Perpetual inventory
2. Estimated inventory
3. Physical inventory

## Perpetual Inventory

All the information required in setting up a system of finished goods stock requirements is contained in a merchandise account that shows the quantities of each merchandise item received at cost contra to the amounts of the item sold, the sales being also computed at cost. The resulting balance shows the amount of each item of merchandise on hand at cost. Such a merchandise account is commonly known as a *perpetual* inventory.

If a perpetual inventory is maintained on the goods in stock, it will show the cost of such goods as they are shipped from the vendor, and will also show the value at cost of goods shipped under sales invoices. The net figures in such an inventory will indicate at all times the goods on hand.

It is possible to keep the inventory record in terms of quantities rather than in terms of value, if desired. A form of inventory record suitable for use in connection with raw materials is shown in Figure 9 (page 153). The record for general merchandise is usually more simple than this form, but the same principles govern its construction and use.

## Estimated Inventory

The experience of merchants is that perpetual inventories are often expensive in their operation. This is especially true where many small items are bought and sold, and where the average turnover of the stock is high. Many merchants content themselves with estimated inventories of merchandise on hand, and these estimates are proven as to their accuracy by actual inventory once or twice a year.

The estimated inventory is determined on the basis that the actual inventory at the beginning of the period, plus purchases for the period, plus the estimated gross profit subtracted from the sales at sales price, equals the ending inventory. The method of arriving at this formula will be seen easily if the organization of the trading section of the pro forma statement of profit and loss is considered.

It may be assumed that the trading section of the statement of profit and loss of the Brown Mercantile Company for the month of December appears as follows:

THE BROWN MERCANTILE COMPANY

STATEMENT OF PROFIT AND LOSS

For Month Ended December 31, 192–

| | | |
|---|---:|---:|
| Sales.................................................. | | $51,000.00 |
| Inventory, December 1......................... | $16,500.00 | |
| Purchases for month........................... | 34,100.00 | |
| Total Merchandise in Stockroom during month..... | $50,600.00 | |
| Inventory, December 31........................ | 13,200.00 | |
| Cost of Goods Sold.................................. | | 37,400.00 |
| Gross Profit on Sales............................. | | $13,600.00 |

From the foregoing statement, it is possible to prepare the following equation:

Sales — Beginning Inventory — Purchases + Ending Inventory
= Gross Profit

Ordinarily when a statement of profit and loss is made, the only unknown quantity is the gross profit, and it is obtained by this equation. When it is desired to use this formula for estimating the ending inventory, there are two unknown quantities—the ending inventory and the gross profit. One of these must be determined before the equation can be solved. This is accomplished by estimating the gross profit. To make the estimate, the ratio of the average gross profit to sales during the past periods is determined, and this percentage is applied to the sales of the current period to obtain the estimated gross profit for this period.

To illustrate, it is found that the average gross profit of the Brown Mercantile Company during the past three years has been 26.66 per cent of sales. It is thought that the average gross profit of these years is indicative of the gross profit of the month of December of the current year. By taking this percentage of the sales for this month, the estimated gross profit is calculated to be $13,600. By using this figure, the equation given above can be stated as follows:

$$\$51,000 - \$16,500 - \$34,100 + \text{Ending Inventory} = \$13,600$$

By transposition and solving, the ending inventory is determined to be $13,200. Since the gross profits on different lines of goods varies, it is necessary to perform the foregoing calculation for each line of goods if an accurate estimated inventory is to be obtained.

It should be evident that estimated inventories can be only approximately correct. If the merchandise manager has before him only estimated inventories as at the close of each month or fiscal period, he must use his judgment in basing his actions on them. In any case frequent tests should be made to verify the accuracy of the estimate.

## Physical Inventories

In those businesses where it is not feasible to maintain a perpetual inventory because of the cost involved, and where it is impossible to obtain an accuraté estimated inventory because of the widely varying rates of gross profit, it may be necessary to resort to actual inventories taken at frequent intervals. This necessitates the taking of a physical count of the goods on hand.

Some department stores take an inventory in certain departments every two weeks. Such a check-up at frequent intervals is especially desirable in the case of variety goods, where fashion and styles play an important part. Practically all businesses take a physical inventory yearly, and there is a decided tendency towards semiannual and quarterly inventories. It has been found that if a standardized procedure for the taking of inventories is properly worked out, the task is not so great as it was formerly thought to be.

## Relation of Inventory Planning to Statistics of Past Periods

In estimating inventory requirements it is necessary to refer to the statistics of previous periods as shown by the accounting records. As to how many past periods should be considered will depend on the circumstances of each case. The statistics desired are those which will most nearly indicate the probable condition of the current year. It may be that conditions have changed so rapidly that it is deemed wise to use only the statistics available for the preceding period, or, on the other hand, the preceding period may be considered as abnormal and may be disregarded entirely.

In some cases a weighted average of three or more past

periods is taken. In any case, the object is the same—to obtain the statistics with reference to past operations which will be most helpful in planning future operations. For the sake of brevity in the following discussion, reference will be made to the "past period" or "past periods" without defining the length of this period, or periods, unless such definition is necessary to make the meaning of the discussion clear.

## Determination of "Normal" Inventory

In the preceding discussion it has been explained that the next step in merchandise planning after the sales estimate is prepared, is to determine the "average" or "normal" inventory which is necessary to meet sales demands. To accomplish this it is necessary:

1. To determine the average inventory during past periods.
2. To determine the ratio of the average inventory of past periods to the sales of those periods, that is, determine the merchandise turnover of those periods.
3. To apply the turnover of past periods to the estimated sales of the current period to obtain the average inventory for the present period.

## Determination of Inventory of Past Periods

If any rational control has been exercised over stock investments during the past periods, inventory of stock on hand must have been taken at frequent intervals. This inventory may have been obtained by any of the methods discussed in the preceding paragraphs.

If it was deemed necessary to know the value of the stock on hand only at the beginning and the end of the period a physical inventory may have been taken. If it was deemed desirable to have the value of the stock on hand at more frequent intervals, it is probable that either an estimated inventory was determined at regular intervals or stock records established which made possible a perpetual or continuous inventory.

It is apparent that the more frequently the inventory is determined, the more useful are the statistics obtained thereby in determining average inventory and in planning stock investment control. In any case the desire for accuracy must be balanced against practicability.

## Calculation of Turnover

Whatever method of taking inventory has been followed during the past periods, it should be possible to determine at least approximately the average inventory and the ratio of the average inventory of each period to the sales for the same period. In other words, the turnover for each of the past periods can be determined. If the turnover computations are to be of value, it is necessary that care be exercised to calculate them properly.

In practice it will be found that several methods are used in the determination of merchandise turnover. There are in fact but two methods of determining turnover accurately. They are as follows:

1. Divide the cost of the goods sold during the year by the cost of the average inventory of the year. For instance, a retail store carries on the average a stock of goods the cost price of which is $20,000 and makes during the year sales of $100,000 on which a gross profit of twenty per cent is made. The cost of the goods sold is $80,-000 and the turnover is four.

In other words, in this store, on an average, the articles sold remain in stock three months after they are purchased before they are sold. It will, of course, be realized that it is rather dangerous to try to determine the average turnover on all goods carried in stock. It is more accurate to determine if possible the turnover for each kind of goods, since the turnover varies on each kind.

2. The turnover may be determined by dividing the average inventory for the year at sales price into the sales at sales price. For instance, taking the illustration given above, where the average inventory at cost is $20,000 and the sales for the year are $100,000 on which an average gross profit of twenty per cent is made; if the inven-

tory is taken at sales price, it will be seen that it will amount to
$25,000, and dividing the sales of $100,000 by $25,000, a turnover
of four will be obtained.

It will be seen that the same result is obtained as in the first case
where the inventory at cost is divided into the sales at cost. Either
method can be used, whichever is the more convenient.[1]

The error is sometimes made of dividing the sales at
selling price by the inventory at cost. This obviously gives
a turnover larger than the actual one.

When a firm relies on a physical inventory taken once a
year, it may determine its average inventory by taking one-
half of the sum of the beginning and ending inventories. If
the sales of the business are subject to seasonal fluctuations,
this method will not give satisfactory results, since it does
not give effect to the fluctuations in inventory which must
inevitably result from the fluctuations in sales. The proper
method is to obtain the average of the monthly inventories.

### Use of Turnover Figures

Turnover figures are very useful in merchandise control.
As Nystrom, in his "Economics of Retailing," very aptly
says:

One of the productive factors of a retail store is the capital invested in its stock of goods. When this capital is borrowed for use in
the store, interest must be paid for it, and interest should be entered
as an expense charge in any case regardless of whether the manager of
the store borrows or supplies capital from his own funds. Efficiency
in its use depends upon its activity. By activity is meant the number of times it can be used over and over again in the course of a
year. Each complete use of the capital invested in merchandise is
known as a "turnover." If expenses and profits per sale remain
the same, the greater the number of turnovers within a year, the
greater the net profit resulting. This fact has long been recognized.
There is an old maxim that expresses the idea exactly: "A nimble
sixpence is better than a slow shilling."

---

[1] McKinsey, Bookkeeping and Accounting, Vol. I.

From the viewpoint of our present discussion we are interested in turnover primarily as a basis for determining inventory requirements. After the turnover of past periods is calculated, it is necessary to give it careful consideration before using it as a basis for merchandise planning. Whether or not the turnover of past periods will be used as a basis for planning stock control for the current period, will depend upon whether the average inventory of the past periods is deemed to be satisfactory or not for the purpose.

It may be that the inventory during the past periods was too large and the turnover too slow. Or it may be that the inventory was too small for the volume of sales which were possible.

The merchandise manager may know that in the case of many articles a much larger inventory was carried than was necessary to meet the volume of sales, and he estimates that a smaller inventory may be carried during the coming year and the same volume of sales be obtained.

On the other hand, he may know of many articles the sales of which could have been increased if a larger variety or assortment had been carried, or if the goods desired by the customer had always been on hand when called for. He may rightly decide that the turnover of past periods must be modified before it can be used as a basis in determining the average inventory to be maintained during the current year.

The foregoing discussion indicates two facts of importance in connection with inventory and turnover. First, it indicates that it is unsafe to take average turnover, that is, the average turnover of all lines carried, especially if goods of many different varieties are carried in stock. As previously suggested, it is usually necessary to determine the turnover of each different class of merchandise carried.

Secondly, it indicates the need for the intelligent consideration of statistics with reference to past operations and their modification in the light of past experience before they are used as a basis of future plans.

Whether the turnover of the past periods is deemed satisfactory or is modified as suggested above, a figure is finally determined which is used in connection with the estimated sales of the current period, to arrive at the average inventory deemed necessary to meet these sales. The process involved is illustrated by the following steps:

1. Sales for the past period........................... $500,000
2. Average inventory for the past period.............. $100,000
3. Turnover for the past period....................... 5
4. Estimated sales for the current period.............. $600,000
5. The estimated average inventory for the current period is $120,000

It is, of course, assumed in the foregoing illustration and discussion that the inventory and sales are both stated at the same price, either both at selling price or both at cost price.

### The Buying Budget

When the estimated inventory has been determined, it is then necessary to make a schedule of deliveries and purchases which will maintain this inventory. If the sales of the period fluctuate to any great extent, it will probably be necessary to determine the inventory desired at the beginning of each month. Then, to determine the deliveries to stock which must be made during the month, it will be necessary to add the estimated sales at cost for the month to the estimated inventory at the end of the month, and subtract the inventory at the beginning of the month.

It can be seen from the foregoing that the *normal* inventory, that is, the inventory which it is estimated will have to be carried to meet the sales demands, may not be an average or uniform inventory, but may fluctuate from

month to month as the sales fluctuate owing to seasonal
demands, etc.   It should also be realized that in many cases
it may be desirable to make the finished goods schedule in
terms of the number of items required rather than in terms
of value.

To illustrate the preparation of a schedule of deliveries of
finished goods, it may be assumed that the New York Department Store, which makes a specialty of high-grade

| NEW YORK DEPARTMENT STORE |
| :---: |
| Furniture Department |
| X-Y PIANO |

| Month | Stock Beginnings | Sales | Stock End | Deliveries to Stock | Memorandum |
| :---: | :---: | :---: | :---: | :---: | :---: |
| *Nov.* | *16* | *34* | *14* | *32* | *Xmas season begins Nov. 15* |
| *Dec.* | *14* | *21* | *10* | *17* | *Xmas season ends Dec. 18* |
| *Jan.* | *10* | *17* | *15* | *22* | *Jan. Bargain sales begin Jan, 1920* |
| *Feb.* | *15* | *32* | *8* | *25* | *Bargain sale ends Feb. 20* |

Figure 18.   Schedule of Deliveries to Stock

pianos in its furniture department, desires to set up a schedule of deliveries to stock of a certain grade of piano during
the months of November, December, January, and February.   Such a schedule may be in the form shown in
Figure 18.

A similar schedule of finished goods deliveries will need
to be prepared for each item of finished stock.   If the sched-

ule is made in terms of value, the only difference will be the method of stating the quantity in each column.

## Responsibility for Preparation of Estimate of Purchases

As to the unit of the organization which should be held responsible for the preparation of the estimate of purchases, no arbitrary rule can be established. The nature, size, and organization of the business must be considered in each case. In so far as possible the purchases estimate, like all other estimates, should be made by those who are responsible for its enforcement.

In a business with branches which handle resale material, the branch manager may make the purchases which his branch needs, under the supervision and functional control of the general purchasing agent of the company. In this case each branch manager should be held responsible for making an estimate of the purchases of his branch. These original estimates of the branch managers will be gone over by the general purchasing agent, who will transmit them with his approval to the executive in charge of the budgetary procedure, who in turn will transfer them to the budget committee for consideration and approval.

Although revisions may have to be made in the estimates submitted by the branch managers, it is desirable that they prepare these for two reasons:

1. They will take more interest in their execution if they are responsible for their preparation. If they receive an estimate prepared by someone else, they may not feel the proper amount of responsibility for any variations between the actual and the estimated figures.

2. In the making of their estimates the branch managers must study past operations and plan future ones. This study and planning will be of much value to them; it will bring to their attention many things which they would otherwise not notice.

In a department store the head of each department is responsible for the preparation of the estimate of purchases for his department. In preparing this, he may employ the assistance of the various buyers in his department. After being prepared, these departmental estimates will be examined by the merchandise manager, who will make such revisions as he deems necessary.

In a business where all purchases are made by a central purchasing department under the control of a general purchasing agent, the estimate of purchases may be prepared under his direction, but he will usually obtain the assistance and advice of subordinates in its preparation, and his estimate will be based on the estimated requirements submitted by the various departments.

Whatever is the origin of the original estimate, it will be transferred to the executive in charge of the budgetary procedure, and by him submitted to the budget committee for consideration and approval.

### Purchases Budget Control

The purchases budget provides a working program for the current period. But this program is based on estimates which, however carefully made, may prove inaccurate because of market conditions that could not be foreseen at the time these estimates were made. If the estimates prove incorrect, it is necessary to change as soon as possible the plans which were based on them. If it is estimated that the sales for the current year will be 25 per cent more than they were for the past year, a purchases budget will provide for a corresponding increase in purchases. But if at the end of the first month the sales have not increased and market conditions indicate that the anticipated increases will not materialize, it would be very unwise to continue to follow the original purchases budget. It is necessary, therefore, to have certain records and reports to make possible a revision of the purchases budget throughout the year, if the results during the year make such a revision necessary.

A revision of purchase quotas to meet changing trade conditions is not a simple task in the case of a department store where quotas are made out months in advance on thousands of different items. Perhaps the simplest way to make changes on numerous quotas is to compute the percentage that the delivery quota for the month is to the estimated sales for the month. Thus, if the estimated sales are 43 units and the delivery quota is 38 units, we may express the quota as 88.3, so that if the actual sales are 51 units we may permit, without being criticized, the delivery into stock of 88.3 per cent of 51 units, or 45 units. For reasons that are obvious, this percentage method does not give us a quota that will result in the exact inventory at the end of the month for which we originally planned. But this use of percentages is decidedly useful for revising large numbers of quotas to meet discrepancies between estimated and actual sales.

There should be prepared monthly for the use of the executives responsible for the purchasing program and for the budget committee, a report similar in form to Figure 19.

### Interpretation of Illustration

The amounts given for each item or line of goods in the first money column will be taken from the last revision of the sales program. In columns (4) and (5) a comparison is given between the delivery to stock quota on each item and the estimated sales at cost for the item. It must be remembered that estimated sales are taken at cost so that there may be this comparison between sales at cost and purchase quotas at cost. In column (6) a percentage of the quota to sales at cost is shown for each item. The data for column

## MONTHLY REPORT ON PURCHASES BUDGET

| ITEMS | Estimated Sales for Month | Less Gross Profit Estimated | Estimated Sales for Month at Cost | Purchase Quota for Month | Per Cent of Quota to Sales at Cost | Actual Sales for Month Less Gross Profit | Revised Quota | Delivered to Stock during Month (Taken from Purchase Account) | Balance in Quota Not Delivered Or Excess Delivered over Quota | Purchase Orders Outstanding under Quota Not Delivered | Balance in Quota Not Ordered or Excess of Ordered over Quota |
|---|---|---|---|---|---|---|---|---|---|---|---|
| (1) | (2) | (3) | (4) | (5) | (6) Per Cent of (5) to (4) | (7) | (8) Per Cent in (6) to Actual Sales in (7) | (9) | (10) | (11) | (12) |

Figure 19.   Monthly Report on Purchases Budget

15

(6) is not taken from the accounts, but is the result of dividing estimated sales at cost into quotas.   The actual sales for the month shown in column (7) will be taken from the sales as reported in the sales accounts of the month.   From the sales, as reported in the sales accounts, estimated gross profit is subtracted.   When actual inventory has been taken at the end of the month, actual gross profits, as shown by the accounts, should be subtracted.   The revised quotas given in column (8) may be made by applying the quota percentage given in column (6) to actual sales at cost as given in column (7).   The amounts of deliveries into finished stock, as shown in column (9), will be taken from the purchase accounts.   The orders outstanding as shown in column (11) will be taken from an order register if a book record of orders is maintained, or they may be found by adding the unfilled orders on file.

If a monthly quota system is maintained on stock deliveries, the unfilled orders at the end of a month furnish useful information to use as a basis for purchase control. It may be that unfilled orders represent poor buying, or it may be that they represent a lack of coordination of the activities between the purchase and other departments of the business.   In any case, the reason for such unfilled orders should be determined and such executive action taken as is necessary to remedy the condition.

### Use of Control Reports

Control reports are a necessity to the head buyer of a store if the activities of the various assistant buyers are to be coordinated so that they may all work towards a common end.   He makes use of purchase quotas and the subsequent reports on these quotas for the unification of the plans of his buying organization.   The quota set up on article S485, a shoe, is coordinated with the quotas set up on article H563, a silk stocking, because both the shoe and silk stocking are of a certain color, shade, and quality, and are expected to be sold together in many cases. In like manner, there will be planning on quotas of staple articles with reference to certain proposed bargain sales, and also on quotas of certain specialties with reference to their use as liners. In the same manner, quotas on various lines and variety of goods are considered in connection with each other to the end that a well-coordinated sales and purchase program may be formulated. And then reports are made on these quotas which serve as a means of correcting errors of judgment on the original quotas and of detecting failures to execute properly the program based on these quotas.

# CHAPTER XV

## THE PURCHASES BUDGET (CONTINUED)

### Disbursements for Purchases

The discussion in the preceding chapter has dealt primarily with the method of securing a coordination between purchases and sales. This is essential, but in addition it is necessary to provide for the coordination of purchases with finances. To do this it is necessary to determine the monthly expenditures in payment of purchases.

The finished goods budget shows the deliveries to stock. From the viewpoint of financial requirements, it is necessary to determine when the goods delivered are to be paid for. The method of doing this will depend on the volume of purchases to be made, and the terms on which they are to be purchased. It may be necessary to classify all purchases made by credit terms so as to obtain the data by means of which an estimate can be made as to the amount of the estimated purchases which will be made on such terms. It will then be possible to estimate the disbursements which will be made for the purchases made on each kind of terms.

To illustrate, if it is found that 50 per cent of the purchases during the past three years have been on terms 2/10, n/30, and that the payment is always made within the discount period, it may be estimated that 50 per cent of estimated purchases for the next period will be paid within ten days after the receipt of the invoice. On this basis it may be estimated that two-thirds of the merchandise purchased on these terms which is to be delivered during the next month, will be paid during that month, and that in addition it will be necessary to pay during the month for one-third of the merchandise purchased on these terms during the preceding month.

In the same manner, estimates can be made for disbursements to be made in payment for merchandise purchased on each class of terms. The errors which may arise in making such estimates are apparent. There are a number of factors which influence their exactness. It is well to remember, however, that cash receipts and disbursements can never be estimated with absolute exactness. The cash balance is maintained to provide for this inaccuracy in the same way as the inventory of finished goods is carried to provide for the inaccuracy of the sales and purchases estimates. Further discussion of the method of estimating disbursements will be found in Chapter XIX in connection with the treatment of the financial budget.

### Report on Disbursements for Purchases

As a means of controlling the disbursements for purchases and of providing data for the financial budget, it is well to have an estimate made as shown in Figure 20.

The form as given is premised on a budget period of three months in length. It can of course be adapted for use for a budget period of any length, but the longer the period, the more inaccurate the estimates for the latter part of the period are apt to be. In any case, it should be revised monthly on the basis of the monthly reports, showing actual sales, actual purchases, and actual disbursements.

### Use of Estimate of Disbursements for Purchases

The report shown in Figure 20 provides information which is of value not only in judging the advisability of the contemplated purchasing program, but also the advisability of the contemplated sales and financial programs. The most important items of information which it shows are the following:

1. The estimated deliveries to stock during the month. This can be checked against the same item on the schedule of deliveries to finished goods to determine the accuracy of the amount.

2. The estimated orders to be placed during the month. This provides a check on the amount of orders which are to be placed for future delivery. This enables the executives to know the plans of the merchandise or purchasing department so that they can curtail these plans if they deem this necessary. It indicates to the treasurer the possible demand for funds for the payment of vendors' claims.

3. It shows the estimated inventory at the end of the period. By comparing this with the inventory at the beginning of the period, it can be seen whether the purchasing program contemplates an increase in inventory. If so, the reason for this increase can be ascertained. It may of course be desirable for the inventory to be increased for several reasons which are no doubt apparent to the reader, but it is well for the contemplated increase to be called to the attention of the principal executives for their approval.

4. It shows the disbursements to be made during the month for purchases made during previous months. These are disbursements which presumably must be met, since the contracts are already made. This is useful information for the treasurer.

5. It shows the estimated disbursements for purchases made during the month. This amount is of course subject to change in case the estimated purchases are changed.

The estimate of purchase disbursements as a whole provides information which is useful in estimating the financial requirements of the contemplated sales program. If such requirements are too great, a revision of the sales program may be necessary.

### Classification of Purchase Data for Control Purposes

The discussion in the preceding chapter has pointed out the necessity for records and accounts for purchases, and

## ESTIMATE OF PURCHASES DISBURSEMENTS

| ITEMS | FIRST MONTH | | | | | | SECOND MONTH | | | | | | | THIRD | | MONTH |
|---|---|---|---|---|---|---|---|---|---|---|---|---|---|---|---|---|
| | Inventory at Beginning of Month | Estimated Deliveries to Stock during Month | Estimated Orders to be placed during Month | Estimated Inventory at End of Month | Estimated Cash Disbursements for Purchases made during Previous Month | Estimated Cash Disbursements for Purchases made during the Month | Inventory at Beginning of Month | Estimated Deliveries to Stock during Month | Estimated Orders to be placed during Month | Estimated Inventory at End of Month | Estimated Cash Disbursements for Purchases made during Previous Month | Estimated Cash Disbursements for Purchases made during the Month | Inventory at Beginning of Month | | Estimated Cash Disbursements for Purchases made during the Month |
| | | | | | | | | | | | | | | | |
| | | | | | | | | | | | | | | | |

Figure 20.  Estimate of Purchases Disbursements

the need for records and files for unfilled orders if information is to be available for the preparation and control of the purchase program. But this information must not only be available, it must be available in such form as to make this control comprehensive and not unduly burdensome. For that, it is necessary that a proper classification of purchase accounts and purchase orders be maintained. The classification which is necessary for the preparation of the monthly report shown in Figure 19 (page 225) is indicated by the report itself.

For the purpose of this report the purchase accounts must analyze the purchases into the same classes by which they are shown on the purchases budget, and outstanding orders must be classified in the same manner. For instance, if the purchases budget states a separate quota for twenty different types of purchases, there must be twenty different accounts maintained with purchases, or some supplementary record must be kept which provides for such a classification if the monthly report shown in Figure 19 is to be used effectively. The outstanding orders must also be subject to such a classification if the desired information for column (10) is to be obtained. But if this report is to be properly interpreted after it is made, additional information with reference to purchases made and orders issued is necessary, and to obtain this information other classifications must be maintained.

### Classification of Purchase Invoices

Purchases, in addition to being classified to correspond to the analysis shown on the purchases budget, may be analyzed as follows:

1. By departments or units of responsibility
2. By terms of credit
3. By buyers

In a business where there is any attempt toward functional organization and control, both sales and purchases are usually classified according to the units of organization for responsibility. Expenses are classified similarly, and consequently the efficiency of the functional managers can be judged in terms of profit and loss. For instance, in a department store the departmental managers are held responsible for the operations of their departments, and consequently the sales and purchases are analyzed by departments so that departmental profit and loss can be determined. In such a business the sales estimates and purchasing estimates are usually made separately for each department, so that the departmental analyses serve a double purpose in that they serve not only as a check upon the efficiency of departmental heads, but also as a basis for the preparation and control of the departmental estimates. In a business with branches, the responsibility for the management of each branch is imposed on the branch manager, and in order to determine his efficiency an analysis of purchases, sales, and expenses by branches is necessary.

In planning the financing of a firm's operations, it is of considerable value to the financial executive to know the terms on which the estimated purchases will be made. It has been explained above that the terms of purchase must be taken into consideration in the preparation of the estimate of purchases. If that is done, the purchase invoices may be analyzed by terms of credit so that statistics will be available to show the purchases made on each kind of terms. This analysis can then be used in estimating the proportion of the total estimated purchases which will be made on each kind of terms during the budget period. Often this classification is not shown on the ledger accounts, but only in a supplementary record. In a large business where several analyses are to be made, it will probably be obtained by a tabulating equipment.

Sometimes it is desirable to know the quantity of purchases made by different buyers, and the purchase invoices are analyzed accordingly. Such an analysis may be of value in assigning quotas to buyers and keeping a check on the amount purchased by different buyers or judging as to the wisdom of continuing the services of particular buyers.

There may be various other classifications of purchases under different circumstances, such as commodity classification, classification by vendors, etc. The classification shown on the purchase budget is usually by commodities or by groups of commodities.

### Classification of Unfilled Orders

The unfilled purchase orders, in addition to being classified according to the analysis shown on the purchases budget, should be classified so as to show the following:

1. Month of delivery
2. Contract orders
3. Orders subject to cancellation

It should be apparent that it is quite important to know the month of delivery of the goods for which orders are outstanding. Without this information, it is impossible to determine the proper delivery dates of goods still to be ordered. If orders are outstanding for goods to be delivered six months hence, this can have no effect on purchases necessary to satisfy the needs of the current month. The time of delivery is also of value to the financial executive in arranging for the payment of the goods delivered, and to the operating superintendent in planning to store and handle them.

It is also important in planning future deliveries to

know the amount of contract orders, the period covered thereby, and the extent to which deliveries under such contracts are subject to shifting. It may be desirable to speed up deliveries or to delay them, depending on the extent to which the sales program may exceed or fail to reach the estimated program.

The amount of those orders that are subject to cancellation is also quite important, especially if it becomes necessary to reduce the buying quota because of a failure of the sales program to attain the estimated goal.

In order that the amount of each class of purchase orders mentioned may be readily available, supplementary records may be kept which classify the orders as issued and show them as filled when goods are received. But if these records are to be of the greatest service, they must be accurate, and to this end periodical audits should be made to test their accuracy. Oftentimes, because these records are not a part of the general financial records, proper care is not given to their operation and verification.

### Relation of Purchasing Budget to Merchandise Policies

The discussion in the preceding chapter has explained the method of determining the "normal" inventory and the formulation of a purchasing program based on this inventory. A brief consideration of the method employed in determining the normal inventory will show that it represents what would be a satisfactory inventory under the conditions of the preceding period. It should be apparent to the reader that it is not always safe to assume that these same conditions will continue during the current period. Consequently the estimated average inventory, as determined by the method shown in the preceding chapter, may be modified by a consideration of the anticipated market conditions of the current period.

There are many considerations which may make such modifications desirable. It may be thought desirable to purchase a large amount of stock early in the period because of an anticipated increase in price, or because it is anticipated that there may be congested traffic later, or because of other conditions. On the other hand, it may be thought desirable to let the reserve stock fall below normal because of an anticipated fall in the market price. The merits of this procedure have been considered in Chapter X, in discussing the raw materials budget.

In some cases, changes in personnel of customers may be expected to increase turnover, making a smaller inventory possible. For instance, a large inflow of war workers during the war period increased the sale of certain grades of goods in some cases, and made a more rapid turnover possible. On the other hand, an attempt to cater to a more fastidious trade may tend to necessitate a large inventory in order to provide the proper variety.

The foregoing are but a few of the many changes in market conditions which may affect the purchasing program. Comparisons of statistics of past years by lines of goods, territories, and personnel of trade will help in determining the modifications necessary to arrive at the proper estimated inventory for the current period.

## Use of Purchases Budget to Control Conditions of Stock

The purchases budget may be used in many ways to assist in the control of various conditions of stock. If the warehousing facilities are limited, the purchases budget, by providing for a more or less uniform inventory, and consequently uniform deliveries into stock, will prevent the arrival of stock to an amount greater than can be properly stored. It can be seen readily that if there is not cooperation between the purchasing department and the operating or warehouse department, very undesirable situations may arise.

Again, if the purchases budget is properly made and is faithfully followed, it will be possible to have a well-formulated system of reserve and forward stocks, and there will be little danger of the reserve stocks being exhausted when it is necessary to replenish the forward stock. In some lines of business, such as mail-order houses and wholesalers of standard lines of clothing, this is a matter of prime importance.

A properly controlled buying budget will eliminate the necessity of making omissions or substitutions in filling orders. The demands of the orders are anticipated in the sales estimate and the correlated buying budget, and the goods are on hand when the orders arrive. Such a budget will also eliminate the need for holding unfilled sales orders until goods are purchased with which to fill them.

In short, the purchases budget, like the sales budget, is one of the connecting links between the various departments and serves as a basis for coordination of all the activities of the business.

## Relation of Purchasing Program to Merchandise Policies

The purchasing program is but one part of the merchandise program and in the formulation of the latter a number of factors must be considered. Some of these factors are external to the business organization, while others are matters of internal policy. Illustrations of the former were given in the discussion of the relation of market conditions to the purchases budget. Some of the most important internal factors which must be given consideration in merchandise planning are:

| | | |
|---|---|---|
| 1. Sales | 3. Turnover | 5. Mark-downs |
| 2. Inventory | 4. Purchases | 6. Expense |

Each of these factors must be given careful consideration in making the merchandise plans of each department, and the policy of the firm with reference to each given proper emphasis.

It may be said, by way of caution, that "external" and "internal" factors which affect the merchandise plans are closely related. Each may have an effect on the other. For instance, the market conditions may be such that the company may find it necessary to alter its usual policy with reference to inventory, purchases, or expense.

## Importance of a Consideration of Expense

In the preceding discussion it has been assumed that all the plans of the business are based on the sales program. It has been explained, however, that the sales program is based not alone upon sales possibilities, but also upon production or purchasing capacity, expense requirements, and profit potentialities. As the expense factor is an important one in a mercantile business, it seems worth while to emphasize again the importance of giving it very careful consideration in forming the sales program and the relative purchasing program.

It is important to see the anticipated expenses of each department and to determine if the sales program is sufficient to warrant the expenses planned. If that program is not sufficient, it is necessary to plan either for an increase in sales or for a decrease in expense. It is beneficial to the department head to have the relationship between his sales and expenses brought forcibly to his attention. After the estimated expenses of the department are determined, it is well to show the amount of sales which are necessary to make possible the incurrence of these expenses with a satisfactory margin of profit.

To make this calculation it is necessary to consider (1)

DEPT. #1

## PRELIMINARY SIX MONTHS' PLANS

Period from ___Jan. 1, 1922___ to ___July 1, 1922___

**Retail Stock**

On Hand at
Beginning of Period_____

Desired at
End of Period_____

**Retail**

Maximum Stock_____

Minimum Stock_____

Mark-Downs Allowed_____

**Initial Mark-Up Required**

| MONTH | Jan. July | Feb. Aug. | Mar Sept. | April Oct. | May Nov. | June Dec. | TOTAL |
|---|---|---|---|---|---|---|---|
| **SALES:** | | | | | | | |
| Last Year | | | | | | | |
| Estimated | | | | | | | |
| Result | | | | | | | |
| **INVENTORY** | | | | | | | |
| Last Year | | | | | | | |
| Estimated | | | | | | | |
| Result | | | | | | | |
| **TURNOVER:** | | | | | | | |
| Last Year | | | | | | | |
| Estimated | | | | | | | |
| Result | | | | | | | |
| **PURCHASES:** | | | | | | | |
| Last Year | | | | | | | |
| Estimated | | | | | | | |
| Result | | | | | | | |
| **MARK-DOWNS:** | | | | | | | |
| Last Year | | | | | | | |
| Estimated | | | | | | | |
| Result | | | | | | | |
| **EXPENSE:** | | | | | | | |
| Last Year % | | | | | | | |
| Estimated % | | | | | | | |
| Result % | | | | | | | |

**REMARKS**

Figure 21. Showing Merchandise Plan of Each Department of a
Department Store

the estimated sales, (2) the average mark-up, (3) the average mark-down, and (4) the expected profit.  If we assume that the estimated expenses of Department A are $7,000, the average mark-up 40 per cent, the average mark-down 2 per cent, and the expected profit 3 per cent, then the necessary sales will be obtained by the following calculation:

$$\$7,000 \div [40\% - (2\% + 3\%)] = \$20,000$$

If the sales program of Department A calls for sales of less than $20,000, it must be revised or else the expense or profit estimate must be revised.

If a merchandise plan is made based on a close correlation between the sales, purchasing, and expense program, there will be less likelihood of disappointments at the end of the period.

### Report on Merchandise Plan

The merchandise plan of each department of a department store or wholesale house can be very effectively presented for executive consideration by the use of a report made in the form shown in Figure 21.

The information shown on this report is self-explanatory. It serves not only as a basis for formulating plans, but can also be used as a means of checking their performance since it provides for a comparison of the estimated and the actual.  If desired, sufficient space may be left in connection with each section so that at the end of each month revisions may be shown for each of the following months.

It will of course be understood that this general report will be supplemented by a number of detailed reports which will serve to explain the summary figures shown on it.  If desired, this report may be so designed as to show comparisons by percentages.

## Review and Summary

In Chapters V and VI the formation and execution of the sales budget has been discussed. In Chapters XIV and XV an attempt has been made to outline the procedure involved in the correlation of purchases with sales, and in the preparation and execution of the purchases budget.

In summary form this procedure may be stated as follows:

### I. PREPARATION OF PURCHASES BUDGET

*First.* An estimate of sales is made for the period. To recapitulate what has been said in a preceding chapter, this requires:

1. An analysis of the sales of preceding periods. The sales accounts should furnish this analysis. But several analyses may be of value in arriving at the final sales program, and it may be necessary to refer back to sales tickets or other vouchers for data in making this analysis. Thus if the sales accounts lead to a report of sales by lines of goods, it may be of value to refer to analyses of sales by terms, by territories, etc.
2. Use of sales analysis comparisons in estimating sales under existing or future trade conditions.
3. Revision of original sales estimates in the light of purchasing possibilities, expense requirements, and profit potentialities.
4. Comparison of estimates of sales with actual sales accounts during the period, and correction of first estimate as actual sales accounts show errors of judgment in setting up the sales program.

*Second.* An estimate of turnover for the period is made. To do this requires:

1. Use of inventory accounts and sales accounts of past periods in arriving at average turnover for each line of goods in comparable past periods.
2. Use of past average turnover in estimating probable turnover under the existing or future trade conditions.

*Third.* Estimated average inventory for the coming period is computed for each item or line of finished stock to be sold in the period. For control purposes, these estimates are set up in schedules of finished stock inventory

16

requirements. As the period advances, comparisons are made between schedules and the amounts shown by the inventory accounts, and the schedules are corrected where errors of judgment are apparent through such comparisons.

*Fourth.* A schedule of deliveries of finished stock is made. To be effective as a basis for management control, this schedule or estimate of deliveries should specify the amount of each line of goods that is to be placed in stock each week or each month of the period. If the period covers six months commencing on January 1, the delivery quotas may be computed as follows:

> Estimated sales for the month of January at cost.
> Plus inventory expected on January 31.
> Less actual inventory on December 31.
> Equals delivery into stock quota for the month of January.

> Then for the month of February.
> Estimated cost of sales for February.
> Plus inventory expected on February 28.
> Less estimated inventory on January 31.
> Equals delivery into stock quota for month of February.

And so on for each of the six months. If the volume of sales is large and fairly constant, as in a mail-order furniture line, such a monthly quota will furnish reasonably close limits on purchases. But if the volume of the sales in the line is subject to great seasonal variations, as in a department store wall-paper line, a weekly quota should be set up for deliveries into stock during rush seasons.

*Fifth.* An estimate of purchases which will satisfy the schedule of finished goods deliveries is set up. This will show estimated orders to be placed each month, estimated deliveries to be made, and estimated disbursements to be made in settlement of vendors' claims.

*Sixth.* The schedule of finished goods deliveries and the estimate of purchases is approved by the controlling executive authority with whom final approval rests.

## II. Reports Used in Preparation and Execution of Purchases Budget

If it is assumed that the buying budget for 1922 is under consideration, the name of each report with the money column headings of each which would be used in its preparation and execution may be as follows:

*First.* Weighted Average of Sales for three years for each class of goods:
1. Sales for the year 1919.
2. Sales for the year 1920.
3. Sales for the year 1921.
4. Arithmetical average.
5. Weighted average—to be used as a basis for the sales estimate.

*Second.* Sales program for the year 1922 for each item sold:
1. Weighted average for the three years preceding.
2. Per cent of 1922 estimated increases and decreases.
3. Sales estimate for 1922 on each item.

*Third.* Monthly Report of Actual Sales under sales program:
1. Sales estimated for period to date.
2. Actual sales for period to date.
3. Per cent of increase or decrease of actual over estimated.
4. Add or deduct from sales program for the rest of the period.

*Fourth.* Estimated Average Inventory by Classes or Goods and Items:
1. Actual sales for 1919, 1920, 1921.
2. Less actual gross profit for 1919, 1920, 1921.
3. 1919–1920–1921 sales at cost.
4. Rate of turnover on each item for 1919, 1920, 1921.
5. Estimated sales for 1922.
6. Estimated gross profit for 1922.
7. Estimated sales at cost for 1922.
8. Estimated turnover rate for 1922.
9. Estimated average inventory for 1922.

*Fifth.* Estimate of Finished Goods:
1. Month.
2. Estimated inventory at beginning of the month.
3. Estimated sales at cost.
4. Estimated inventory at the end of the month.
5. Estimated deliveries to stock during the month.
6. Comments.

*Sixth.* Estimate of Purchases:
1. Item.
2. First month:
   (a) Estimated inventory at beginning of month.
   (b) Estimated deliveries to stock during the month.

(c) Estimated orders to be placed during the month.

(d) Estimated inventory at the end of the month.

(e) Estimated cash disbursements for purchases made during previous months.

(f) Estimated cash disbursements for purchases made during the current month.

3. Second month:

The same as for first month, and so continued for each month.

*Seventh.* Monthly Inventory Comparison Report:

1. Estimated sales.
2. Actual sales.
3. Per cent of increase or decrease.
4. Estimated average inventory.
5. Actual inventory.
6. Per cent of increase or decrease.

*Eighth.* Monthly Report on Quotas:

1. Estimated sales for month.
2. Estimated gross profit.
3. Estimated sales at cost.
4. Purchase quota.
5. Ratio of (4) to (3).
6. Actual sales for month.
7. Revised quota, per cent shown in (5) taken of actual sales shown in (6).
8. Delivered into stock during the month—taken from the purchase accounts.
9. Balance of quota not delivered or excess of quota delivered.
10. Purchase orders outstanding under quota, not delivered.
11. Balance in quota not ordered or excess ordered over quota.

*Ninth.* Report on Merchandise Plans of Each Department:

This report may be made in the form in Figure 21.

# CHAPTER XVI

## THE PLANT AND EQUIPMENT BUDGET

### Need for Consideration

In every business there is need for certain equipment to be used in carrying on its operations. The amount and nature of this equipment depends on the size and the nature of those operations. The professional firm needs little equipment and very rarely owns the building in which it is housed. The mercantile firm uses a limited amount of equipment, depending on its size, and in many cases does not own the building in which it operates. The manufacturing firm usually employs a large amount of equipment, and in most cases owns the plant in which it carries on its manufacturing operations. Consequently a large part of the capital of most manufacturing firms is invested in their plant and equipment.

It can be seen, therefore, that expenditures for plant and equipment are most important in connection with an industrial concern, but that they are of some significance in the case of all businesses. The following discussion will be devoted primarily to a consideration of the control of expenditures for the plant and equipment of a manufacturing business, but the same principles will apply to the control of expenditures for plant and equipment of any other type of business.

### Classification of Plant and Equipment Expenditures

The expenditures made in connection with the plant and equipment of a business may be classified into the following general groups:

245

1. Expenditures which are necessary to maintain the present plant and equipment at its normal efficiency. No matter how carefully equipment is selected or how carefully it is used, certain expenditures must be made from time to time to keep it in such condition that it can be operated efficiently. Such expenditures are called "repairs."

2. Expenditures which are made to replace with new equipment, old equipment that is worn out and discarded. Regardless of the amount spent in the way of repairs, equipment will in time be in such a condition that it can no longer be operated profitably. It is necessary to purchase new equipment to take its place. Such expenditures are termed *replacements*.

3. Expenditures in connection with present equipment which add to its life or efficiency. For instance, a machine may be entirely overhauled; old and worn parts are replaced by new ones, with the result that it will continue in use longer than was originally estimated. Or a new patent may be added to the machine which will not prolong its life but will increase its efficiency during its life. Such expenditures are termed "betterments."

4. Expenditures which are made to obtain new equipment which does not replace other equipment but which represents an addition to the sum total of the equipment employed by the business. As a business expands, it is necessary to secure additional equipment to carry on the increased volume of business. Expenditures for this purpose are termed "additions."

## Treatment of Different Classes of Expenditures

From the viewpoint of both accounting and financial management, the classes of expenditures explained in the foregoing discussion are distinctly different and must be recorded carefully to show properly their effect on the financial condition and operating efficiency of the business. A proper record is necessary also for use as a basis in planning and executing an effective control of these expenditures. It will be necessary to discuss separately the method of recording and reporting each class.

## Repairs

Repairs are usually considered as a current expense of the business, which must be provided for out of the income of the fiscal period in which they occur. This is on the theory that repairs are necessitated because of the operations of the period when they occur and that consequently their cost should be borne by that period.

In opposition to this theory it is sometimes urged that repairs are not the result necessarily of the operations of the period when they occur, but may be necessitated because, in part at least, of the operations of previous periods. In other words, the operations of one period may cause a machine to be so worn that it is almost ready to break down at the end of the period, but the break with the consequent repair may not actually occur until the beginning of the next period. The customary practice assumes, however, that repairs "even up" from period to period, since each period suffers repairs caused in part by the operations of previous periods, and in turn transfers "potential repairs" to the next period. Consequently, it is argued that the cost of repairs tends to be approximately uniform from period to period.

If, for any reason, the cost of repairs fluctuates to any extent from period to period, and it is desired to distribute their cost evenly, this may be accomplished by estimating the average cost of repairs on the basis of past experience and future plans, and setting up a reserve for repairs. Under this method there will be charged to expense and credited to a reserve for repairs an amount equal to the estimated cost of repairs. As the repairs take place they are charged to the reserve for repairs.

If standard rates for repairs are established, the preparation of the manufacturing expense budget is facilitated.

This procedure also assists in the establishment of standard expense rates such as were discussed in Chapter XIII.

## Replacements

The cost of replacements is not an expense of the period when the replacement takes place, but is an expense of all the periods during which the equipment which is replaced has been used.   If a machine costing $1,000 is purchased in 1921, the year 1921 should not bear the entire cost of the new machine, neither should it bear the difference between the cost and the scrap value of the old machine.   Each of the six years during which the machine has been used has received a benefit from its use, and consequently, each of the six years should be charged with a part of its cost.   If the scrap value of the machine is $100, the six years during which the machine has been used must be charged with $900 for its use.

As to whether each year should be charged an equal amount, there is no unanimity of opinion.   It depends upon the method of "depreciation" that is adopted.   It is not deemed desirable at this time to enter into a discussion of the different methods which may be employed.   It is important to see, however, that the estimated decrease in value of the asset due to the operations of the business each year must be charged against the income derived from these operations.

Since the actual expenditures for any particular equipment take place at one time, and not during each year of its use, it is customary to credit the estimated depreciation of each period to a reserve for depreciation account and to debit an expense account for the same amount.   When the asset is sold or discarded, it is charged against the reserve account.   By this means the cost of equipment is charged against the income of the periods which benefit from its use.

The new equipment which is purchased to take the place of the old is charged to the asset account.

## Betterments

When betterments are made, future periods will be benefited either through the increased efficiency of the equipment concerned, or through its longer life, and hence replacement costs are postponed. In either case, since future periods are to receive the benefit of such betterments, they should bear the cost of the betterments. Hence betterments are charged to asset accounts and are not reflected in the expense accounts of the period in which they are incurred.

It is often difficult to distinguish between a betterment and a repair. In many cases an expenditure is partly one and partly the other. To take a classic illustration, if a wooden roof is replaced by a slate roof, so much of its cost as would have been incurred if a wooden roof had been used will be treated as a repair, while the excess of the cost of the slate over a wooden roof will be treated as a betterment. In case of doubt, it is the practice of accountants to be conservative and treat the expenditure as a repair.

## Additions

Additions to plant and equipment are made for the benefit of future periods. Hence their cost is not charged to the period in which they are obtained but is distributed, by means of the periodical depreciation charge, over the periods during which they are used. Consequently, additions are a capital and not a revenue charge.

It must be realized, however, that as soon as additions are secured they give rise to revenue charges, since a charge for depreciation must be made at the end of each fiscal period to provide for their replacement.

## Capital vs. Revenue Charges

From the foregoing discussion it can be seen that from the viewpoint of accounting, plant and equipment gives rise to two kinds of charges:

1. Those which are made to *maintain* the present equipment. Repairs and replacements are included in this group. These may be termed "maintenance" costs. They must be included in the periodical expense accounts; or to use technical terminology, they are "charged against revenue." Many authorities do not include provision for replacements (that is, the periodical depreciation allowance) as an item of maintenance cost. From the viewpoint of a maintenance budget, this inclusion is desirable and no difficulty arises if the definition of maintenance precedes its use.

2. Those charges which represent an addition to the assets of the business. Betterments and additions are included in this group. These are termed "plant and equipment costs." They are charged to the asset, or to use technical terminology, they are "charged to capital."

## Method of Handling Maintenance Charges

The preceding discussion has dealt with the method of recording these two classes of charges. The following discussion will deal primarily with the method of exercising control over their amount.

Maintenance charges on plant and equipment used in production are a part of manufacturing expenses and should be included in the manufacturing expense budget. This is necessary in order to judge the effect of the contemplated production program on the amount of the manufacturing expense. It is also necessary in determining costs of manufacturing product and in the establishment of standard rates.

It is desirable that the maintenance costs also be shown on the plant and equipment budget, since this makes it possible to obtain a comprehensive picture of the plant and equipment program as a whole.  Their appearance on the plant and equipment budget also facilitates the establishment of appropriations for them.  If the manufacturing expense budget and the plant and equipment budget are prepared by different units of the organization, which is usually the case, the maintenance charges appearing on the two budgets can be checked against each other, which will tend to correct errors made by either party in making the estimate.  If there is a disagreement between the estimates shown on the two budgets, this should be reconciled, if possible, by the parties responsible for it.   If this cannot be done, it will be necessary to submit the disagreement to the budget committee for settlement.

It must of course be remembered that in preparing the financial budget and also the estimated statement of profit and loss, the cost of maintenance must be taken from only one budget.

### Requirements for Plant and Equipment Control

To exercise effective control over disbursements for plant and equipment, three things are necessary:

1. There must be available data which will show results of past operations and serve as the basis of future plans.
2. After all the available data have been considered, the plans which have been formulated must be expressed in workable form by means of a budget on plant and equipment.   Sometimes two budgets are made, one on maintenance costs and one on the cost of betterments and additions.   The requirements for each are sufficiently similar to make their joint discussion possible.
3. After the budget is made, it is necessary to have records and reports prepared which will make possible the control of such expenditures and the enforcement of the budget plans.

### Data Required as Basis of Control

The data required to serve as a basis for control of plant and equipment expenditures may be classified as follows:

1. That which is obtained from the accounting and statistical records with reference to past experience.
2. That which is obtained by a mathematical calculation based on predetermined factors.
3. That which is determined by a consideration of future plans.
4. That which is obtained as a result of the investigation and study of experts.

## Accounting and Statistical Data

To make plans which will serve to control expenditures for plant and equipment, it is necessary that a proper classification of the plant and equipment be made and that proper records be maintained which reflect this classification. This classification is necessary to make an accurate estimate of plant and equipment expenditures.

To illustrate, in a manufacturing business the plant and equipment expenditures will vary with the production program. If production is to be increased it will be necessary to do one or both of two things: (1) secure additional equipment; (2) use present equipment more intensively. In either case, additional expenditures will be incurred, and to estimate accurately the amount of these expenditures it is necessary to consider carefully the various kinds of equipment used in production.

If additional equipment is to be secured it will be necessary to determine the units of equipment used in the past and the amount of production which has been accomplished with this equipment. On this basis, the additional equipment required to secure the increased production capacity can be estimated. That the past production capacity may be obtained accurately, a record of each unit of equipment is necessary.

If the present equipment is to be used more intensively, this will increase the maintenance cost, and an estimate of this increase must be made. It should be obvious that a change in the production program will not affect all the equipment of the business to the same extent. For instance, it may be planned to increase the output of one department, while the output of all the remaining departments is to remain the same. This increase in the output of one department is very apt to increase the maintenance expense of this department, and if the previous expense is shown separately from that of all the other departments, a more accurate estimate of the increase can be made. It will be necessary, however, to know more than the total cost of the maintenance of the department. The new program will probably affect some units of equipment in the department more than it will others. It is desirable, therefore, to have records which will show each unit of equipment in the department, and the maintenance expense incurred on it. This is accomplished by keeping a plant ledger.

## Plant Ledger

A plant ledger is a record which contains an account with each unit of plant and equipment. It serves as a subsidiary record to the controlling account or accounts with plant and equipment which are kept on the main ledger. The plant ledger is usually kept on cards or loose-leaf sheets, each card or sheet providing a record of one unit of equipment. The size of this unit will vary, depending on conditions. There may be a separate account for each machine, or if several machines of the same pattern and size are purchased at the same time, they may all be recorded in one account.

Each account in the plant ledger should show at least three things:

1. The original cost of equipment and the date of purchase.
2. The amount of depreciation which has accrued on the equipment to date.
3. Its present book value.

In addition the account may show the amount of the repairs which have been made on the equipment to date.

It will be understood that the repairs entered on the plant ledger account will not affect the value of the equipment, since they are treated as an expense and are never

| PLANT LEDGER | | | | Our Plant No._____ | |
|---|---|---|---|---|---|
| Name of Item_____ | Made By_____ | | Maker's No._____ | | Acct. No._____ |
| _____ | | | Bldg._____ | | Dept._____ |

| Indicate below whether machine proper, accessories, foundation, or additions, etc. | FIXED ASSETS | | DEPRECIATION RESERVE | | | |
|---|---|---|---|---|---|---|
| | Detail | Total | Date | Rate | Annual | Total |
| | | | | | | |
| | | | | | | |
| | | | | | | |
| | | | | | | |
| | | | | | | |
| | | | | | | |
| | | | | | | |

Figure 22.   Plant Ledger

added to the asset.   It is useful to have them entered on the plant ledger account for memorandum purposes, so that in making future estimates it will be possible to obtain information of the past costs of repairs, not only in total but also by departments and by units.   It is not within the province of this discussion to treat of the accounting features involved in the operation of a plant ledger, but it is necessary to emphasize its usefulness in making plans for the control of maintenance cost.

Figure 22 shows a typical form of plant ledger.

## Data Calculated from Predetermined Factors

Later chapters will show that the various departmental estimates are combined for two purposes:

1. To determine the estimated cash receipts and the estimated cash disbursements, and thereby formulate a financial budget.
2. To determine the estimated revenues and the estimated expenses, and thereby formulate an estimated statement of profit and loss.

In making all the departmental estimates, it should be borne in mind that every business desires to formulate a program which it is capable of financing and which will result in the greatest possible profit. A financial budget and the estimated statement of profit and loss are the statements which answer the two questions which are most significant with reference to the budgetary program. And all departmental estimates must be made so that these two statements can be prepared. In the preparation of the estimated statement of profit and loss, the periodical depreciation charge is an important factor. Consequently it must be given careful consideration in the preparation of the plant and equipment budget.

All equipment wears out in time and its replacement must be provided for. This provision is accomplished by charging a certain amount to the expenses of each budget period, and crediting a like amount to a reserve for depreciation. The accounting technique involved in the operation of such a reserve account need not be dealt with here. It is sufficient at this time to see that the amount of such depreciation is an important element of the expense of operation and must be included in the plant and equipment budget.   In the calculation of the depreciation charge, three things are considered: the original cost of the asset, its antici- pated life, and its estimated scrap value.   By subtracting the scrap value of the asset from its original cost, it is possi- ble to determine the cost of the use of the asset during its period of life.   This cost must be distributed over the period of its life in such a way that each budget period will be charged with its equitable share.

### Distribution of Depreciation Cost

There is a difference of opinion as to how this cost should be distributed.  Some contend that each budget period should be charged an equal amount; others contend that the earlier period should be charged more than the later periods, since the equipment is more efficient when it is new and the cost of repairs is less, while, when it becomes older, its efficiency decreases and the cost of repairs becomes greater.  Other methods are also suggested, but it is not thought advisable to discuss them here.  Whatever method of determining the periodical charge is used, once adopted it should be followed throughout the life of the equipment.

The determination of the periodical charge is, therefore, merely a mathematical calculation.  If it is decided to charge each period a uniform amount, it is only necessary to take the figures of past periods as a basis of the present period budget charge.  If some other method is followed, the charge for the current period may be more or less than that of the previous period, but it will be a uniform increase or decrease and can be determined by a consideration of the predetermined factors previously mentioned.

### Effect of the Budget Program

The accounting and statistical records show the past expenditures for plant and equipment, but as suggested by the preceding discussion, a change in the volume of production affects both the maintenance charges and the charges for additions and betterments. It is necessary, therefore, to consider the effect of the budget program on each of these.

There are many plans which may affect cost of maintenance. If a large increase in production is planned, the increased cost of maintenance arising from this increased production must be estimated. If new methods of manufacture are to be employed, the consequent change in maintenance cost must be calculated. If new equipment is to take the place of old, the maintenance cost will be affected. If it is planned to inaugurate a policy of keeping the equipment in better repair so as to make it more efficient and to prolong its life, this change must be considered. These as well as other factors affect the cost of maintenance, and all these factors must be considered.

In considering the relation of maintenance cost to future plans, various comparisons should be made. This is due to the fact that some items of maintenance cost will vary in proportion to certain factors, while others will vary in proportion to different factors. To estimate these, it is necessary to determine the ratio of the volume of production to these costs during the past period or periods. By applying this ratio to the estimated volume of production for the current period, an estimate of these items of maintenance expense for this period can be obtained. Some items of maintenance cost will vary more nearly with the floor space used than with the production volume. Therefore, the ratio of floor space used in the past period to these items of maintenance expense during the same periods will be obtained, and this ratio applied to the estimated floor space of the current period. Other items of maintenance costs may vary in proportion to the number of units of equipment

17

which are used. Hence the amount of these items will be increased as the number of the units of equipment are increased.

In the same manner in which the general plans of the business, as reflected in the departmental estimates, affect the cost of maintenance, they determine the amount of new equipment to be purchased. In a manufacturing business the amount of equipment required is determined primarily by the volume of production. If records are available which show machine capacity, such as were discussed in connection with the production budget, it is not difficult to estimate the requirements of the increased production in terms of number of machines or units of equipment. If proper records are maintained, it is possible to estimate the total requirements of the production program and the total production capacity of the factory. By a comparison the excess of requirements over capacity can be determined, and from this the new equipment required can be calculated.

### Information Obtained by the Investigation and Study of Experts

It is desirable that a periodical check be made on the accuracy of the value of the plant and equipment as shown by the records. If a plant ledger is maintained in the form described in the preceding discussion, it is possible to obtain the original cost, the accrued depreciation, and the repairs incurred on each unit of plant and equipment. The depreciation shown as accrued is only an estimate, however, and the expenses which have been incurred may have been more or less than those required to maintain the equipment in an efficient condition. Unless some steps are taken to determine the accuracy of the estimated depreciation and the sufficiency of the repairs which have been made, it may be determined in the future that both the depreciation and the repairs have been inadequate, and consequently there will be an unduly heavy charge against the earnings of future years.

To avoid this it is desirable that a periodical inventory or appraisal be made of plant and equipment and used as a means of checking the plant ledger and as a basis for budgetary plans. By this means inaccuracies in depreciaton estimates and inadequate repairs can be discovered and corrected. It is also possible that too liberal depreciation may be allowed or too extensive repairs are being made. Such appraisals will serve to disclose this. They will also show when it is better to purchase a new machine rather than repair an old one.

Although an appraisal of plant and equipment is quite valuable to use in the way indicated in the preceding paragraph, it must be used with discretion, especially if it is made by professional appraisers. The viewpoint of the professional appraiser is not always that of the accountant or that of the financial executive. The appraiser tries to determine the present value of the article he is appraising. He is concerned with its original cost and past use, only as they assist him in determining present value. As a consequence, market fluctuations are apt to be reflected in his appraisal. The accountant and financial executive, on the other hand, are not interested in the market value of the equipment. They are interested only in apportioning the original cost and the cost of repairs over the periods which will benefit from its use, in as equitable a manner as possible. An increase in the market value of the asset does not increase its life or its efficiency; neither does a decrease in its market value decrease its life or its efficiency.

Because of these reasons, the value of the appraiser may not agree with the book value, and yet the book record may be satisfactory. The chief importance of the appraisal is not the value which it places on the asset, but rather the appraiser's estimate of the length of life and efficiency of the asset as reflected in the value placed on it.

## The Plant Engineer

Many manufacturing companies have on their staff a plant engineer, who is responsible for the production, use, and maintenance of plant and equipment. As indicative of the function of the plant engineer, the following responsibilities may be mentioned:

1. The study of improved methods of factory construction.
2. The study of present factory layouts, and presentation for the approval of the executive in charge of production, of proposals for improvements based on costs involved and savings made.
3. The study of machinery, equipment, and tools, and the presentation for the approval of the executive in charge of production, of proposals for changes, based on costs involved and savings to be made.
4. The presentation of a periodical plant and equipment program, based on studies made in collaboration with the works planning department and the works engineering department.
5. The presentation of the plant and equipment program to the executive in charge of production, for approval and transmission to the budget committee.
6. The preparation of a periodical maintenance program as prepared by the works maintenance department and detailed by the works engineering department.
7. The presentation of the maintenance program to the executive in charge of production, for approval and transmission to the budget committee.
8. The supervision over the execution of the plant and equipment and the maintenance programs as approved by the budget committee.

Where there is an efficient plant engineer performing the functions suggested in the above outline, the services of professional appraisers can usually be dispensed with under normal conditions.

# CHAPTER XVII

## THE PLANT AND EQUIPMENT BUDGET
### (Continued)

### Preparation of Plant and Equipment Budget

The preceding discussion explained in considerable detail the data which serve as a basis for the preparation of the plant and equipment budget. It is now necessary to see how these data are formulated into a budgetary program which serves as a means of controlling plant and equipment expenditures. This involves a consideration of:

1. The contents of the plant and equipment budget.
2. The responsibility for its preparation.
3. The form in which it is made.
4. The manner in which it is used.

### Contents of the Plant and Equipment Budget

The plant and equipment budget can be made to show any information which the executives think is desirable for their use. It is usually thought desirable that it contain the following:

1. The value of present equipment at the beginning of the period.
2. The estimated depreciation and repairs on present equipment.
3. The estimated cost of new equipment which should show:
    (a) Cost of factory equipment, and
    (b) Cost of equipment for administrative and selling units of the business.
4. Estimated depreciation and repairs on new equipment.
5. Total depreciation and total repairs on both old and new equipment.
6. Value of total equipment at end of period.

261

### Responsibility for Preparation of Plant and Equipment Budget

The executive in charge of production is responsible for the preparation of the plant and equipment budget so far as it relates to the factory. This responsibility he will delegate to the plant engineer, who in turn will employ the assistance of the works maintenance department and the works engineering department. In calculating the depreciation charges he will avail himself of the services of the accounting department as well. The cost records will also be of service in estimating the cost of repairs and construction of new equipment. The purchasing department will assist in estimating the cost of new equipment which it is planned to purchase.

In estimating the amount of equipment required it is necessary to make use of the estimate of production, since the quantity of production will affect the equipment requirements. If a plant engineer is not employed, the plant and equipment budget may be prepared by the staff of the production manager or by the planning department. The cost of repairs and depreciation will be estimated by the cost accounting department in the estimate of manufacturing expense, and this estimate may be used in preparing the estimate of plant and equipment, but it is preferable that a separate estimate be prepared by some unit of the production department.

The office manager is responsible for the preparation of the estimate of equipment for the administrative and selling units. In its preparation he will employ the assistance of the heads of the departments and executive units. Each of these will submit a request to the office manager for the equipment which he desires during the next budget period. The office manager will consolidate these into one estimate and transmit it with his recommendations to the executive in charge of the budgetary procedure.

## PLANT AND EQUIPMENT BUDGET

| GROUP | OLD EQUIPMENT | | | NEW EQUIPMENT | | | | | Total Depreciation | Total Repairs | Value of Total Equipment at End of Period |
| | Amount at Beginning of Period | Estimated Depreciation | Estimated Repairs | New Equipment Required | When Needed | Estimated Depreciation | Estimated Repairs | | | | |
| (1) | (2) | (3) | (4) | (5) | (6) | (7) | (8) | | (9) | (10) | (11) |

Figure 23.   Plant and Equipment Budget

The production manager will transmit the estimate of manufacturing plant and equipment to the executive in charge of the budgetary procedure, and the latter will transmit it together with the estimate of the office manager to the budget committee. After the committee has approved these estimates, they will be returned to the production manager and the office manager, respectively.

### Form of the Plant and Equipment Budget

No standard form for the plant and equipment budget can be described, for its form will depend upon the method employed in its preparation and use. Figure 23 is indicative of the information that the budget should contain. A separate form may be used for factory equipment and for office equipment, but the information desired in the two cases is sufficiently similar to make the same form satisfactory in most cases.

In filling in columns (4) and (8) the plant engineer will consult the works engineering department with reference to the cost of repairs. The works maintenance department will supply information with reference to the amount of repairs to be made. If the company produces its equipment, the works engineering department will supply the data needed for column (5). If the new equipment is to be purchased from outside vendors, the purchasing agent will supply these data.

Column (6) on the plant and equipment budget states when the new equipment is desired. With this as a basis the purchasing agent will state the terms on which the goods will be purchased and show the date of payment. This information is necessary for the preparation of the financial budget. If the equipment is to be produced by the company, an estimate must be made of the disbursements necessary for its production. The date given in column (6)

is the date when the complete equipment is desired.   It
may require a considerable period of time for its production.
During the process of its construction expenditures for
labor and possibly for materials will need to be made.
Under such circumstances, the estimated expenditures preceding the completion of the equipment must be determined
and allocated to the proper period for the purpose of the
financial budget.

## Execution of the Plant and Equipment Budget

The budget for plant and equipment consists of an estimate of the expenditures necessary for maintaining the
present equipment and the securing and maintenance of
the additional equipment demanded by the budget program.
Its approval is followed by the making of various appropriations for the necessary amount to cover the cost of the various items included in the budget.   After these appropriations are made, it is necessary to establish a procedure which
will effect their enforcement.   This procedure usually
requires the following:

1. That expenditures under any appropriation be made only after
   requisitions for these expenditures, accompanied by proper
   estimates of cost, have been submitted and approved by the
   proper authority.
2. That careful costs be kept on all work done under appropriations.
3. That reports be prepared showing a comparison between the
   estimated and actual cost of all such work performed.
4. That reports be prepared monthly showing the status of all
   appropriations.

## Requisitions for Expenditures

It is customary to delegate to some official of the company the authority to grant expenditures under each appropriation.   In many cases the expenditures are divided
into two groups, known as "minor" and "major."   For

instance, any expenditure of less than $100 may be termed a "minor" expenditure, and any expenditure of more than $100 may be termed a "major" expenditure. The head of the production department may be given the authority to approve all minor expenditures for the production department, and the office manager to approve all minor expenditures of the other departments. For the major expenditures the approval of the budget committee may be required.

That the proper executives may exercise effective control over the disbursements made under appropriations, it is necessary that the disbursements be made only as a result of a requisition or request on the part of the one desiring that repairs be made or additional equipment secured. When repairs or additions to plant or equipment are desired by any department, the head of this department should transmit a requisition to the production manager or the office manager, as the case may be.

Such requests should be accompanied by an estimate of the cost of the repairs or additions. If equipment is to be purchased from outside vendors, it is easy to obtain the purchase cost and submit it with the requisition. If additions to plant or equipment are to be constructed by the company, an estimate of the cost of the construction must be made.

The estimate of the cost of repairs or construction which is to be done by the company can be made in two ways. If the business maintains an engineering department, this department can be asked to make an estimate. A competent engineer learns by experience to estimate costs accurately. His estimates should be checked by statistics of past costs. If it is not possible or not desirable to have engineers make the estimate, it can be made by the cost accounting department, which will make the estimate on the basis of the statistics obtained from the records of previous costs. These estimates may be erroneous if the one making them is not trained in mechanics. If cooperation between the accounting department and the engineering department is secured, more accurate estimates will be obtained.

### Costs of Construction and Repairs

If the requisition calls for construction of repairs or equipment by the factory, there should be careful records kept of the cost of the construction. The method of determining these costs is very similar to the method of determining the cost of goods manufactured for sale. Each requisition, after it has been approved, is given a number, and a construction order is issued authorizing the construction called for by the requisition. The construction order has the same number as the requisition. An account is opened on the cost records for the construction order and all costs incurred in the construction are charged to this account.

It must be remembered that in arriving at the cost of construction a business cannot derive a profit from work done for itself. Hence no profit must be allowed on construction work performed by the company for itself. It may be possible that the company performs this work for less than it can secure it from outsiders. This results in a *saving* to the company, but it does not result in a profit.

### Reports on Construction Costs

When a construction order is completed, a report is made to the executive having supervision over the expenditures for construction, showing the estimated cost and the actual cost. If there is any considerable variance, it is due to inaccurate estimates or excessive cost. With the comparative figures available it is possible to determine the cause of the variation. Unless such comparisons are made, it is impossible to exercise any effective control over the cost of construction work.

A copy of these reports should go to the controller or head accountant, as well as to the production manager and budget committee. This procedure will provide a comprehensive check on the costs of construction.

### Report on Appropriations

To exercise effective control over the plant and equipment budget, it is necessary to have periodical reports which will make possible a comparison between the amount appropriated for each class of expenditures and the actual amount expended. A report should be made monthly, giving this comparison. This report should provide the information shown in Figure 24.

A report made in this form is of service not only to the executive who is exercising control over the purchases and construction of plant and equipment, but also to the financial executive. It shows the former the amount which he has available for future construction, and the latter the amount which he must plan to finance. The tenth column gives the treasurer information of special value, since it states the payments which must be made in the near future. Column (13) shows the amount which may be diverted to some other purpose in case of financial stringency. If the budget committee receives this report each month, it can exercise an effective control over all disbursements for plant and equipment.

### Reserve for Contingent Expenditures

It is usually not possible to estimate exactly each item of plant and equipment cost which must be met during the budget period. There will usually be need for expenditures

MONTHLY REPORT ON APPROPRIATIONS FOR PLANT AND EQUIPMENT

MONTH OF____________192__

| NAME OF APPROPRIATION | No. | Period | Per Cent of Completion | Original Amount | Additions | Deductions | Final Amount | Cash Disbursed | Accounts Payable | Undisbursed Balance | Contract for Labor & Supplies | Balance Available for Future Contracts |
|---|---|---|---|---|---|---|---|---|---|---|---|---|
| (1) | (2) | (3) | (4) | (5) | (6) | (7) | (8) | (9) | (10) | (11) | (12) | (13) |

Figure 24. Monthly Report on Appropriations for Plant and Equipment

which cannot be foreseen. It is desirable to anticipate these additional costs and include an item in the plant and equipment budget of each period to cover them. Since these additional costs vary in amount from period to period, it is well to credit a reserve account for the amount provided for them in each budget. When the costs are incurred, they can be charged against the reserve. These additional costs may be due to rising costs of material and equipment, labor emergencies, accidents, increased production, and similar causes.

By employing the method outlined above, these costs can be taken care of when they arise. It is obvious that this reserve has a limited use and must not be used as a means of hiding excessive amounts paid for construction or repairs during certain periods. If it is too large, it prevents the control being exercised for which the plant and equipment budget is intended.

### Use of Standardized Equipment

There is a modern tendency to use standardized equipment throughout a business. Such standardization is especially desirable for furniture, fixtures, and office equipment. To that end businesses frequently select a standard type of desk, standard typewriters, and standard calculating machines to be used in all offices. Any other type of equipment which is in general use should be standardized, if possible. Factory equipment should be standardized if practicable.

There are several advantages in having standardized equipment, among which the following may be mentioned:

    1. By buying all equipment from one company, it may be possible to obtain more favorable terms. At least such buying prevents the purchasing of unduly expensive equipment by some departments when less expensive equipment would do as well.

2. It facilitates the purchasing of new equipment, since a requisition can be made for one unit of equipment and sent to the general purchasing agent who knows what to purchase, from whom to purchase, and the cost of the same. This eliminates the preparation of specifications for the use of the purchasing agent and relieves him of the task of obtaining quotations on special types of equipment.

3. It facilitates the production of equipment which the company produces for its use, since standard specifications can be prepared and the necessary materials and tools can be procured in advance. It also facilitates the making of repairs, since piece parts can be kept on hand, and mechanics will become more skilled in making repairs.

4. It facilitates future planning, for it is only necessary to estimate the number of units required and the cost can be easily obtained.

5. It tends to promote the most economical use of equipment, since equipment can be moved from one office or one department to another, thus preventing a probable surplus in one and a shortage in another.

6. In case of equipment which requires technical skill to operate, it facilitates the transfer of employees from one department to another.

## Review and Summary[1]

In the preceding pages, the procedure necessary for the preparation and execution of the plant and equipment budget has been outlined. In summary form, this procedure is as follows:

I. REQUIREMENTS FOR CONTROL OF PLANT AND EQUIPMENT:

1. A proper analysis of plant and equipment expenditures to determine their classification and a record of them which will show correctly their effect on the financial condition of the business.

2. A proper control of the amount expended for plant and equipment to the end that sufficient will be expended to provide a

---

[1] In this brief summary no attempt is made to indicate the organization necessary for plant and equipment control, this having been discussed in the preceding pages.

well-equipped and efficient plant, and at the same time prevent the expenditures of more than is necessary to secure this
result.

II. Control of the Amount of Expenditures Required:

1. That data be available which will show results of past operations
and serve as the basis of future plans.

2. That plans be formulated on the basis of these data and be expressed in workable form by means of a plant and equipment
budget.

3. That records be maintained and reports be made which make
possible the enforcement of the budget formulated.

III. Data Required as Basis of Control:

1. Those which are obtained from the accounting and statistical
records with reference to past experience.

2. Those which are obtained by mathematical calculations based
on predetermined factors.

3. Those which are determined by a consideration of future plans.

4. Those which are obtained as a result of the investigation and
study of experts.

IV. Plant and Equipment Budget Shows:

1. The anticipated repairs and estimated depreciation on the present plant and equipment.

2. The estimated cost of new equipment including (a) cost of factory
equipment, and (b) cost of equipment for administrative and
selling units.

3. The anticipated repairs and estimated depreciation on the new
equipment to be secured.

V. Records and Reports for Control of Plant and Equipment
Budget Include:

1. Requisitions for all purchases of equipment and for all construction of equipment or repairs.

2. Estimates of cost of purchases or construction which accompany
the requisitions.

3. Records of the cost of all construction or repair work performed
by the company.

4. Reports showing a comparison of estimates and costs.

5. Reports showing a comparison of expenditures with budget
allotments.

# CHAPTER XVIII

## THE EXPENSE BUDGETS

**The Expense Problem**

In the operation of a business it is necessary to incur numerous expenditures which in accounting and business practice are designated by the general term "expenses." Expenses are incurred in connection with the operations of all the functional departments of a business. In the securing of sales, expenses are incurred for salaries of salesmen, wages of clerical help, postage, stationery, supplies, and advertising. In the production of goods, heat, light, power, supplies, and miscellaneous labor must be purchased. In the maintenance of plant and equipment, repair and replacement costs must be borne. In the general administration of the business, expenses of various kinds are necessary.

Although many expenses are incurred in small amounts, the sum total of all expenses in most businesses is sufficiently large to absorb a large percentage of the returns from sales. The amount of the expenses of a business is apt to determine whether it operates at a profit or a loss. Its sales and its purchases are presumably made in a competitive market where it has the same advantages as its competitors. In so far as this is true, the gross profit of competing businesses should tend to be the same. But the expense element in different businesses varies widely, and in this fact lies to a large extent the explanation of the wide variations in the net profits.

Because expenses are incurred by all departments of a business, are largely intangible in nature, and the individual items are small, their control is difficult. They have a tendency to increase constantly, and as they increase, the profits of the business tend to decrease.  To secure a control of expenses which is effective and yet not unduly burdensome is one of the most important and difficult tasks of business management.

### Classification of Expenses

One of the first steps in effecting a proper control of expenses is the establishment of a proper classification or grouping of them.  It is obvious that administrative attention cannot be given to each separate item of expense, and this fact necessitates that a classification be made which will make possible the focusing of executive attention on groups of related items.

Expenses may be classified in many ways, depending on the purpose for which the classification is to be used.  From the viewpoint of administrative control the following classification is helpful:

1. Manufacturing expenses, or those which are incurred in the operation of the factory and the production of the commodity or service which is offered for sale.
2. Selling expenses, or those which are incurred in the marketing of the product produced or purchased for sale.
3. Financial expenses, or those incurred in planning and controlling the receipt, custody, and disbursement of funds.
4. Auxiliary expenses, or those incurred by the various auxiliary or "service" departments of the business, such as the accounting department, personnel department, purchasing department, and office manager's department.
5. Executive expenses, or those which are incurred in the general administration of the business and cannot be charged to any of the foregoing groups.  This group includes the expenses of the general manager and his staff.
6. Corporate expenses, or those which are not incurred as a result of the operations of any particular department, but which are necessary that the business exist and operate as an entity. Directors' fees and expenses, capital stock tax, and income taxes are illustrations of such expenses.

This classification is different both in grouping and terminology from the usual accounting classification of expenses. The reasons for these differences will be explained when each class of expense is discussed.

### Relation of Expense Classification to Form of Organization

The foregoing classification of expenses will be more readily seen if it is considered in connection with the chart of

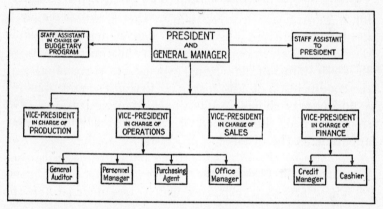

Figure 25. Organization Chart for a Manufacturing Business

a typical organization of a manufacturing business which is shown in Figure 25.

It will be understood that the chart of organization shown in Figure 25 is intended to be suggestive and not arbitrary. Scarcely any two businesses will have the same plan of organization. This is due to the differences in size, volume, nature of operations, and nature of personnel. In a mercantile business a merchandise department will take the place of the production department shown in the illustration. In many businesses there will not be a vice-president in charge of operations to which some of the auxiliary departments report. Where the administration of personnel is regarded as a major function, the personnel manager may be given a more prominent position than is indicated in this chart. If the standards and record function is developed properly, there may be a controller who will combine under his jurisdiction several of the functions given in the fore-going chart.

A form of organization which the author thinks is pref-erable to that given in Figure 25 is shown in Figure 26. The less preferable form is used as a basis for this discussion for it more nearly corresponds to the situation found in most medium-sized businesses. The primary purpose of introducing a chart of organization at this time is to indicate the desirability of classifying expenses to correspond with the classification of administrative activities maintained by a business as shown by its chart of organization. The significance of this method of classification will be more apparent as the discussion proceeds.

### Direct and Indirect Expenses

There are some expenses which are incurred for the benefit of only one department, and these can be charged directly to that department. For instance, the salaries of the sales clerks can be connected directly with the opera-tions of the sales department and charged to selling expense. The repairs on factory equipment can be connected directly with the operations of the production department and charged to manufacturing expenses. These are known as "direct" expenses.

There are other expenses which are incurred for the benefit of two or more departments and which cannot be charged directly to the expenses of any one department. For instance, the expenditures for light and heat are for the benefit of all the departments of a business. It is neces-sary to allocate these expenditures to the various depart-

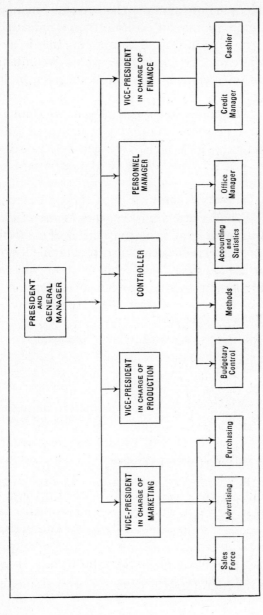

Figure 26. Another Form of Organization for a Manufacturing Business

ments which are benefited by them. These are known as "indirect" expenses.

The expenses which are here termed *indirect* expenses are referred to by various names by writers and practitioners. They are called "overhead," "burden," "non-productive," and by other terms. The terminology of accounting and business management is not standardized. It is impossible to use terms which have a uniform meaning and usage. The most that can be done is to define clearly those used and to limit their use to the definition given.

### Allocation of Indirect Expenses

In most businesses the indirect expenses are of sufficient amount to make their allocation a matter of major importance if a proper classification of expenses is to be maintained, and accountants and industrial engineers have given much thought to this problem of allocation. Two questions arise from a consideration of the problem:

1. What expenses should be allocated and to what departments?
2. On what basis should the allocation be made?

In answering the first question it is necessary to consider the purpose for which the allocation is being made; or to carry the inquiry one step farther, it is necessary to know for what purpose the data with reference to expenses are to be used.

### Allocation of Manufacturing Expenses

Most of the discussion of allocation of indirect expenses in the past has dealt with the allocation of manufacturing expenses to classes of product, or to specific "jobs" or order lots. The purpose of this allocation is to obtain unit costs. The problem here is one of intra-departmental distribution. It is a question of distributing the total manufacturing expenses over the total product produced so that each unit of the product will bear its proportionate part of these expenses. Sufficient consideration is given to this problem in the chapter on the manufacturing expense budget.

There is some question as to what should be included under manufacturing expenses, but this is not very important. Because of the attention given to factory costs during the past few years, which has led to a careful consideration of what elements should be included in the determination of those costs, there has developed a fairly uniform opinion as to what expenses should be classified as manufacturing expenses. There are some items, such as interest on investment and rent, which are yet the subject of controversy.

## Allocation of Commercial Expenses

Until recently there has been little attempt to apply the principles of costs, as developed in connection with production, to the determination of selling or "administrative" costs. There has been much attention given to the unit cost to produce, but little attention given to the unit cost to market or the unit cost of "administration." There are certain inherent difficulties which make the determination of such unit costs quite difficult, and in some cases there may be doubt of their usefulness.

As a consequence of the failure to develop "commercial" costs, there has been much less attention given to the classification of "commercial" or non-manufacturing expenses, than has been given to the distinction between manufacturing and non-manufacturing expenses.

Usually the "commercial" expenses which represent the difference between gross profit on sales and net operating profit, are grouped under the two general headings of "selling" and "administrative." All items which are not clearly selling expense are usually placed under administrative expense. In case of doubt with reference to any particular item, it is placed in the latter group which consequently comes to contain a great many items of a miscellaneous nature. Subclasses may be maintained under each of the major groups of selling and administrative expense, but usually no great care is exercised in the allocating of expenses between the subclasses.

As a consequence of these practices, there has been a decided tendency to slight the question of allocating indirect commercial expenses. When such allocation has been made, it has frequently been on an unscientific basis. Department stores and some few other businesses have broken away from the traditional policy and given careful consideration to the allocation of these expenses, but such a practice has been the exception rather than the rule.

### Relation of Expense Allocation to Organization of Business

It can be seen from the foregoing discussion, that the consideration of expense allocation has been confined largely to manufacturing expenses and has here been limited in the main to a consideration of their allocation as a basis for unit costs. Unit costs are useful and desirable, but in the desire to obtain them there has sometimes been a tendency to overlook one of the important purposes of cost statistics. It is not sufficient to know what costs *are*—in addition it is necessary to control costs so that they will be as small as possible.

In the modern business organization, control is exercised through individuals who compose the organization. If control of expenses is to be effected through members of the organization, it is necessary that they be classified so as to show the responsibility for each class. If responsibility is taken as the controlling factor in an expense classification, each department will be charged with those expenses over which the executive head of the department exercises control. In addition it may be charged with some items of expense the amount of which is fixed or at least is beyond the control of any officer.

To illustrate, the production department will be charged for the supplies used in production, for these are under the control of the production manager, and in addition it will be charged with the depreciation on production equipment, the estimated amount of which is determined in most cases by others than the production manager. The depreciation should be treated as a manufacturing expense, for it is a direct result of the operations of the production department and is necessary to the proper performance of the production function. The production manager could not affect its amount if the duty of determining it was left to him, for its amount is determined by definite factors such as cost, scrap value, and estimated life.

### Expenses Which Should Not Be Allocated

As an illustration of the type of expenses which it seems better not to allocate to a department, the salaries and expenses of the president and his staff may be mentioned. It is sometimes contended that as the president supervises and directs all the departments of a business, his salary and that of his staff should be allocated to the functional departments. For instance, a portion of these expenses should be charged to selling expense. It seems that such a policy is unwise, since such salaries are variable amounts, subject to the wishes of the president and the board of directors and are not directly or indirectly under the control of the sales department. If these salaries are increased, the sales expense will be increased and the sales manager is powerless to prevent it.

The author can recall one case in which the compensa-

tion of the sales manager was affected by the ratio of selling
expense to sales. After the passage of the income and
excess profits tax law of 1917, the corporation increased the
salaries of some of its executives. The corporation is a
close one and certain of the executives are the principal
stockholders. Large salaries were thought to be better
than large profits. The sales manager had put forth an
unusual effort to increase his sales for the year 1918 with
unexpected success. But when the increased salaries had
been allocated to the departments, the sales expense was so
increased that the bonus of the sales manager was smaller
than the year previous, despite the unprecedented increase
in sales.

It is admitted that the foregoing is an extreme case, but
it illustrates an important principle. If a department is
charged with variable expenses over which its executive
head and his assistants have no control, the value of the
departmental expense reports as a basis of administrative
control is largely destroyed. Expenses, like sales, production, and purchases can be adequately controlled only when
estimates are made by those responsible for their amount
and these held responsible for the attainment of these estimates. Such a procedure is greatly weakened if executives
are held responsible for expenses over which they do not
exercise control.

The first question asked with reference to expense
allocation may be answered by saying that no expense
should be allocated to a department if such allocation
will affect in a material way the fixing of responsibility
for the expenses of the department on its executive head.
There are of course cases where expediency will dictate
a variation from the application of the general principle,
but such variations should be permitted only for good
reasons.

## Basis of Allocating Expenses

With reference to the basis of allocation, it is beyond the province of this discussion to enter into any detailed discussion of this question. Cost accountants have given much consideration to the allocation of manufacturing expenses to factory departments and manufacturing orders. The reader will find in the standard works on cost accounting able discussions of the various methods employed. Much less attention has been given to the proper basis for the allocation of commercial expense, although, as already stated, considerable has been done in this connection by department stores.

The factory cost accountant in the early development of factory costs found the easiest method of distributing manufacturing expenses to be on the basis of direct labor. In a similar manner the mercantile cost accountant found the easiest method of distributing commercial expenses to be on the basis of sales. Consequently, sales have been used very extensively by department stores as a basis for allocating expenses to the various departments of the store. But the factory cost accountant has found that the distribution of expenses on the basis of labor often gives incorrect results, and the commercial cost accountant has found that the distribution of commercial expenses on the basis of sales may give results equally unsatisfactory.

To illustrate, one of the largest items of expense to be allocated in a department store is advertising. Formerly the usual method of allocating this to the various departments of the store was on the basis of sales. This practice leads to two undesirable results. First, some departments profited much more than others by the advertising, since it was devoted to articles sold by some departments much more than to articles sold by other departments. For instance, the advertising of ladies' ready-to-wear clothing will

usually be much more extensive than the advertising of
groceries.   Yet the sales of the grocery department may be
larger than the sales of the ladies' ready-to-wear department;
hence, according to the system of allocation based on sales,
it may be charged more for advertising.   This gives inaccurate figures, and if the departmental heads are paid a
bonus on profits, it leads to an unfair charge against the
profits of the head of the grocery department.   Secondly,
if advertising is distributed on the basis of sales, each departmental head will try to secure as much advertising as
possible, since he will feel that each of the other departments
must pay part of its cost which results in his department's
paying only a small part of the total.   He naturally con-
cludes that he must certainly get more benefit from the
advertising than it costs him; therefore he will request and
urge it.   He will be the more apt to do this because he
knows every other department is seeking advertising, for
which his department must pay its proportionate part.

To be more concrete, the head of Department A may be
contemplating a certain amount of advertising of the articles sold by his department, which will cost $500.   If the
entire $500 were to be charged against his department, he
might decide immediately not to request its expenditure.
If, however, there are ten departments and he knows that
on the basis of sales only $60 of the cost of the advertising
will be charged against his department, he will feel that it
must certainly be worth more than that to him; so he will
urge that it be done.   The tendency, therefore, will be for
the ratio of advertising to sales to increase constantly.   Of
course, a capable advertising manager or merchandise manager may check this tendency, but it will have to be guarded
against constantly with a strong probability that the advertising will be larger despite this vigilance.

The brief consideration given to the method of allocating indirect expenses affords a basis for the statement of the general principle that care should be exercised to allocate them in such a manner as to attain two results:

1. Greatest possible accuracy.
2. The fixing of responsibility in such a manner that those responsible for the expense will desire to decrease and not to increase it.

## Selling and Manufacturing Expenses

The foregoing discussion has stated the general classifications or groups into which expense may be divided for purposes of administrative control, and the general principles which should govern the allocation of expenses between these groups. It is now necessary to discuss briefly the contents of each of these groups.

The composition of selling expenses and manufacturing expenses, and the method of exercising control of their amount, have been discussed in connection with the selling expense budget and the manufacturing expense budget respectively. It is not necessary to discuss these classes of expense further. They are included in the classification given at the beginning of this chapter in order that the reader might have a comprehensive picture of the expense problem.

## Financial Expenses

The financial department, of which the treasurer is usually the executive head, incurs expenses in planning and executing the financial program. In many cases the credit and collection departments are under the control of the treasurer, in which case the expense of maintaining these departments will be treated as a financial expense. Financial expenses can usually be grouped under two major classes: (1) office expense, and (2) credit and collection ex-

pense. The first will include the salaries of the treasurer and
his assistants, including the cashier, and the cost of maintaining his office. The latter will include the cost of the
services and supplies of the credit and collection department.

There has been a tendency in the past to place the cost
of maintaining the financial department under the general
heading of "administrative" expense. This tendency is
probably due to the fact that the president in many small
companies acts as treasurer. Even when a treasurer is
appointed, he is often regarded as assistant to the president.
It seems that, regardless of whether there is a separately
organized financial department, the financial function is of
sufficient importance to merit the showing of its costs as a
separate expense. This is particularly important from the
viewpoint of budgetary control where the aim is to have a
budget prepared for each functional department.

### Auxiliary Expenses

The expenses which will be included in this group will
depend on the organization of each particular business. In
a business organized in accordance with the chart in Figure
25, the expenses incurred in maintaining the accounting,
personnel, office manager's, and purchasing departments will
be included in this group. In a business organized in accordance with Figure 26, this group of expenses would not
appear, since there are no auxiliary departments. Instead,
there will appear the two major groups, controller's expense
and personnel expense.

Where the auxiliary departments exist, the expenses
charged to each department will include the cost of the services and supplies used by the department. Sometimes the
expense of maintaining these departments is allocated to the
major departments of sales, production, and finance. From
the viewpoint of budgetary and administrative control it is

desirable, if these departments exist as separate units of organization, that the expense of each be shown as a separate group, in order that the responsibility for this expense may be placed on the executive head of the department.

## Executive Expenses

The "executive" expenses should include those which are incurred by the executives of the business who do not devote their services to any particular department, but render service to all the departments in the way of direction and supervision. This will include the salaries of the president and his staff assistants and the cost of maintaining their offices. Where a general office is maintained which is separate and distinct from the functional departments, these expenses are frequently termed "general office" expenses.

Unless care is taken to exercise control over such expense, there is a tendency for it to increase unduly. One reason for this tendency is that the president of the company is usually vested with the control of the expenditures incurred in the general office and it is somewhat difficult for him to act as criterion of his own expense. It is desirable that the amount of this expense be presented to the board of directors in such form that they can easily judge of its advisability. The board of directors is the immediate superior of the president and therefore is the proper party to pass on his expenses.

The need for presenting these expenses to the board of directors for careful inspection is another argument against allocating them to the various operating departments, since this tends to obscure their amount and to prevent a careful control of them. The treatment of these expenses as a separate and distinct classification also facilitates their budgeting in the same manner as the other expenses of the business.

## Corporate Expenses

"Corporate" expenses, as that term is used in this discussion, include those which must be incurred not because of any functions which the corporation exercises, but because of its existence as a corporate organization and its relation as such an organization to governmental bodies and parties outside the corporate organization. These expenses comprise corporation fees paid to the state government, capital stock taxes, directors' salaries and fees, expenses connected with the maintenance of stock registers and dividend records, and fees paid for professional counsel in connection with appraisals, business reports and audits required by creditors. The laws of most states impose on corporations obligations in the way of making reports, the maintenance of records, and the payment of fees. In the preparation of some of these reports, such as income tax returns, and also in the preparation of reports to creditors, it may be necessary to obtain professional counsel from attorneys, accountants, and industrial engineers. These costs are obtained for the benefit of the business as a whole and should be shown as a special group.

In many businesses a general group of expenses known as "administrative" expenses, is maintained, and in this group are placed what in this discussion are classed as (1) financial expenses, (2) auxiliary expenses, (3) executive expenses, and (4) corporate expenses. In such cases the items here termed "corporate" expenses are usually shown under the heading of "general administrative expense." This method does not provide for an effective control of expense on the basis of responsibility, which we have previously seen is necessary for both administrative and budgetary purposes. The terminology suggested in the foregoing discussion may not be the best possible, but the general procedure outlined is one which will provide a proper basis for effective administration of the expense problem.

## Relation of Stores Budget and Pay-Roll Budget on the Expense Budgets

In previous chapters the stores and pay-roll budgets have been discussed. When these budgets are prepared it is possible to eliminate the departmental expense budgets, with the exception of the manufacturing expense budget and the possible exception of the general office expense budget and the selling and advertising expense budget. The supplies used by each department will be included in the stores budget, and the salaries of the employees will be included in the pay-roll budget.

Both the advantages and disadvantages of this procedure have been discussed in previous chapters and need not be repeated here.

## Budgetary Control of Expenses

To provide an effective control of the expenses of the various departments as well as to provide the necessary data for the financial budget, it is necessary to adopt a procedure which contains the essentials of the following:

1. Before the beginning of each budget period, an estimate is prepared by the executive head of each department or unit, showing the anticipated expenses of this department or unit for the next budget period. It is sent to the executive in charge of the budgetary procedure.

2. All these estimates are used by the executive in charge of the budgetary procedure, probably with the assistance of the treasurer, in preparing a financial budget and an estimated statement of profit and loss.

3. The estimates are submitted by the executive in charge of the budgetary procedure to the budget committee or to the board of directors, or to both, and after they are revised by the budget

19

committee or board of directors where deemed necessary, an appropriation is made to meet the expenses called for by each estimate.

4. The amount of each appropriation as determined by the budget committee or by the board of directors, is communicated to the executive responsible for the original estimate.

5. A monthly report is made to the budget committee or the board of directors through the executive in charge of the budgetary procedure, showing the status of each appropriation.

6. The original appropriation must not be exceeded by any department without the permission of the budget committee or the board of directors.

## Responsibility for the Preparation of Expense Estimates

To insure the effective operation of the budgetary program, it is necessary that definite responsibility for the preparation and enforcement of the expense budgets be fixed. The sales manager and the production manager will be responsible for the preparation of the estimate of selling and advertising expense and the estimate of manufacturing expense, respectively. Their responsibility in this connection has been explained in previous chapters.

The treasurer will be responsible for the preparation of the estimate of expenses for the financial department. He will require the preparation of estimates by the head of the credit and collection department and by the cashier, which he will use in preparing the estimate for the whole department.

The head of each of the auxiliary departments, such as the accounting, personnel, purchasing, and office manager's departments, will be responsible for the estimate of his department. He may employ assistants in its preparation at his discretion, but the responsibility for its preparation will rest upon him.

The president is responsible for the preparation of the estimate of executive expenses. This duty he probably will delegate to his staff assistant, and this assistant may employ the aid of other officers in the office of the president.

The estimate of corporate expenses will be prepared by the official designated by the president. This estimate may be prepared by the secretary of the corporation, since he is conversant with the relations which give rise to these expenses. In some cases this estimate is prepared by the treasurer; but if this practice is followed, care must be exercised to keep the estimate entirely separate and distinct from the estimate of expenses of the financial department as prepared by him.

## Form of Estimate

The work of the executives who are responsible for the consideration of the departmental estimates is greatly facilitated if these estimates are presented in a form which shows comparisons between the estimates and past expenses. Usually it is desirable that the form provide at least the information called for by the columnar headings shown by Figure 27.

By a consideration of the estimates when submitted in this form, the executives can see whether an increase of expenditures is called for, and if so, they can investigate to see if this increase is justified. The estimates as submitted by the various departments will show the salaries to be paid to the employees of these departments and the amount of supplies to be consumed during the budget period. The supplies used by all the departments of the business are usually purchased by a central purchasing department. The purchasing agent buys these in the quantities which he thinks are most economical, and consequently there may be at any time a considerable inventory of supplies on hand. The supplies consumed during any period, therefore, will not correspond with the supplies purchased in that period.

After the departmental estimates are made, it is necessary that these be sent to the purchasing agent, who, on the
basis of the estimated consumption by the various departments, will estimate the purchases which must be made,
taking into consideration the terms on which these will be

| | | | | | DISTRIBUTION | | | |
|---|---|---|---|---|---|---|---|---|
| **EXPENSE BUDGET** | | | | | | | | |
| ITEM | Expenses for Past Budget Period | Estimated Expenses for Current Period | Per Cent of Increase or Decrease | Average Expense for Past Four Periods | First Month | Second Month | Third Month | Etc. |
| | | | | | | | | |
| | | | | | | | | |

Figure 27.   Expense Budget

secured, and will thus determine the disbursements for supplies for each period.   The estimated disbursements are
necessary as a basis for the preparation of the financial
budget.

## Monthly Reports

To effect a proper control of the appropriations made for
each department, it is necessary to have prepared monthly a
report which will show for each department a comparison
between the expenditures of the department to date and the

appropriation for expenses of the department. Usually the accounting department prepares a report showing the actual expenditures of each department, and the executive in charge of the budgetary procedure prepares the report showing a comparison of the expenditures with the appropriation.

A difficulty which may arise from this method is the failure of the accounting department to prepare the monthly

### MONTHLY REPORT ON EXPENSE APPROPRIATION

| ITEM | No. of Appropriation | Original Amount | Additions | Deductions | Final Amount | Cash Disbursed | Accounts Payable | Undisbursed Balance |
|------|------|------|------|------|------|------|------|------|
|  |  |  |  |  |  |  |  |  |
|  |  |  |  |  |  |  |  |  |

Figure 28. Monthly Expense Appropriation Report

report in sufficient time to provide for a current check upon the monthly expenditures of the departments. To be of service, the budget committee should receive these comparative reports shortly after the end of the month. If undue delay is caused by depending on the accounting department, it may be necessary to have each department keep a special record of its expenditures and report these at the end of the month to the executive in charge of the budgetary procedure.

It is desirable that the monthly report on departmental expenses contain at least the information shown in Figure 28.

## Review and Summary

In the preceding pages the procedure necessary for the preparation and execution of the expense budgets has been outlined. In summary form the procedure is as follows:

I. CLASSIFICATION OF EXPENSES:

    1. The setting up of an expense classification which corresponds to the classification of activities maintained by the business as shown by its organization chart.

    2. The allocation of indirect expenses in such a manner as to indicate the responsibility for their incurrence.

    3. The establishment of subclassifications under the major classes, which will enable the definite fixing of responsibility and a comprehensive explanation of variations.

II. PREPARATION OF BUDGETS:

    1. The preparation of an estimate of the expenses of each department for each budget period by the executive heads of the department.

    2. The transmission of this estimate to the budget committee or the board of directors for consideration and approval.

    3. The making of an appropriation by the budget committee or the board of directors to meet the estimate as approved.

III. CONTROL OF BUDGETS:

    1. The preparation of a monthly report showing a comparison between the actual and estimated expenditures.

    2. The consideration of this report by the budget committee or the board of directors, and the making of such revisions in the original appropriations as may be found necessary.

# CHAPTER XIX

## THE FINANCIAL BUDGET

### Importance of Financial Planning

Financial planning is the essence of financial administration. Without such planning the success of a business
is a matter of accident. Many businesses, especially small
ones, fail to plan ahead with reference to their finances and
to this fact many of the business failures are due.

The reports of the credit agencies show that the principal cause for failure of business firms is "lack of capital."
This lack of capital in many cases could have been prevented
if financial requirements had been estimated and plans made
in advance to meet these requirements. The failure of
these firms was due to the fact that they waited until the
capital was urgently needed before attempting to secure it,
and then they were unable to get it. In many cases its
urgent need arose from the undertaking of plans which were
beyond the capital capacity of the businesses and which
would not have been undertaken if the managers had known
in advance the financial requirements to which they would
give rise.

Mr. Walter H. Cottingham, President of the Sherwin-
Williams Company, writing in the May, 1920 *System*, very
aptly says:

> The small business does not raise additional funds easily. In
> fact, no money is raised "easily"—it has to be bargained for. But
> I think a part of the smaller man's difficulty may be traced to two
> reasons. The first is a lack of planning ahead and of a consequent
> scheduling of money requirements for at least several years in ad-
> vance. This carelessness naturally results in a panicky getting of
> money, only when it is urgently needed. The second difficulty is in

analogy: because he has not planned the owner has no clear, comprehensive idea of just what he can afford to pay for money and is
likely to insist upon too low a price until suddenly he finds himself
"up against it." Then he pays too high a price—if he gets the
money at all.

The foregoing quotation emphasizes the necessity of
financial planning for the small business, but its need in the
large business is no less imperative. The *principles* discussed in the following pages are applicable equally to the
small and the large business, although in discussing *procedure* a business of sufficient size to make expedient a functional division of administrative duties is assumed.

### Need for Financial Program

The operations of all the departments of a business
necessitate the use of services and supplies, and the purchase of these necessitates the expenditure of funds. As
a result of the operations, a service or commodity is purchased or produced, and this commodity or service is sold.
From these sales, funds are received either immediately or
at the expiration of the period of credit which is granted to
customers. The typical cycle may be stated as follows:
cash–supplies and services–sales–accounts receivable–cash.

It can be seen, therefore, that the operations of a business result in the constant receipt and disbursement of funds.
These funds are in the form of cash or the equivalent. Since
a business cannot continue to operate unless it is able to
pay its obligations, it is necessary for its operations to be
so planned that its cash receipts will be equal to its cash
disbursements.

The ideal financial program would be one which provided for the receipt each day of the same amount of cash
which must be disbursed on that day. It is impossible to
make plans which are sufficiently exact to make possible

such a schedule of receipts and disbursements, and so it is necessary to maintain a "cash balance" which will insure against a discrepancy between the cash receipts and the cash disbursements. The cash balance in financial operations serves a function similar to that performed by the merchandise inventory in merchandise operations.

The custody of the cash receipts, the maintenance of the cash balance, and the control of the cash disbursements, are among the most important functions of a business. To accomplish these functions it is necessary that the cash requirements of a business be determined in advance and that well-formulated plans be made for the satisfaction of these requirements.

## Long-Time vs. Short-Time Financial Planning

In the foregoing discussion it has been stated that a business should follow a far-sighted policy and plan its financial requirements several years in advance. This is undoubtedly true, but it must be obvious that such long-time plans can be made only in a general way and that they will indicate the capital requirements only by setting up certain maximum and minimum limits. For instance, a manufacturing firm may plan on the expansion of its business over a period of five years and estimate the additional plant, equipment, and working capital which it will need if the contemplated expansion is realized. It may secure the authorization of sufficient stocks or bonds to provide the maximum amount of capital required by its program, and may take such steps as are possible to assure itself that it will be able to issue these as capital is needed. But if its program fails of realization, it will not issue all the stocks and bonds authorized; or if conditions change so that their issuance is impossible or unprofitable, it will curtail its program.

On the other hand, a business can plan its immediate capital needs with fair exactness, and it must estimate these needs if it is to assure itself that the capital to meet them will be available. It may be impossible for a business to know exactly the capital it will need to finance the sales which it expects to obtain three years hence, but it can know quite definitely that if bank loans are falling due during the next month which are in excess of its possible cash receipts from customers, it must renew these loans or obtain sufficient funds from other sources to pay them.

For the present we shall be interested in a consideration of the short-time financial plans of a business. But the general principles discussed are in the main applicable to the planning for long-time capital needs.

## Determination of Cash Requirements

In the past most business executives prepared their estimates of financial requirements on the basis of the requirements of previous years, taking into consideration in a rough way such factors as the amount of business expected for the coming year, business conditions, and any plans that may be under way for the extension of plant, equipment, etc. The method by which these factors were taken into consideration is perhaps not improperly to be described as "expert guesswork" in the majority of cases. The length of time for which any such estimate is made will depend on the conditions in the particular line of business in question, though six months and a year have been the most usual periods.

Such a plan as this is about all that is possible where a thoroughgoing departmental budget system has not been established, under which each department makes up a formal estimate of requirements and possible achievements, all to be organized by the chief executive in consultation with the departmental heads, into a single consistent plan for the budget period. Where such a budget system is in existence, each departmental budget can be made to show, among other things, the estimated cash requirements and estimated cash receipts.

It is important to bear in mind that all budgets, from the point of view of executive control, fall roughly into two classes, though the budget made by one department may be composed of elements of both. One of these types is an estimate of requirements for conducting the activities of the department along the line proposed, that is, a requisition for supplies, materials, labor, equipment, etc. After it is approved it is in the nature of an allotment, that is, not to be exceeded without permission. The various expense budgets are good illustrations of this type. They request a certain amount of services and supplies to carry on the operations of the departments for which they are made.

The other type is a statement of the proposed accomplishments of the department, a tentative promise to deliver materials, services, etc., which, upon being accepted as a part of the general plan of the business, comes to be a quota to be attained. The sales budget, which states the sales which the sales department agrees to secure, and the production budget, which states the volume of production which the production department promises to deliver, are illustrations of this type.

That which from the point of view of one department is a quota, from the point of view of another may be an allotment, and it is through this dovetailing of quota and allotment that a budget system seeks to coordinate the activities of all the departments of an organization into a single unified policy. For instance, the volume of finished goods stated on the production budget is a quota for the production department, but it is an allotment to the sales

department, since it states the goods which the latter has
for sale. The materials budget is an allotment to the
production department, since it states the materials it will
have available for use, but it is a quota for the financial
department, since it states the funds which the latter must
procure to meet the disbursements called for by the budget.

Applying this distinction to the financial budget, each
departmental estimate of cash requirements, when approved, comes to be an allotment of cash to that department. In the same manner a departmental estimate of
cash receipts becomes a cash quota for that department.
In many businesses the sales estimate is the only one which
represents anticipated cash receipts.

### Relation of Financial Budget to Departmental Budgets

Sometimes the financial budget is wrongly regarded as
a departmental budget. This may probably arise from
the fact that it is often prepared by the treasurer. From
the foregoing discussion it can be seen that this view is
clearly erroneous. The financial budget is not a budget
of the treasurer's department, but a combination of the
budgets of all the departments. The financial budget
must state the funds which are needed to finance all the
activities of a business, and these activities are stated in
the departmental budgets.

Some business firms have attempted to make a financial
budget without making careful departmental budgets.
In these cases the treasurer or controller prepares estimates
of cash receipts and disbursements based on past operations
and such contemplated changes of which he is cognizant.
This procedure has usually resulted in unsatisfactory results for two reasons:

1. The financial budget cannot be made accurately without the
   use of the departmental estimates, for it is impossible for

the treasurer or controller to know accurately the plans of all the departments.

2. It is necessary to control the activities of the various departments in order to enforce or carry out the financial budget, and this can be done only through the departmental budgets. It is obvious that if the disbursements of any department are shown on the financial budget, a departmental budget must be established so that the disbursements of this department will not exceed the amount stated.

## Determination of Cash Receipts

In estimating the cash receipts of a business, it is necessary to determine all sources from which cash may be obtained. The number and nature of these sources will depend on the nature of the operations of the business. In a mercantile or industrial business the principal source of cash receipts is its sales. At the beginning of any budget period there will be certain accounts receivable outstanding from which funds will be received during the next budget period, and there will be additional accounts receivable resulting from the sales during the period from which collection will be derived during the period. In a retail store there will also be receipts from cash sales.

The method to be employed in estimating the receipts from accounts receivable and sales depends on the number of customers and the terms on which they are sold. In a small business or in a business which has few customers, it is possible to take each customer and estimate the amount which will be obtained from the accounts receivable which he owes at the beginning of the budget period, and also the amount of the sales which will be made to him during the budget period and the collections which will be made during the period from the accounts receivable arising from these sales. In a large business which has many customers, this method is impracticable. In such a case the method to be followed will be determined largely by the terms on which the sales are made.

In a retail department store a considerable part of the sales are for cash. The sales on account are due at the end of the month and presumably are paid during the first few days of the following month. In such a business it is necessary to estimate separately the cash sales and the sales on account. The records will show the ratio of cash sales and account sales to total sales during the past, and these ratios can be used in estimating the amount of the total estimated sales which will be made on each of these terms. The cash sales will result in cash receipts for the month in which they are made, while the sales on account will result in cash receipts during the following month. In the case of the account sales, allowance must be made for the bad debts and also for those accounts which will not prove bad but will not be paid promptly. The amount of both these accounts can be estimated on the basis of past experience.

In some businesses sales are made on terms which result in the payment for all the sales of each month on the same day. For instance, a customer is sent a statement at the end of each month for his purchases during the month and he pays on the fifteenth of the following month. In such cases it is not difficult to estimate when the cash receipts from the sales will be obtained.

If a business sells on terms of 1/10, n/30; 1/20, n/30, etc., which result in the receipt of cash from accounts receivable throughout the month, it is necessary to resort to ratios to estimate the cash receipts from estimated sales. A study of past records will show in many businesses that there is a fairly uniform ratio between sales and collections. This ratio may vary during different months or seasons of the year, and it may vary during different years owing to trade and market conditions. But by careful study it is often possible to obtain a ratio which is approximately correct.

After the ratio of collections to sales for past periods is obtained, it is applied to the estimated sales for each month of the next period to determine the estimated cash receipts for each month. The inaccuracies which may arise from this method are apparent. It, of course, will be understood that it is never possible to obtain exact estimates of cash receipts or disbursements. We carry a cash balance primarily to provide for these inaccuracies.

Because of the wide and unforeseen fluctuations in the volume of sales during the past eighteen months, some firms have found it impossible to use the ratio of sales to collections as a basis of estimating their cash receipts. Various other methods have been devised. One business has found that they receive no cash receipts during the month from sales made after the twentieth of the month. Accordingly they add the estimated sales for the first twenty days of the month to the accounts receivable outstanding at the beginning of the month, and use the sum as the basis of their estimate of cash receipts for the month. Experience has shown that they can expect to collect a fairly uniform percentage of this amount during the month.

### Estimate of Cash Receipts Based on Lag of Collections on Sales

Another method of handling this problem is suggested by Mr. Morris A. Copeland in the December, 1920 issue of the *Journal of Political Economy*. At the author's request, Mr. Copeland has submitted the following statement in explanation of this method:

> One method of handling the problem is to calculate the average turnover or collection period, and use this directly as a lag on sales. The average turnover period of accounts receivable in fractions of a

year is the average of accounts receivable at the end of each month
divided by the amount of the collections for the year.   In case this
should prove to be one-twelfth, the sales estimate for March
would be the collections estimate for April, etc.   But if it were
twenty days, instead of a month, the collections for May would be

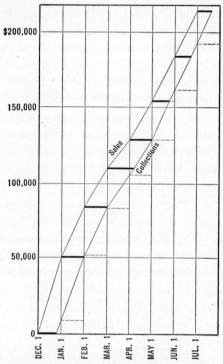

Figure 29.   Graph Showing Accumulated
Sales and Collections

approximately equal to the sales from April 11 to May 11, a figure
which cannot be obtained conveniently from the sales estimate if it
states the sales by calendar months.

Partly on this account and partly because the collections period
may vary from season to season, and is sure to vary according to
business conditions, the whole thing may be shown more easily
graphically.   It is evident that if the collections period varies, the

collections for one month will not correspond to the sales during an interval of equal length. For a good mathematical reason which we need not go into here, it is best to show the sales and collection in cumulative form, i.e., to show the total sales from January 1 to each succeeding date.

Figure 29 illustrates the graphical method. The dates are shown in the horizontal scale (Sundays and holidays should be omitted); the amounts are shown on the vertical. This diagram is based on the following data:

| Month | Sales Estimate | Estimated Collection Period |
|---|---|---|
| December............................ | $50,000 | 20 days |
| January.............................. | 35,000 | 30 " |
| February............................ | 25,000 | 28 " |
| March.............................. | 20,000 | 35 " |
| April............................... | 25,000 | 30 " |
| May................................ | 30,000 | 25 " |
| June................................ | 30,000 | 20 " |
| | $215,000 | |

The estimated collection period is measured from the first of each month, and is the horizontal distance from the sales graph at that time to the collections graph. The collections graph is obtained by connecting the right-hand ends of these horizontal lines. From it we can read off the collections estimate for any month, as January $37,500 and May $32,500.

## Cash Receipts from Miscellaneous Sources

After the estimate of collections from sales is made, it is necessary to determine whether cash may be received from any other source. In many cases interest is received on bank balances. If notes are taken from customers, these will often bear interest. If stock or bonds of other companies are owned by the company, the probable income from dividends or interest must be considered. If a company maintains a restaurant for employees, cash receipts will result therefrom. If a company owns houses which it

20

rents to employees, the cash receipts to be received from
these must be included. In some businesses there may be
other sources of income. In any case, all these sources
must be carefully considered and recorded in the estimate
of cash receipts. It is not difficult to estimate the cash
receipts from any of these sources.

It may be well to add a word of caution to the effect
that a careful distinction must be made between cash
receipts and accrued income. For instance, interest on
bonds owned may accrue in one period but not be paid
until a subsequent period. On the other hand, interest
may be received during one period which has accrued over
several past periods. It will be seen, therefore, that the
amount of interest and similar items recorded on the
financial budget during any period will in all probability
not agree with the amount of these same items as entered
in the financial records.

### Estimating the Cash Receipts for Different Types of Business

In a professional firm the principal source of cash receipts is from the sale of services to clients, and an estimate
of the cash receipts from this source can be made in a
manner similar to that in which the estimate of receipts
from the sale of commodities is determined in a mercantile
firm. In this connection it must be remembered that an
engagement may not be completed until a considerable
time after it is sold, and if the engagement is not unduly
long the client may not be invoiced until it is completed.
It may also be worth mentioning that clients are often
dilatory in paying for professional services. Usually there
is no discount offered for prompt payment, nor even are
specific terms stated on the invoices of professional firms.
Consequently a firm is apt to postpone payment of the
invoice for professional services and pay an invoice for

merchandise on which a discount is offered. These factors must be considered in preparing the estimate of cash receipts of a professional firm.

In a financial institution, such as a bank, the principal sources of cash receipts are entirely different from those of a mercantile or industrial firm, but the method of determining the amount of these in the two cases is not greatly dissimilar. A bank derives its chief income from interest on loans, and the amount of the receipts from this source is not difficult to determine. The receipts from exchange, investments, etc., are not difficult to estimate. Care must be exercised here as in other businesses to distinguish carefully between accrued income and cash receipts.

In other types of businesses there are still other sources of cash receipts, but if the general principles developed in the foregoing discussion are kept in mind, it should not be difficult to develop a procedure for making an estimate of cash receipts for any type of business.

### Form of the Estimate of Cash Receipts

In making up the estimate of cash receipts, a careful record should be made of the amount estimated to be received from each source. A form should be designed to show the estimated receipts for each month of the budget period as well as the total for the period. This enables the budget committee to judge better the financial program which is proposed, and enables the treasurer to see the cash available each month, so that he can plan his cash disbursements and loans. It also makes possible a check on the financial program at the end of each month, since the estimated receipts can be compared with the actual receipts. These comparisons are valuable both in controlling the present estimates and in the preparation of future ones.

A simple form of the estimate of cash receipts is shown in Figure 30. This form assumes a budget period of three months in length. If a longer period is used additional columns can be added.

### ESTIMATED CASH RECEIPTS
#### For Quarter Ending March 31, 192__

| SOURCE | JANUARY | FEBRUARY | MARCH | TOTAL |
|---|---|---|---|---|
| **Accounts Receivable:** Customers-Class A Schedule No. 1 | | | | |
| Customers-Class B Schedule No. 2 | | | | |
| Customers-Class C Schedule No. 3 | | | | |
| **Notes Receivable:** Not Discounted Schedule No. 4 | | | | |
| **Sales:** Customers-Class A Schedule No. 5 | | | | |
| Customers-Class B Schedule No. 6 | | | | |
| Customers-Class C Schedule No. 7 | | | | |
| **Miscellaneous:** Income from Investments Interest on Bank Balances | | | | |
| Total | | | | |

Figure 30. Estimate of Cash Receipts

## Determination of Cash Disbursements

It is necessary that an estimate of cash disbursements be prepared to be used in connection with the estimate of cash receipts in order to complete the financial budget. To do this it is necessary to prepare an estimate of the expenditures necessary to carry on the operations of every department of the business. A discussion of the various departmental estimates has been given in previous chapters, and the method of estimating the cash disbursements required by each has been explained.

A brief review of the discussion in the previous chapters will be given here to show the relation of these estimates to the estimate of cash disbursements.

### Disbursements for Purchases of Mercantile Store

The principal disbursements of a mercantile business are for merchandise. The purchases budget, if prepared in the form explained in Chapters XIV and XV, will show the following information for each month of the budget period:

1. Inventory at beginning of month.
2. Estimated deliveries to stock during month.
3. Estimated orders to be placed during month.
4. Estimated inventory at end of month.
5. Estimated cash disbursements for purchases made during previous months.
6. Estimated cash disbursements for purchases made during the month.

Items (5) and (6) will be added for each month and entered in the estimate for cash disbursements.

It is usually easier to estimate the disbursements for purchases than to estimate the receipts from sales. The purchases are made in large quantities and consequently there are fewer creditors than there are customers. A business controls the payment of its liabilities and knows whether it will take its discounts or wait until the end of the credit period. It does not control the receipts from customers and can judge what they will do only by what the past indicates. After the purchasing department knows the purchases which must be made to meet sales demands, it should not have any particular difficulty in preparing the purchases budget so that it will show the information stated above.

## Disbursements for Production Purposes by Manufacturing Business

The principal disbursements of a manufacturing business are for materials, labor, and manufacturing expenses. The method of estimating the amount of each of these and the form in which the estimate of each should be prepared, has been discussed in the chapters on the materials, labor, and manufacturing expense budgets.

In estimating the disbursements for materials, a procedure similar to that followed in estimating the disbursements for the finished goods of a mercantile firm is necessary. First, the materials which are to be purchased must be determined, and then the date of payment for these purchases must be calculated.

The disbursements for labor are ordinarily made during the same period in which the labor is consumed. If the estimate of disbursements is made on the basis of calendar months this may not be true, for labor may be paid on a weekly basis. In this case there is apt to be an accrued pay-roll at the end of the month which will need to be paid during the following month. Some firms use a four-week period instead of a calendar month as the basis for both their accounting and budgetary records. This procedure eliminates the difficulty of accrued pay-roll but may give rise to accruals for expenses for which invoices are rendered on the basis of the calendar month.

A large part of the manufacturing expense will consist of supplies which may be purchased in one period and paid for during the next period. Consequently, the disbursements for these must be determined in a manner similar to the disbursements for materials and finished goods. Indirect labor will also be included in the manufacturing expense estimate, and will usually be paid for during the period in which it is consumed. The re-

## ESTIMATED CASH DISBURSEMENTS

### For Quarter Ending March 31, 192____

| PURPOSE | January | February | March | Total |
|---|---|---|---|---|
| NOTES PAYABLE | | | | |
| | | | | |
| ACCOUNTS PAYABLE | | | | |
| Outstanding, Jan. 1 | | | | |
| Estimated Cash Dis- | | | | |
| bursements for | | | | |
| Purchases | | | | |
| | | | | |
| FACTORY PAYROLL | | | | |
| Department A | | | | |
| Department B | | | | |
| Department C | | | | |
| | | | | |
| FACTORY EXPENSE | | | | |
| Department A | | | | |
| Department B | | | | |
| Department C | | | | |
| | | | | |
| DEPARTMENTAL EXPENSE | | | | |
| President's Office | | | | |
| Treasurer's Department | | | | |
| Auditor's Department | | | | |
| Purchasing Department | | | | |
| Office Manager's Department | | | | |
| Traffic Department | | | | |
| Sales Department | | | | |
| Production Department | | | | |
| | | | | |
| NEW EQUIPMENT | | | | |
| | | | | |
| CORPORATE | | | | |
| Taxes (Non-property) | | | | |
| Attorneys' Fees | | | | |
| Directors' Fees | | | | |
| Miscellaneous | | | | |
| | | | | |
| TOTAL | | | | |

Figure 31. Simple Estimate of Cash Disbursements

marks with reference to direct labor are equally applicable
here.

In a manufacturing business there will be disbursements
for manufacturing plant and equipment, and in all businesses there will be disbursements for furniture and office
equipment. The preparation of the estimate for plant
and equipment has been discussed in Chapters XVI and
XVII. This estimate shows the plant and equipment
desired and the date when needed. The purchasing agent
will need to use this as a basis for estimating the date of
payment for the equipment purchased.

## Disbursements for Expenses

After the expenditures necessary to obtain the goods
needed to supply the sales demands, and the disbursements
necessary to secure the required amount of plant and equipment, are determined, it is necessary to estimate the disbursements which must be incurred in operating the business so as to secure the sales and deliver the goods to the
customers. This requires the preparation of an estimate
of selling expenses by the sales department, an estimate of
executive expenses by the general office, an estimate of
corporate expenses by the secretary or some other official
designated by the president, and an estimate of auxiliary
expenses by each of the service departments, such as the
personnel department, purchasing department, etc.

The content and form of the various expense estimates
have been discussed in Chapter XVIII.

## Form of the Estimate of Cash Disbursements

In making up the estimate of cash disbursements, a
careful record should be made of the estimated amount to
be disbursed for each purpose. A form should be designed
to show the estimated disbursements for each month of the

MONTHLY REPORT ON ESTIMATED CASH DISBURSEMENTS

Month of December, 1921

Estimated Disbursements at the General
Office:

| | |
|---|---|
| General Office Pay-Roll.................... | $10,311.45 |
| General Office Building Rental............. | 3,541.67 |
| Interest Payable on Notes................. | 6,700.00 |
| Interest Payable on Bonds................. | 50,000.00 |
| Dividends................................. | 25,000.00 |
| South X Real Estate Tax.................. | 48,800.00 |
| A State Tax............................... | 3,145.00 |
| Equipment (General Office)................ | 210.00 |
| Other General Office Purchases, etc........ | 6,425.00 |
| Advertising............................... | 6,411.00 |
| Eastern Division and X Works—Pay-Roll.... | 133,166.46 |
| Eastern Division and X Works—Purchases (except Pipe)......................... | 94,000.00 |
| X Branch Pay-Roll........................ | 10,500.00 |
| Branch Pay-Rolls Paid from General Office except X Branch....................... | 4,998.34 |
| X Branch Purchases....................... | 14,500.00 |
| Consigned Pipe Purchases................. | 68,350.00 |

                                                          $486,058.92

To Western Division..............................          75,000.00

Estimated Disbursements at Western Divi-
sion and Y Works............................          310,500.00

Estimated Disbursements of Branches:

| | |
|---|---|
| A Branch.............................. | $36,500.00 |
| B Branch.............................. | 30,000.00 |
| C Branch.............................. | 65,000.00 |
| D Branch.............................. | 25,000.00 |

                                                          156,500.00

Estimated Disbursements of M Company
of Oregon:

| | |
|---|---|
| Outside Purchases and Pay-Roll........... | $75,000.00 |
| To M Manufacturing Company............ | 20,000.00 |

                                                          95,000.00

Estimated Disbursements of M Interna-
tional Company:

| | |
|---|---|
| Outside Purchases and Pay-Roll........... | $39,000.00 |
| To M Manufacturing Company............ | 80,000.00 |

                                                          119,000.00

Total..................................          $1,242,058.92

Figure 32.  More Elaborate Estimate of Cash Disbursements

budget period as well as the total for the period. This enables the budget committee to judge better the financial program which is proposed and enables the treasurer to see the cash required each month, so that he can make plans to secure the necessary amount. It also makes possible a check on the financial program at the end of each month, since the estimated disbursements can be compared with the actual disbursements. These comparisons are valuable both in controlling the present estimates and in the preparation of future estimates.

A simple form of the estimate of cash receipts is shown in Figure 31. This form assumes a budget period of three months in length. If a longer period is used, additional columns can be added.

## Estimating the Cash Disbursements for Different Types of Businesses

In different types of businesses the method of estimating the cash disbursements will vary somewhat because of the different operations they perform, but the same general procedure will be followed in preparing the estimate of cash disbursements.

In a professional firm the principal item of disbursements will be the salaries of the staff. The amount of these will be easy to obtain. In addition there will be the disbursements necessary for maintaining the office. These also can be estimated easily.

In a financial institution, such as a bank, there will be three principal items of disbursements: (1) the interest paid on deposits, (2) the salaries of the employed staff, and (3) the office expenses. None of these are difficult to estimate. In estimating the cost of supplies used in the various offices the same problems arise as in the estimating of the disbursements for purchases of a mercantile or industrial firm.

In other types of businesses there are still other purposes for which disbursements must be made, but if the general principles developed in the foregoing discussion are kept in mind, it should not be difficult to develop a procedure for making the estimate of cash disbursements for any of these.

## Various Items Appearing on Estimate of Cash Disbursements

The estimate of cash disbursements shown in Figure 31 is purposely made quite simple. In many businesses more numerous items would appear on this estimate. As an indication of some of the items which may appear on such an estimate, Figure 32 shows the estimate of cash disbursements of a large manufacturing firm for the month of December, 1921.

The amounts have been changed since these are immaterial for our purposes. This company has two factories and seven branches. The classification of items shown on the estimate is not the most desirable, but is the one found most expedient by the company at its present stage of development in financial control.

# CHAPTER XX

## THE FINANCIAL BUDGET (Continued)

### Relation of Financial Budget to Bank Loans

After the estimates of cash receipts and cash disbursements are completed, a statement can be prepared showing the relation of the estimated receipts to the estimated disbursements. If the disbursements exceed the receipts, the excess will usually be met by means of bank loans. If the receipts exceed the disbursements, the excess will usually be used in the reduction of bank loans contracted during previous periods when the disbursements exceeded the receipts.

In determining the amount of the loans necessary, or vice versa, the cash balance at the beginning of the period and the desired cash balance at the end of the period must be taken into consideration. The amount of the cash balance may be determined by what the firm has learned by experience is a necessary minimum, or it may be determined by the minimum requirements of the banks. Banks usually insist that the cash balance be maintained at a certain percentage of the loans obtained from them. Consequently, as the loans at a bank increase, the cash balance must increase accordingly.

A simple form of statement which will provide the information suggested in the preceding discussion is shown in Figure 33.

In this illustration it is assumed that the disbursements are such that loans are required. If the opposite situation exists, the last item on the summary will read "Loans to be Liquidated," instead of "Loans Required."

## Program for Bank Loans

On the basis of the estimated cash receipts (Figure 30, page 308), the estimated cash disbursements (Figure 31, page 311), and the summary of financial requirements (Figure 33), it is possible to prepare a statement showing the program to be followed with reference to bank loans. The contents of such a statement is indicated by Figure 34.

A statement made in this form is useful to the president and board of directors, since it shows them the effect of the contemplated program on the bank indebtedness.   If they

| SUMMARY OF FINANCIAL REQUIREMENTS<br>For Quarter Ending March 31, 192_ | | | | |
|---|---|---|---|---|
|  | January | February | March | Total |
| Cash Balance at the Beginning of Month Receipts |  |  |  |  |
| Total Disbursements |  |  |  |  |
| Excess of Disbursements Cash Balance at End of Month |  |  |  |  |
| Loans Required |  |  |  |  |

Figure 33.   Summary of Financial Requirements

approve the program as suggested, they may authorize the treasurer to carry out its provisions.  The treasurer, in addition to this program, will need a more detailed statement which will show him the exact dates on which additional funds must be obtained, with the consequent renewing of notes, discounting of customers' notes, etc.

## Preparation of Financial Budget

The various departmental estimates as sent to the executive in charge of the budgetary procedure provide the data from which the estimates of cash receipts and cash disbursements are prepared. Some of these estimates provide information which can be transferred directly to

---

SUGGESTED PROGRAM FOR BANK LOANS

FOR QUARTER ENDING MARCH 31, 1922

---

SITUATION AT BEGINNING OF QUARTER:

| | |
|---|---|
| Notes Payable...................................... | $ 500,000 |
| Notes Receivable Discounted........................ | 780,000 |
| Total.......................................... | $1,280,000 |

MONTHLY PROGRAM:

*January:*
Renew $45,000 of $47,500 due

| | |
|---|---|
| Reduction of Notes Payable for Month.............. | $ 2,500 |
| Notes Receivable Discounted Matured............... | 300,000 |
| Total Reduction of Indebtedness to Bank.......... | $ 302,500 |

*February:*
Renew $75,000 of Notes falling due

| | |
|---|---|
| Notes Receivable Discounted Matured............... | $ 290,000 |
| Total Reduction of Indebtedness to Bank.......... | $ 290,000 |

*March:*
Renew $60,000 of Notes falling due
Discount Notes of R. L. S. and J. J. S. for $71,000

| | |
|---|---|
| Increase of Indebtedness.......................... | $ 71,000 |
| Notes Receivable Discounted Matured............... | 100,000 |
| Net Reduction for Month.......................... | $ 29,000 |

SITUATION AT END OF QUARTER:

| | |
|---|---|
| Notes Payable...................................... | $ 531,500 |
| Notes Receivable Discounted........................ | 90,000 |
| Total.......................................... | $ 621,500 |

Figure 34. Financial Program for Bank Loans

the cash estimates. For instance, the estimate of purchases, if prepared in the manner suggested in Chapter XV, will show the estimated disbursements for purchases for each month. Other estimates show only the volume of the operations of the department for which they are made and an estimate must be prepared of the effect of these operations on the cash balance. The sales budget is an illustration of this type. It states the estimated sales for the budget period, but there is a lag between the sales and the collections therefrom, which necessitates that an estimate of collections must be prepared, based on the sales estimate.

In some cases the cash estimates are prepared by the executive in charge of the budgetary procedure, while in other cases they are prepared by the treasurer. Probably the best plan is to have these officials cooperate in their preparation. The executive in charge of the budgetary procedure can easily obtain most of the items of disbursement directly from the departmental estimates. The treasurer will prepare an estimate of the disbursements of his department. He also usually prepares the estimate of collections, since he has available the data necessary for its preparation. In some cases he makes the estimate of disbursements for corporate expenses.

In any case, after the cash estimates are completed they should be submitted to the treasurer for approval before they are transferred to the budget committee. The budget committee will consider these in connection with the various departmental estimates and make any revisions which it thinks necessary. After they are approved by the budget committee they will be transferred by the executive in charge of budgetary procedure to the departments concerned.

## Control of Financial Budget

After the departmental estimates have been approved by the budget committee, the departmental heads should not be permitted to exceed their estimates without the

permission of the committee.   At the end of each month a
report should be made to the budget committee, showing
a comparison between the estimated expenditures for each
department for the budget period and the actual expenditures to date.   This report enables the committee
to see the tendency in each department and makes it
possible for it to take measures to prevent undesirable
tendencies.

In the same manner a report should be made showing a
comparison between the estimated and the actual collections for the month, since collections are the principal
source of cash receipts.   This report will be more useful if
it also shows comparisons between sales and collections.
The contents of such a report are indicated by Figure 35.
The percentages shown in this report, if obtained for a
number of periods, will be useful in estimating receipts from
collections for future periods.

It is important to emphasize that if effective control is
to be exercised over the financial budget, it is necessary to
control carefully the disbursements and receipts of the
separate departments, since, as previously explained, the
financial budget is but a combination of the departmental
budgets.

Monthly reports should be made showing a comparison
between the estimated receipts and the actual receipts from
all sources and the estimated disbursements and the actual
disbursements from all sources.   These reports will be
submitted to the budget committee together with the other
budgetary reports.   Simple forms for these monthly reports of receipts and disbursements are shown in Figures
36 and 37.   If revisions in the various departmental
budgets are made on the basis of the monthly reports received by the budget committee, these revisions must be
given effect in the cash budget.

## MONTHLY REPORT ON COLLECTIONS

MONTH OF _____ 192____

| SALES UNIT | ESTIMATED THIS MONTH | | Per Cent Estimated Collections to Estimated Sales | ACTUAL THIS MONTH | | PER CENT COLLECTIONS TO DATE | | |
|---|---|---|---|---|---|---|---|---|
| | Sales | Collections | | Sales | Collections | This Month | Last Month | Same Month Last Year |
| EASTERN DIVISION | | | | | | | | |
| WESTERN DIVISION | | | | | | | | |
| A BRANCH | | | | | | | | |
| B BRANCH | | | | | | | | |
| C BRANCH | | | | | | | | |
| D BRANCH | | | | | | | | |
| E BRANCH | | | | | | | | |
| M CO. OF OREGON | | | | | | | | |
| M INTERNATIONAL CO. | | | | | | | | |

Figure 35. Monthly Collections Report

## Length of Cash Period

Although the financial budget may be made for a quarter, a half, or a whole year, it is necessary to make a comparison between the cash receipts and cash disbursements over shorter periods of time than is represented by the budget; otherwise there may be times during the period

### MONTHLY REPORT ON CASH RECEIPTS

MONTH OF_____192___

| SOURCE | Amount Received | Estimated Receipts | Per Cent Increase or Decrease | Comments |
|--------|-----------------|--------------------|-----------------------------|----------|
|        |                 |                    |                             |          |
|        |                 |                    |                             |          |
|        |                 |                    |                             |          |

Figure 36.   Monthly Cash Receipts Report

when there will not be sufficient cash on hand to meet current obligations.   For instance, the cash receipts from accounts receivable and miscellaneous sources from January 1 to April 1 may exceed the cash disbursements for the same period, but there may not be sufficient cash to meet current demands at one or more times during that period. The demand for cash is an imperative one and care must be exercised to see that it is forthcoming at the time needed.

In the preceding discussion it has been assumed that such comparisons will be made monthly. The estimated receipts for each month are compared with the estimated disbursements for the month, and the excess of disbursements which must be financed determined. Usually this procedure is satisfactory, but there may be cases where the

| MONTHLY REPORT ON CASH DISBURSEMENTS | | | | |
|---|---|---|---|---|
| Month of _____192__ | | | | |
| PURPOSE | Amount Disbursed | Estimated Disbursement | Per Cent Increase or Decrease | COMMENTS |
| | | | | |
| | | | | |
| | | | | |
| | | | | |

Figure 37.    Monthly Cash Disbursements Report

receipts and disbursements fluctuate so violently that it is necessary to have a comparison on the basis of ten- or fifteen-day periods. In such businesses the fluctuating demand for cash is usually satisfied by arranging a "reserve line" of credit at banks so that additional funds can be obtained immediately at any time when they are needed.

### Formulation of a Financial Program

In the foregoing discussion the procedure by which the financial budget is prepared has been explained. It should be apparent that this procedure can be effective only when it is exercised as a part of a well-formulated financial program. It is not only necessary to know what the financial requirements of a business *are*, so that plans to meet them can be made, but it is also necessary to know that these requirements are *what they should be*. In other words, it is desirable to know whether the financial program called for by the financial budget is the one which will be the most profitable to the business. A consideration of what constitutes a proper financial program would necessitate a discussion of the whole program of financial management which is beyond the province of this discussion.

There are one or two phases of the financial program, however, which are so vitally connected with the determination of cash requirements that it is worth while to mention them here.

### Constant and Variable Capital Requirements

Bankers have given considerable attention to the analysis of the assets and liabilities of business firms in connection with the granting of loans. From the viewpoint of credit granting, they have found it desirable to differentiate between fixed assets and current assets, and between fixed liabilities and current liabilities. This distinction is made largely on the basis of turnover. An asset with a slow turnover is termed a "fixed" asset, while one with a rapid turnover is termed a "current" asset. Liabilities are classified in the same manner. Since bankers have emphasized this classification in their relations with business men, the latter have come to regard it as fundamental. Many bankers have insisted on the use of the "rule-of-

thumb" financial standard of the "2 to 1" ratio, and business men have come to believe that so long as they succeed
in keeping their current assets twice their current liabilities,
they are successful financial managers.

The classification of assets and liabilities as current and
fixed is very useful in many cases, but it sometimes leads to
a confusion of thought. Because any particular piece of
merchandise will presently be converted into cash again,
it is felt that it is a less permanent form of investment than
a building. From the viewpoint of credit this is true, but
from the viewpoint of capital requirements it may not be so.
If a concern never allows its merchandise inventory to fall
below $20,000 that twenty thousand dollars is as truly a
permanent investment in the business as is the cost of the
longest-lived of its permanent assets. The same may be
true of current liabilities. Many concerns never pay off all
of their short-time loans at once. A business that always
owes at least $50,000 on short-time loans, though it may
clear up its account at each bank once a year, is obtaining
that much permanent capital on commercial loans.

From the viewpoint of financial administration, there is
a distinct difference between *permanent* assets and assets
which involve a *permanent investment*. During any particular period of time a given asset or liability, whether permanent or current, whether an accrued or a deferred item,
may vary in amount. The proprietorship may also change.
Of course the variations in different assets may not all be
in the same direction at the same time, so that some will
serve to offset others and the same is true of liabilities and
proprietorship.

For the purposes of financial requirements, what is of
primary importance are the changes in the totals. Usually
the total of each of these items fluctuates constantly.
These fluctuations may be due to seasonal operations, in

which case they are confined between certain maximum and minimum limits. Or they may be due to the expansion or contraction of the operations of the business, in which case there may be a constant increase or decrease for a certain period of time. Even here a minimum or maximum will sooner or later be reached. In the case of a decrease a minimum will be reached below which the business cannot continue to operate. In the case of an increase or expansion of business, in time a state of diminishing returns will be reached beyond which it will be unprofitable for the business to expand and consequently the assets of the business will cease to increase.

The minimum total of assets of a business during the period under consideration, such as a year, may be termed the "constant" assets of that business, and the amount in excess of this minimum may be termed the "variable" assets. In analogous fashion, constant and variable liabilities and proprietorship may be defined. Thus, if the balance sheet of the King Manufacturing Company on June 1, 1921, shows:

| | |
|---|---|
| Assets................................... | $200,000 |
| Liabilities............................... | 120,000 |
| | |
| Proprietorship......................... | $80,000 |

and the lowest value for the total assets during the year is $160,000, this will be the constant assets and also the constant liabilities and proprietorship. The variable assets will be $40,000 on June 1, and this will be also the amount of the variable liabilities and proprietorship. The variations in the proprietorship total taken by itself will not ordinarily be large. It will usually increase gradually through an accumulation of profits and then drop off at the time when dividends are paid. If the profits are left in the business, there will be a permanent increase in the proprietorship, and if losses are incurred there may be a decrease. Proprietorship may be increased by a sale of stock, but this occurs rarely in the life of any particular business.

The assets of a business at all times are equal to the proprietorship plus the liabilities. Since the proprietorship in most businesses under normal conditions fluctuates but little, it follows that the fluctuations in the assets usually result in like fluctuations in the liabilities. In other words, the variable assets tend to be offset by the variable liabilities. To illustrate, by the foregoing example of the King Manufacturing Company, it is evident that if the proprietorship remains approximately at $80,000 throughout the year and the assets are reduced to $160,000 at the time of the "slack season" of the year, then the liabilities at that time of the year will be reduced to $80,000.

The relation between the variable assets and the variable liabilities is significant in that it points out the relation between the financial budget and the financial condition of a firm as shown by its balance sheet. An illustration will make this clear. It may be assumed that the assets of the King Manufacturing Company reach the minimum amount of $160,000 on January 1, and that they then gradually increase until they reach the maximum amount of $200,000 on June 1, after which they gradually decrease until the minimum is reached again on January 1. The increase in assets between January 1 to June 1 will probably be shown in the main by an increase in accounts receivable and merchandise inventory. To carry the increase in these items the firm will in all probability increase its borrowings from banks, although some part of the increase in inventory may be offset by an increase in accounts due to trade creditors.

In so far as the increase in assets is offset by an increase in bank loans, the financial budget during this period will show an excess of disbursements over receipts, since it is to meet such an excess that bank loans are contracted.

During the period from June 1 to January 1, the accounts receivable and merchandise inventory will be decreasing and the bank loans will be decreasing likewise. During the same period the financial budget will show an excess of receipts over disbursements and with this excess the bank loans are paid.

### Relation of Financial Budget to the Business Cycle

The variable assets, and consequently the variable liabilities, will increase during the busy season of a seasonable business, and will increase for all businesses during the upward trend of the business cycle when the operations of a business are expanding. They will decrease during the dull season and during the downward trend of the business cycle. In the same manner the financial budget should normally show an increase of disbursements in proportion to receipts during the busy season or upward trend of the business cycle, and it should show the opposite condition during the dull season and the downward trend of the cycle.

Because of the non-liquid condition of the variable assets, this "normal" condition may not exist during the downward trend of the business cycle. For instance, during the year 1921 many firms were "hard pressed" for funds because their variable liabilities became due, and their variable assets were not converted. In other words, it was impossible to reduce their assets to the minimum when it became desirable to reduce their liabilities. This condition, however, does not offset the general principle that during the downward trend of the cycle the cash receipts from the operations of the business should exceed the disbursements other than for bank loans and that this excess should be used in paying these loans. The condition during 1921 merely indicates that because of inadequate planning ahead many businesses were in such a condition when the downward trend of the cycle came that they could not do what the conditions of the times demanded.

### Relation of Financial Budget to Estimated Financial Statements

The primary purpose of the foregoing discussion with reference to variable assets and liabilities and the financial budget is to show the close relationship between this budget and the financial condition of the business as shown by its balance sheet. The budget sets forth the results of the contemplated operations of the business in terms of financial requirements. To interpret this budget properly and to judge properly of its desirability, the executives should have before them an estimated balance sheet showing the anticipated financial condition at the end of the period for which the budget is made.

But the purpose of the operations of a business is to secure a profit. A contemplated program of expansion or contraction, as shown by the financial budget and estimated balance sheet, is desirable only if it will produce profitable results. To determine whether this result will be achieved, it is necessary to have an estimated statement of profit and loss showing the anticipated results of the contemplated program in terms of profit and loss.

The financial budget, the estimated statement of profit and loss, and the estimated balance sheet, are the three statements which show the goal towards which the contemplated operations of the business, as reflected in the departmental estimates, are leading. If these statements are properly made and properly correlated, a basis for sound and efficient management is laid. The latter two statements will be discussed in the following chapters.

## Difficult Problems in Preparing Financial Budget

The preparation of the financial budget is not an easy matter. In most businesses, problems of considerable magnitude and difficulty are encountered. Some of these are inherent in the problem of financial control and some are the result of circumstances which exist in particular businesses owing to personnel or to the nature of the operations of the business. The nature of these problems has been indicated to some extent in the previous discussion. In order that it may not be thought that these difficulties have been disregarded or minimized, it is desirable to summarize them here. They may be stated as follows:

1. The financial budget is a budget covering all the activities of the business; therefore it requires the cooperation of all the departments of the business. Without this cooperation it is impossible to prepare an accurate budget or to enforce it after it is prepared.

2. The cash receipts and the cash disbursements in many cases are separated from the activities which produce the receipts or cause the disbursements by a certain interval of time, and it is difficult to estimate accurately the length of this interval. For instance, the collections from sales are not made until some time after the sales take place, and the payments for purchases are not made until some time after the purchases are contracted for.

3. The planning of finances is in most cases in the hands of the principal executive of the company or of the treasurer who acts as his confidential assistant. The financial methods which these executives employ are regarded as highly confidential. Consequently there is little or no exchange of information between companies with reference to financial methods, and no standardized procedure has been developed. In undertaking, therefore, the introduction of scientific

financial planning, each firm is dependent largely on its own
experiences and resourcefulness.

4. The executives in charge of the financial operations of a business
are usually loath to delegate any duties with reference to them
to others, and hesitate to commit their plans to a definite form
for fear that they will be hampered in their freedom of action
and that important information may be divulged.

None of these difficulties is insurmountable, and for-
tunately the present tendency indicates a rapid removal of
the latter two and the development of scientific methods
of overcoming the first two.

### Summary

In the preceding pages an attempt has been made to
outline the procedure necessary for the preparation and
control of the financial budget. In summary form this
procedure may be stated as follows:

1. PREPARATION OF A PRELIMINARY ESTIMATE OF CASH
RECEIPTS. This requires the determination of the probable receipts from all sources. The principal source of cash
receipts is the collections from accounts receivable, and
the estimate of collections must be based on the estimate
of sales which has been prepared in the manner previously
explained.

2. PREPARATION OF A PRELIMINARY ESTIMATE OF CASH
DISBURSEMENTS. This requires the determination of probable disbursements needed to finance the operations of all
the departments of the business. Consequently the estimate of disbursements must be based on the various departmental estimates which have been explained in previous
chapters.

3. PREPARATION OF THE CASH BUDGET. The preliminary estimates of cash receipts and disbursements explained
in (1) and (2) are submitted, together with all the other

estimates, to the budget committee. After the various departmental estimates have been approved, the preliminary estimates of cash receipts and disbursements will be revised, if necessary, to give effect to any changes made in the departmental estimates by the budget committee. After the revised cash estimates are approved, they constitute a cash budget.

4. PREPARATION OF THE FINANCIAL PROGRAM. Based on the preliminary estimates of cash receipts and disbursements, there will be prepared a suggested financial program which will indicate the financial procedure by which the requirements of the proposed financial program are to be met. This program will be revised, if necessary, to correspond to the revised financial budget and will then constitute the working program of the financial department.

5. PREPARATION OF AN ESTIMATED BALANCE SHEET AND ESTIMATED STATEMENT OF PROFIT AND LOSS. These financial statements, discussed in the chapters immediately following, are studied in connection with the financial budget to determine the effect of the contemplated financial program on the financial condition and income of the business.

# CHAPTER XXI

## THE ESTIMATED BALANCE SHEET

### The Need for Financial Statements

Business management can be exercised in a rational manner only when it is based on accurate and comprehensive information with reference to the operations of the business which is to be administered. Not only must information be available, but it should be in the form in which it will be the most serviceable to the business manager. A large part of the information used by the business executive is in the form of statistical data, and experience has shown that these data are most useful when presented by means of reports which show them in a summarized and classified form. Consequently, business men have long been accustomed to using statistical reports.

The nature of these reports has been determined largely by necessity. When the executive has found that he must have certain information to carry on some activity which it has been necessary to perform, he has devised, or has had devised, a report which will provide him with this information. The balance sheet and the statement of profit and loss are the two reports with which the executive is most familiar and which are most widely used. The reason for the extensive use of these reports is not difficult to see if the development of accounting records and reports is considered.

### Balance Sheet

Every business finds it necessary in the course of its development to borrow funds from banks and to purchase merchandise on account. In the not distant past both bank and merchandise creditors often granted credit on the basis of the general reputation of the applicant and the information which they could obtain from him in an informal manner. During recent years, however, they have found it necessary to have more exact information and, to obtain this, have required a formal report showing the financial condition of the business. Consequently, the standard form of balance sheet has been developed for their use. The executive, being required to prepare this report for his creditors, gradually learned to make some use of it himself.

## Statement of Profit and Loss

For many years creditors satisfied themselves with the information obtained from the balance sheet, but recently they have found it expedient to ask for additional information which will show the nature of the operations of the business and the result of these operations. They have found it desirable to have this information because they realize that, though the balance sheet shows the financial condition of the business at the time credit is requested, what the creditor is primarily interested in is its financial condition at the end of the period of credit. For instance, if a bank grants a loan for three months, it desires to know that the business will be able to pay the loan at maturity; hence it is interested to know its financial condition three months from now.

If it knows its present financial condition and the result of its past operations, it can estimate roughly the effect of its future operations on its present condition and arrive at an estimate of its financial condition three months in the future. The standard form of the statement of profit and loss has been designed to present to creditors and others the information with reference to the past operations of the business which they desire. Since the executive must prepare it for the use of others, he has learned, as in the case of the balance sheet, to use it for his own purposes.

## Standard Forms of Financial Statements

The balance sheet and the statement of profit and loss have become, therefore, the two standard reports which are usually prepared by all businesses and which are used by the creditors, stockholders, and executives of the business in the making of decisions and the formulation of policies with reference to the business. Through the influence of national associations, such as the American Bankers' Association and the National Association of Credit Men, as well as the writings and teachings of accountants, more or less standard forms for these statements have been developed. It is assumed that the form and content of these widely used and orthodox statements are familiar to the reader.

## Use of the Financial Reports

The standard form of balance sheet and the standard form of statement of profit and loss show respectively the present financial condition of a business and the results in terms of profit and loss of its operations over a certain period of time. This information serves two purposes:

1. It indicates the efficiency with which the business has been managed during the past, and
2. It indicates the possible result of its future operations.

The second purpose of the information provided by the financial reports has not been emphasized by writers and practitioners, and yet a little thought will show that it is the primary purpose for which this information is desired. It is true that these reports are usually discussed in terms of past results, but the principal purpose of studying past results is to be able better to control future results. Just as the creditor desires a statement of profit and loss, so that he can estimate the changes in financial condition which will probably take place as a result of the future operations for a certain

period of time—in the same manner the executive is primarily interested in both the balance sheet and statement of
profit and loss in order that he may be able to judge whether
future operations will result in favorable changes in the
financial condition of the business.

It is true that both the creditor and the executive make
their estimates informally and incompletely.   Neither one
may be conscious that he is making such an estimate at all.
His thought may proceed no farther than to reason that the
operations for the past period have resulted in a profit and a
favorable financial condition, and if the same policies are
followed during the next period, equally favorable results
will follow.   If the results of the past period are undesirable,
he may try to locate the cause and determine some means to
remove it.   If he succeeds in making changes which he
thinks will remove the difficulties of the past period, he may
assume that the results of the next period will be more satisfactory without working out in detail what these results
will be.

For instance, the executive may find that his small profits
for the year are due to increased production cost, and that
the increased cost is the result of wasteful and inefficient
methods of handling materials and supplies in certain departments of the factory.   He changes the methods of these
departments so as to lower the cost of materials and supplies,
and assumes that as a result he will have a satisfactory profit
without determining just what the change in profits will be.
If he finds that the small profits are due to decreased sales,
and the decreased sales are due to the failure of salesmen in
specific territories, he may replace these salesmen with
those who are thought to be efficient and estimate that as a
result of these changes favorable profits will be made.

In both of these cases the executive may carry his thinking a step farther.   He may estimate the reduction in cost

of materials which will be effected by the new methods, and then calculate what the profits of the business will be for the next fiscal period if the other results of operation are the same as for the past period. In the same manner he may estimate the increased sales which will be secured from the changes in sales personnel and the consequent results in profits. If he makes a number of changes and estimates the results of each of these, he is led to make a more or less detailed estimate of the result of future operations.

## Need for Estimated Financial Statements

The foregoing discussion and illustrations should be sufficient to show that the standard forms of balance sheet and statement of profit and loss are used as a basis of planning future operations and estimating the results of these operations. It should also be apparent that these plans and estimates are usually made in a very informal manner, and consequently are apt to be incomplete and inaccurate. In fact, they are little more than "expert guesswork."

In the discussion of the various departmental budgets, it has been emphasized that if estimates are to be made they will be most serviceable if they are prepared in a systematic, complete, and formal manner. In pursuance of this policy, it is desirable that there be prepared an estimated balance sheet or "budget" of assets, liabilities, and proprietorship, and an estimated statement of profit and loss, or "budget" of income and expense, in the same manner that there is prepared a budget of sales, purchases, expenses, etc.

It is the purpose of the present chapter to discuss the construction and use of the estimated balance sheet. The estimated statement of profit and loss will be discussed in the chapter immediately following.

22

### Relation of the Departmental Estimates to the Estimated Financial Reports

The departmental estimates show the contemplated operations of the several departments. The profits of the company and its financial condition are dependent on these operations. After the departmental estimates are prepared, it is then necessary to prepare a preliminary estimated balance sheet showing the effect of the contemplated program on the financial condition of the business, and a preliminary estimated statement of profit and loss showing the result of the program in terms of profit and loss.

By studying these two statements and comparing them with the statements at the beginning of the period, it is possible to judge the desirability of the proposed program. If the execution of the proposed program will lead to undesirable results, it will be necessary to revise the departmental estimates. After these revisions are made, the preliminary estimated financial reports should be revised, to give effect to the changes in the departmental budgets. Although the budget period may be three, six, or twelve months in length, it is desirable that the estimated balance sheet and statement of profit and loss be made so as to show the anticipated results at the end of each month. Monthly comparisons can be made, then, between the estimated and the actual results.

In the following discussion the method by which the estimated financial reports are made will first be considered, and then the method by which they are studied to see if they show the necessity of a revision in the departmental budgets will be explained.

### The Estimated Balance Sheet

To make the discussion of the preparation of the estimated balance sheet more concrete, a simple balance sheet

## NATIONAL MANUFACTURING COMPANY
## BALANCE SHEET
### December 31, 1921

CURRENT ASSETS:
| | | | |
|---|---|---|---|
| Cash.................................... | | $ 48,000 | |
| Notes Receivable......................... | | 80,000 | |
| Accounts Receivable............... | $200,000 | | |
| Less: Reserve for Bad Debts..... | 4,000 | | |
| | | 196,000 | |
| Inventory: | | | |
| Raw Materials.................. | $ 40,000 | | |
| Goods in Process............... | 120,000 | | |
| Finished Goods................ | 560,000 | | |
| | | 720,000 | |
| Accrued Items......................... | | 500 | |
| Total Current Assets.................. | | | $1,044,500 |

FIXED ASSETS:
| | | | |
|---|---|---|---|
| Office Equipment................. | $ 40,000 | | |
| Less: Reserve for Depreciation.... | 8,000 | | |
| | | $ 32,000 | |
| Machinery and Equipment......... | $200,000 | | |
| Less: Reserve for Depreciation.... | 40,000 | | |
| | | 160,000 | |
| Buildings........................ | $160,000 | | |
| Less: Reserve for Depreciation.... | 48,000 | | |
| | | 112,000 | |
| Land.................................... | | 240,000 | |
| Total Fixed Assets.................... | | | 544,000 |
| Deferred Charges to Expense........................... | | | 27,000 |
| Good-Will............................................ | | | 80,000 |
| | | | |
| TOTAL ASSETS............................. | | | $1,695,500 |

CURRENT LIABILITIES:
| | | |
|---|---|---|
| Notes Payable........................... | $ 100,000 | |
| Accounts Payable........................ | 150,000 | |
| Accrued Liabilities....................... | 10,000 | |
| | | |
| Total Current Liabilities......................... | | $ 260,000 |

FIXED LIABILITIES:
| | | |
|---|---|---|
| Mortgages Payable........................ | $ 80,000 | |
| Bonds Payable........................... | 80,000 | |
| | | |
| Total Fixed Liabilities.......................... | | 160,000 |

PROPRIETORSHIP:
| | | |
|---|---|---|
| Capital Stock Outstanding................... | $1,000,000 | |
| Surplus................................ | 275,500 | |
| | | |
| Total Proprietorship............................ | | 1,275,500 |
| | | |
| TOTAL LIABILITIES AND PROPRIETORSHIP........ | | $1,695,500 |

Figure 38.   Balance Sheet

showing the financial condition of a business at the beginning of a fiscal period will be given, and on the basis of assumed departmental budgets an estimated balance sheet, as
of the end of the period, will be prepared.   For the sake of
simplicity a budget period one year in length will be assumed,
and only the estimated balance sheet at the end of the year
will be given.   The reader will understand that an estimated
balance sheet at the end of each month is desirable.

The balance sheet of the National Manufacturing Company as of December 31, 1921, is shown in Figure 38.

To show the preparation of the estimated balance sheet
as of December 31, 1921, it will be necessary to take each
item which appears on the balance sheet at the beginning of
the period and see the method by which the changes which
will occur in it are determined.

## Cash

The cash which it is estimated will be received from the
operations of the business during the budget period, will be
shown by the estimate of cash receipts (Figure 30, page 308)
which is prepared as part of the financial budget.   The estimate of cash receipts does not show the cash to be received
from bank loans, for the purpose of the estimate of cash receipts and disbursements is to show the loans required.   The
amount of these loans can be determined from the financial
program (Figure 34, page 318), which is prepared on the
basis of the financial budget.   The estimate of cash receipts
also does not show the cash which may be received from new
financing such as the sale of stock or bonds.   The amount
of such cash must be obtained by a consideration of the
plans of the directors.

The estimated disbursements for operating purposes
can be obtained from the estimate of cash disbursements
(Figure 31, page 311).   The estimate of cash disbursements

does not show the disbursements for paying bonds or retiring long-term notes. Such disbursements can be easily determined from the plans of the directors and the terms under which the bonds or notes were issued.

After the estimated cash receipts from all sources and the estimated cash disbursements for all purposes are determined, the estimated cash balance can be determined. Although this is the method by which the estimated cash balance is finally obtained, it is customary to decide what cash balance is deemed necessary and use this in preparing the summary of financial requirements (Figure 34, page 318), from which the bank loans required are determined. Of course, if the bank loans required as shown by the preliminary summary of financial requirements are larger than it is thought desirable or possible to obtain, revisions are necessary, and in making these revisions the estimated cash balance may be cut down.

Based on the financial budget of the National Manufacturing Company, it is estimated that its cash balance on December 31, 1922, will be $20,000.

### Notes Receivable

To determine the amount of the notes receivable which will be on hand at the end of the period, it is necessary to consider the following:

(a) Notes receivable on hand at the beginning of the period.
(b) Estimated notes receivable which will be received in payment of goods sold during the period.
(c) Estimated notes receivable which will be received in payment of accounts during the period.
(d) Estimated cash receipts from notes receivable during the period.

It should be apparent to the reader that $a+b+c-d$ equals the notes receivable on hand at the end of the period. If a business has but a few customers, it will be possible to determine the amount of b, c, and d by considering each customer separately.  If there are numerous customers, it may be necessary to obtain the ratio between accounts receivable and notes receivable for the past several years, and assume that this ratio will continue during the current year if no changes in terms or of general business conditions are anticipated.  If new lines are to be introduced, which are to be sold on different terms, or if business conditions are such that clients are apt to give notes in payment of accounts in greater quantities than usual, these facts must be considered, and the estimated ratio between notes receivable and accounts receivable revised accordingly.  After this ratio is determined, it will be applied to the estimated balance of unpaid claims against customers at the end of the period to obtain the estimated notes receivable outstanding.

The National Manufacturing Company sells several classes of products.  Some of these are sold on account, and some are sold on terms which provide for the receipt of trade acceptances and notes in payment.  The tendency for the past three years has been for an increase of the sales of the latter in proportion to the former.  The sales program for the year 1922 calls for an increase in this tendency during the next year.  It is also anticipated that general business conditions are such that more than the usual number of notes will be received from customers in settlement of due accounts.  It is estimated that under these conditions the notes receivable on hand on December 31, 1922, will amount to $120,000.

### Accounts Receivable

The amount of the accounts receivable at the end of the budget period is estimated in a manner very similar to that employed in determining the amount of the notes receivable as explained in the preceding paragraph.  It is necessary to consider (a) the balance outstanding at the beginning of the period; (b) the accounts receivable resulting from the sales during the period; (c) cash receipts from accounts receivable during the period.   It is apparent that $a+b-c$ is equal to the accounts receivable at the end of the period.

On this basis it is estimated that the accounts receivable of the National Manufacturing Company on December 31, 1922, will be $180,000.

## Reserve for Bad Debts

The reserve for bad debts at the beginning of the period is 2 per cent of the accounts receivable, and it is estimated that the same ratio will exist at the end of the year.   Consequently it is estimated that the reserve will be $3,600.

## Inventories

The inventory of raw materials at the end of the period can be obtained from the materials budget, since this budget shows not only the deliveries to stock for each month, but also the balance on hand at the end of each month.   The inventory of goods in process can be determined by a consideration of the following: (a) inventory at beginning of period; (b) cost of the materials, labor, and manufacturing expense put into process during the period; (c) finished goods transferred from factory to stock during the period.   The inventory of goods in process at the end of the period is equal to $a+b-c$.   The items in (2) will be obtained from the estimate of raw material requirements, the labor budget, and the manufacturing expense budget.   Item (c) will be obtained from the finished goods budget.

The inventory of finished goods can be obtained by a consideration of the following: (a) inventory at the beginning of the period; (b) finished goods transferred from factory to stock during the period; (c) stock sold during the period.   The inventory of finished goods at the end of the period is equal to $a+b-c$.   Usually, in making up the estimate of finished goods required, the inventory desired of each separate item at the end of the period is estimated, since this inventory constitutes a part of the requirements for the period.   If the inventory of the separate items which it is planned to have is extended at cost price, the total inventory can be obtained.   In some cases it may be easier to reduce the sales estimate by the amount of the average gross profit and substitute the result in the equation given above.   Either method may be followed and approximate accuracy obtained.

On the basis of the present inventories and the various budgets, it is estimated that the inventories of the company on December 31, 1922, will be as follows:

|  |  |
|---|---:|
| Raw materials. | $ 70,000 |
| Goods in Process. | 230,000 |
| Finished Goods. | 1,100,000 |
| Total. | $1,400,000 |

## Accrued Income

The chief source of accrued income is accrued interest on notes receivable.   The estimated increase in the amount of the notes will cause a corresponding increase in the amount of this item.   Accordingly it is estimated to be $1,000 on December 31, 1922.

## Fixed Assets

The plant and equipment budget shows the following for each class of fixed assets:  (a) balance of asset and reserve for depreciation accounts at the beginning of the period; (b) estimated cost of assets to be acquired during the period; (c) estimated depreciation for the period on both old and new assets; (d) balance of asset and depreciation accounts at the end of the period. It is very easy, therefore, to obtain from the plant and equipment budget the desired information for the estimated balance sheet with reference to both the fixed assets and the depreciation thereon.

From the plant and equipment budget it is estimated that the fixed assets and reserves for depreciation of the company on December 31, 1922, will be as follows:

| | | |
|---|---:|---:|
| Office Equipment......................... | $ 60,000 | |
| *Less:* Reserve for Depreciation........... | 14,000 | |
| | | $ 46,000 |
| • Machinery and Equipment................ | $280,000 | |
| *Less:* Reserve for Depreciation........... | 100,000 | |
| | | 180,000 |
| Building............................... | $200,000 | |
| *Less:* Reserve for Depreciation........... | 58,000 | |
| | | 142,000 |
| Land.................................... | | 240,000 |
| Total Fixed Assets........................ | | $608,000 |

## Deferred Charges to Expense

The deferred charges to expense consist of organization expenses, unexpired insurance, and prepaid interest. The organization expenses disappear from the balance sheet, since this is the last year of the period over which they are being allocated. The unexpired insurance can be determined by a consideration of (a) the insurance which it is planned to place during the year, and (b) the insurance unexpired at the beginning of the year. The latter can be obtained from the insurance policy record, while the former must be obtained from the estimate on insurance. Usually there is one officer who is responsible for all insurance contracts. In many cases this responsibility is placed on the treasurer. The responsible official will prepare an estimate of the contracts to be made and their length of life. The prepaid interest will arise largely from the notes of customers which are discounted. The amount of the notes to be discounted can be determined from the financial program, which is prepared in connection with the financial budget.

It is estimated that the deferred charges of the company on December 31, 1922, will be $35,000.

### Good-Will

The book value of the good-will will not change during the year.

### Notes Payable

The amount of the notes payable at the end of the year will depend on the following: (a) notes payable at beginning of the period; (b) notes issued in payment of merchandise; (c) notes issued in payment of accounts; (d) notes issued to bank for loans; (e) notes paid during the period. The notes outstanding at the end of the period equal $a+b+c+d-e$. The notes to be issued to merchandise creditors in payment for merchandise can be determined by a consideration of the materials budget. This budget shows the purchases to be made during the period, classified under at least major groups or classes. Usually it is for only certain classes of merchandise that notes are given or trade acceptances issued, and the amount of these classes of merchandise which is to be purchased can be obtained from the materials budget.

If notes or trade acceptances are issued for part of the purchases in different lines, it is then necessary to obtain the ratio between the purchases made for notes and the total purchases during past periods, and apply this percentage to the estimated purchases for the current period. In most businesses few, if any, notes are issued in payment of accounts. If such notes are issued, it is necessary to obtain the ratio between them and the total purchases on account, and apply this ratio to the estimated purchases on account for the current period.

The amount of the notes to be issued to banks can be obtained from the financial program (page 318), prepared in connection with the financial budget. The disbursements made in the payment of notes payable are shown in the financial program and in the estimate of cash disbursements. In addition to the notes discussed above, notes payable may be issued to officers, employees, and friends of a company. A separate estimate must be made of their amount. On the balance sheet it is desirable to state the notes issued for separate purposes and to different parties as separate items. For the sake of brevity they will be stated as one item in the present case.

The notes payable of the company as of December 31, 1922, will be $450,000, according to the estimate.

## Accounts Payable

The amount of the accounts payable at the end of the period will be determined from the following: (a) accounts payable at the beginning of the period; (b) purchases on account during the period; (c) payments made on account during the period. The accounts payable at the end of the period equal a+b−c. The amount of the purchases on account will be obtained from the materials budget. The amount of the payments on account will be obtained from the estimate of cash disbursements.

The accounts payable of the company as of December 31, 1922, are estimated to be $200,000.

## Accrued Liabilities

The principal items of accrued liabilities are accrued interest on notes payable and accrued wages. Since the company is planning to increase greatly the amount of its notes payable, this will result in an increase in the accrued interest. Since it also plans to increase very much its inventory of finished goods, this will result in an increase in production, with an enlarged labor force, which in turn will probably result in a larger item of accrued wages. It is estimated that the accrued wages and accrued interest on December 31, 1922, will amount to $20,000.

### Mortgages and Bonds Payable

The anticipated increase in fixed assets will necessitate additional capital, and the treasurer recommends to the board of directors that the mortgages on real estate be increased by $40,000, and that $60,000 additional bonds be issued. Accordingly the fixed liabilities of the company on December 31, 1922, will be as follows: mortgages payable $120,000, bonds payable $140,000.

### Capital Stock

The enlarged operations which are planned for the year will necessitate the procurement of additional capital. The president and the treasurer recommend to the board of directors that $250,000 of additional stock be sold. The estimated capital stock of the company on December 31, 1922, therefore, will be $1,250,000.

### Surplus

The amount of the surplus at the end of the period will be determined from the following: (a) surplus at the beginning of the period; (b) profits for the period; (c) dividends to be declared. The surplus at the end of that period will equal a+b−c. The profits for the period are determined from the estimated statement of profit and loss. The dividends to be paid will be determined by the board of directors. Taking these factors into consideration it is estimated that the surplus of the company on December 31, 1922, will be $170,000.

## Interpretation of Estimated Balance Sheet

On the basis of the information given in the preceding paragraphs, it is possible to construct a preliminary estimated balance sheet for the National Manufacturing Company as of December 31, 1922. The contents of this report is shown in Figure 39.

As previously explained, the purpose of the preliminary estimated balance sheet is to show the effect on the financial condition of the business of the proposed plans for the next period, as expressed in the departmental budgets. After it is prepared, it is necessary to study it to see whether it shows a desirable tendency, and, if it does not, revisions in the budgets should be made, if possible, so as to remedy the undesirable tendency. The easiest way to see the effect of the proposed budgets is to show the estimated balance sheet as of the end of the period in comparison with the actual balance sheet at the beginning of the period. This comparison for the National Manufacturing Company is shown in Figure 39.

The most significant comparisons shown by Figure 39 will be considered.

## Cash

It is estimated that the cash balance at the end of the year will be but slightly more than 40 per cent of the cash balance at the beginning of the year. A decrease in the cash balance is not in itself undesirable. In some cases it may be desirable, for the cash balance at the beginning of the period may have been too large. The important question to determine is whether the cash balance at the end of the year is sufficient. Although this question cannot be answered definitely, since there are no definite standards by which to judge the cash balance which a business should have, there are indications that the estimated balance for the company is too small.

In the first place the current liabilities are $760,000, and it is safe to assume that these are maturing each day. The current assets are also presumably being converted into cash every day, but it is not difficult to conceive of a situation where the liabilities maturing on a particular day may be more than the funds received from current assets on that day, plus a cash balance of $20,000. Then, of course, it is impossible, or at least impractical, to pay out the total cash balance. The primary purpose of the cash balance is to take up the possible slack between cash receipts and cash disbursements, and it is unwise to reduce this balance to too small an amount, especially if, as in this case, the excess of current assets over current liabilities is not large.

A more important indication of the inadequacy of the estimated cash balance is the ratio between the cash balance and the notes payable. The latter item is not analyzed, but it is safe to assume that it is expected that a considerable part of the notes outstanding on December 31, 1922, will be in the hands of the bankers of the firm. Practically all banks require that a customer maintain a bank balance which bears a certain ratio to the loans made to the customer by the bank. Many banks require that the balance shall be 20 per cent of the loans granted to the customer. If such a cash balance is required by the bankers of this company, its maximum bank loans on December 31, 1922, would be $100,000. It is hardly to be conceived that less than one-fifth of the notes issued by the firm are to bankers.

It is probable that the estimated balance sheet calls for an impossible condition by planning for larger bank loans than the cash balance will make possible. In any case a

COMPARATIVE BALANCE SHEET

FOR THE

NATIONAL MANUFACTURING COMPANY

### ASSETS

| | | 1921 | | | 1922 | |
|---|---|---|---|---|---|---|
| **CURRENT ASSETS:** | | | | | | |
| Cash...................... | | $ 48,000 | | | $ 20,000 | |
| Notes Receivable............ | | 80,000 | | | 120,000 | |
| Accounts Receivable......... | $200,000 | | | $ 180,000 | | |
| Less: Reserve for Bad Debts. | 4,000 | 196,000 | | 3,600 | 176,400 | |
| Inventories: | | | | | | |
| Raw Materials............ | $ 40,000 | | | $ 70,000 | | |
| Goods in Process........... | 120,000 | | | 230,000 | | |
| Finished Goods............ | 560,000 | 720,000 | | 1,100,000 | 1,400,000 | |
| Accrued Items.............. | | 2,000 | | | 1,000 | |
| Total Current Assets...... | | | $1,046,000 | | | $1,717,400 |
| **FIXED ASSETS:** | | | | | | |
| Office Equipment............. | $ 40,000 | | | $ 60,000 | | |
| Less: Depreciation.......... | 8,000 | $ 32,000 | | 14,000 | $ 46,000 | |
| Machinery and Equipment..... | $200,000 | | | $ 280,000 | | |
| Less: Depreciation......... | 40,000 | 160,000 | | 100,000 | 180,000 | |
| Building.................... | $160,000 | | | $ 200,000 | | |
| Less: Depreciation.......... | 48,000 | 112,000 | | 58,000 | 142,000 | |
| Land...................... | | 240,000 | | | 240,000 | |
| Total Fixed Assets........ | | | 544,000 | | | 608,000 |
| **DEFERRED CHARGES TO EXPENSE..** | | | 24,000 | | | 35,000 |
| **GOOD-WILL..................** | | | 80,000 | | | 80,000 |
| **TOTAL ASSETS.........** | | | $1,694,000 | | | $2,440,400 |

### LIABILITIES

| | | 1921 | | | 1922 |
|---|---|---|---|---|---|
| **CURRENT LIABILITIES:** | | | | | |
| Notes Payable.............. | $ 100,000 | | | $ 540,000 | |
| Accounts Payable........... | 150,000 | | | 200,000 | |
| Accrued Liabilities.......... | 10,000 | | | 20,400 | |
| Total Current Liabilities... | | $ 260,000 | | | $ 760,400 |
| **FIXED LIABILITIES:** | | | | | |
| Mortgages Payable.......... | $ 80,000 | | | $ 120,000 | |
| Bonds Payable.............. | 80,000 | | | 140,000 | |
| Total Fixed Liabilities..... | | 160,000 | | | 260,000 |
| **PROPRIETORSHIP:** | | | | | |
| Capital Stock Outstanding..... | $1,000,000 | | | $1,250,000 | |
| Surplus..................... | 274,000 | | | 170,000 | |
| Total Liabilities and Proprietorship........... | | 1,274,000 | | | 1,420,000 |
| **TOTAL LIABILITIES.....** | | $1,694,000 | | | $2,440,400 |

Figure 39. Comparative Balance Sheet, with Preliminary Estimate

business doing the volume of business which this balance sheet indicates, should not at any time be in such a condition as to be unable to borrow more than $100,000 from its banks.   The estimated statement of profit and loss which will be given later will confirm the inadequacy of this cash balance.   Revisions in the budgetary program which will accomplish its increase will be discussed subsequently.

### Notes Receivable and Accounts Receivable

The notes receivable show an estimated increase of 50 per cent, while the accounts receivable show a decrease. This is rather an unusual situation, since an increase in the volume of business should produce a corresponding increase in both.   In the preceding discussion of the method of determining the amount of the notes receivable, it has been explained that the statistics of past periods show a tendency for the sales for which notes are received in payment to increase faster than the sales on account.   There may be conditions under which this tendency will not be regarded as undesirable, but usually notes received in payment of merchandise are non-interest-bearing and are for a considerably longer length of time than the usual credit period granted on open account sales.   Consequently the seller is required to borrow funds with which to carry these notes or must discount them to obtain funds.   In either case the interest charge must be borne by him which in turn reduces his profit. Unless a higher sales price is obtained for goods sold on notes, less profit is obtained usually than for goods sold on account.

The estimated balance sheet shows such a radical change in the ratio of accounts receivable to notes receivable, that a careful examination should be made of the tendency shown by the comparisons of past periods to see whether the tendency for the notes receivable to increase more than in proportion to the accounts receivable should be permitted to continue, or whether strenuous efforts should be made to correct it by enforcement of stricter credit terms or by placing more sales effort on other lines.

### Inventories

The estimated inventories of December 31, 1922, are almost twice what the inventories are at the beginning of the year. The estimated increases in the inventories of raw materials and goods in process are no doubt the result of the estimated increase in production which is required to build up and maintain the large increase in finished goods for which the estimated balance sheet calls. Such an estimated increase in finished goods may result from the following:

1. A large increase in sales may be estimated and this calls for an increased inventory. Whether the increase called for is justified can be determined to some extent by considering the turnover shown by the estimated statement of profit and loss, and comparing this turnover with the turnover shown by previous statements.

2. It may be due to careless and inaccurate planning on the part of the production department. This department may not estimate accurately the required inventory of each item to be manufactured, not basing this estimate on the estimate of sales, but rather making a lump estimate of the inventory desired.

A very careful investigation should be made to see (1) whether the estimated inventory is necessary in order to meet the estimated sales; (2) whether it is possible to finance such an inventory, even if it is necessary to meet estimated sales; and (3) whether it is desirable to tie up so much capital in inventory, with the consequent carrying charges and the possibility of a large loss being incurred due to falling prices. It may be found more profitable and better financial policy to reduce sales and carry a smaller inventory.

23

There is usually great danger attendant on such a rapid expansion as the increase in the inventories indicates that this company is contemplating.  It is also significant to note that though the notes receivable and accounts receivable have increased less than 8 per cent, the inventory of finished goods has increased almost 100 per cent.  This would seem to indicate that it is planned to increase the inventory of finished goods faster than is required by the sales program, since increased sales, without a change in terms or collection methods, will result in an increase in the accounts receivable and notes receivable.

A statement of the suggested procedure for the company to follow in connection with its inventories will be postponed until after the estimated statement of profit and loss is considered.

### Fixed Assets

The estimated balance sheet shows a considerable increase in office equipment, machinery and equipment, and buildings.  In determining the propriety of these increases, it is necessary to consider the following:

1. Whether the increases shown represent anticipated expenditures which can properly be chargeable to the asset accounts.  Care must be taken to see that they do not represent estimated appreciation on the assets or estimated expenditures for repairs or replacements.  If these increases are based on the plant and equipment budget, it should be easy to determine their accuracy.
2. Whether the estimated increases in these assets are necessary to carry on the contemplated program of the year.
3. Whether, if they are necessary, it will be possible to finance them.
4. Whether it will be profitable to incur these increases in order to carry on the contemplated program.

The estimated depreciation should be investigated to see if it is calculated at the proper rate.  The figures shown would seem to be reasonable in view of the estimated increase in assets.

### Deferred Charges to Expense

The increase in the deferred charges would seem to be reasonable in view of the estimated increase in value of the assets on which insurance should be carried and the probability of an increase in prepaid interest. To determine the desirability of the amount of the deferred charges to expense, it is necessary to consider the advisability of incurring the expenses which give rise to these charges.

### Notes Payable and Accounts Payable

Turning to the liability side of the comparative balance sheet, it will be noticed that a larger increase in the notes payable is estimated. The notes payable of December 31 are estimated to be almost five and one-half times the amount outstanding at the beginning of the year. An increase in the accounts payable is also estimated, but this increase is by no means in proportion to the contemplated increase in notes payable. An analysis should be made to show to whom it is planned to issue these notes. It is regarded as good financial management to borrow funds on notes issued to banks and to use these funds to discount accounts payable. An inspection of the item of purchases discount on the comparative statement of profit and loss which will be shown in Figure 40 (page 363), will serve to show whether this procedure is contemplated. If it is, the estimated purchases discount should show a large increase over the amount of last year.

There are indications that it is contemplated to contract large bank loans in order to pay accounts payable contracted to secure the large increase in inventories. If this be true, there is considerable doubt of the advisability of the contemplated large increase in bank loans.   In the first place, it is doubtful whether banks would loan the amount called for by the estimated balance sheet on the strength of the financial condition shown by this statement. In the second place it is doubtful if the firm should contract such a large amount of loans in order to carry large inventories.   If the inventories are not converted very rapidly, the firm may be unable to meet the notes at maturity.

### Fixed Liabilities

It is estimated that the bonds payable and mortgages payable will both increase during the year.   Presumably the funds to be secured from these increases are to be used in making the increase to the fixed assets.   If the increases in fixed assets are found to be justifiable, it may not be improper to increase the fixed liabilities correspondingly. However, the more desirable procedure is for a business to increase its permanent assets out of profits.   A rapidly expanding business will often find this impossible, and if there is assurance that a rapid expansion will be profitable, no objection can be made to the procedure contemplated by this company.

It must be remembered, however, that fixed liabilities impose upon a business fixed charges which must be met if the business is to continue to operate, and that fixed liabilities are not subject to rapid contraction as are current liabilities.   A business should therefore be cautious in adopting a program which necessitates an increase in its fixed liabilities.

### Capital Stock

The estimated balance sheet shows an increase in capital stock of $250,000.   This increase strengthens the indications of the other comparisons that the company is embarking on an extensive program of expansion. If its plans are dependent on the sale of stock, it should be assured, before embarking upon its year's program, that the stock can be sold. Otherwise it may find itself greatly embarrassed because the estimated balance sheet shows that the company has used practically every other available source of additional capital.

## Surplus

The estimated balance sheet shows a large decrease in the surplus for the year. This decrease may result (a) from a loss being incurred during the year; (b) from the paying of dividends in excess of the profits of the year. Either condition indicates an undesirable situation. To incur a loss is always undesirable. There are times when it may be desirable to pay dividends from accumulated profits, but the balance sheet of this company does not indicate such a procedure is desirable for it.

In the first place, the surplus of the company is not large in comparison to its capital stock. Secondly, the company is planning to issue new stock and additional bonds to obtain necessary capital. It is also planning to contract large liabilities in the form of notes payable. Under such conditions it is doubtful if it is expedient to use funds to pay dividends which are declared from profits of preceding years.

## Ratio of Current Assets to Current Liabilities

A final comparison which is of considerable significance is that of the ratio of current assets to current liabilities. On December 31, 1921, this ratio is slightly more than 4 to 1, while the estimated balance sheet of December 31, 1922, shows a ratio of only 2⅕ to 1. It can be seen, therefore, that there is a decided decrease in this ratio. Although the ratio on December 31, 1922, does not in itself appear unfavorable, the tendency indicated by the decrease in this ratio during the year is decidedly undesirable. If possible, changes should be made to prevent this decided decrease in this ratio. In any case, care must be exercised to see that this tendency does not continue.

It is of course realized that no standard ratio of current assets to current liabilities can be established. This ratio will vary from business to business, and will vary in the same business at different stages of the business cycle.

# CHAPTER XXII

## THE ESTIMATED STATEMENT OF PROFIT AND LOSS

### Contents of the Estimated Statement of Profit and Loss

The estimated statement of profit and loss is prepared in the same form as the periodical statement. Its contents is classified into the following principal groups:

1. Returns from sales
2. Cost of goods sold
3. Operating expenses
4. Non-operating income
5. Non-operating expense

It is necessary to discuss briefly the method of estimating the amount of each of these.

### Returns from Sales

The estimated sales for the period are shown by the sales estimate. The estimate shows the gross sales, and for the purpose of the estimated statement of profit and loss it is necessary to arrive at the net sales. This makes it necessary to determine the amount of the sales returns and sales allowances. An estimate of these can be made by obtaining their ratio to sales during past periods, and applying this ratio to the estimated sales for the current period. If there are conditions which will affect this ratio during the coming period, these will need to be given consideration.

The estimated sales and the estimated returns and allowance of the National Manufacturing Company are shown in the comparative statement of profit and loss shown in Figure 40.

### Cost of Goods Sold

In calculating the cost of goods sold of a manufacturing business, several items have to be considered. These include the beginning and ending inventories of finished goods, materials, and goods in process. In addition it is necessary to know the purchases of materials, labor, and manufacturing expense. The method of calculating the inventories has been explained in the discussion of the estimated balance sheet. The estimated purchases of materials, labor, and manufacturing expense can be taken from the materials, labor, and manufacturing expense budgets, respectively.

In a mercantile business the problem is much simpler than in the manufacturing business. It is necessary to consider only the beginning and ending inventories and the purchases of finished goods. If a finished goods schedule such as that discussed in Chapter XIV is prepared, all this information can be taken directly from it.

The estimated cost of goods of the National Manufacturing Company is shown in the comparative statement of profit and loss given in Figure 40.

### Operating Expenses

The amount of each class of expense can be obtained from the various expense budgets. The only difficulty which may arise in this connection is that the expense classification shown by the expense budgets may not correspond with that usually shown on the statement of profit and loss. This is particularly true if the expense budgets are made according to the classification of expenses suggested in Chapter XVIII. For instance, under corporate and financial expenses will be included items which are often shown as non-operating expenses.

It is the author's belief that some such classification as that suggested in the discussion of the expense budgets is desirable for control purposes, and that it is preferable that the estimated statement of profit and loss show the same classification. If desirable a different classification may be shown on the financial statements submitted for public use.

The statement presented below shows the estimated expenses of National Manufacturing Company, classified under the principal headings suggested in Chapter XVIII. The expense estimates will supply the supporting data to make possible a judgment as to the propriety of these amounts.

## Non-Operating Income

The non-operating income can be obtained by simple calculations based on the information contained in the various budgets. For instance, the purchases discount can be estimated by applying the ratio of purchases discount to the total purchases of previous years, to the estimated purchases of the current year. Interest earned can be calculated on the basis of the sales estimate and the ratio of interest received to sales during preceding years. This method is based on the assumption that the terms of sales and rate of interest on notes receivable will remain the same. Contemplated changes in policy must be given effect in making these estimates.

Such changes are contemplated by the National Manufacturing Company, which accounts for a decrease in the amount of these items on its estimated statement of profit and loss, as shown in Figure 40.

## Non-Operating Expense

If the expense classification previously suggested is maintained, there will not be many items under non-operating expense. Those that are shown here can be easily estimated.   For instance, if it is desired to show sales discount as a non-operating expense, its amount can be estimated by applying the ratio of sales discount to the total sales during previous years, to the estimated sales of the current year.

### Interpretation of the Estimated Statement of Profit and Loss

The most convenient and effective way to show the effect of the proposed budgets on the profits of the business is to show the estimated statement of profit and loss as of the end of the period, in comparison with the actual statement of profit and loss at the beginning of the period. The statement of profit and loss of the National Manufacturing Company as of December 31, 1921, and its estimated statement of profit and loss as of December 31, 1922, are shown in Figure 40.   The most important comparison shown by the statements will be considered.

### Sales

The estimated sales show an increase of 50 per cent. This in itself looks very favorable, but the result of these sales in terms of profit and loss must be considered before a final conclusion can be made.

### Turnover

The merchandise turnover for the year 1921 is 3.4, while for the year 1922 it is estimated to be only 2.5.   This comparison shows a decided decrease in the rate of turnover which should be given careful consideration.   The relation of this decrease in turnover to the inventories will be explained later in this discussion.

### Gross Profits on Sales

The gross profits on sales in 1921 are approximately 12⅛ per cent of sales, while the estimated gross profits for 1922

COMPARATIVE STATEMENT OF PROFIT AND LOSS

FOR THE

NATIONAL MANUFACTURING COMPANY

|  | 1921 | 1922 |
|---|---|---|
| GROSS SALES | $1,600,000 | $2,400,000 |
| *Less:* Sales Returns and Allowances | 16,000 | 24,000 |
| Net Sales | $1,584,000 | $2,376,000 |
| **COST OF GOODS SOLD:** | | |
| Raw Materials, Beginning Inventory | $ 18,000 | $ 40,000 |
| Purchases | 600,000 | 962,000 |
|  | $ 618,000 | $1,002,000 |
| Raw Materials, Inventory End of Period | 40,000 | 70,000 |
| Raw Materials Used | $ 578,000 | $ 932,000 |
| Labor Used | 625,000 | 1,130,000 |
| Manufacturing Expense | 575,000 | 700,000 |
|  | $1,778,000 | $2,762,000 |
| Work in Process, January 1 | 50,000 | 120,000 |
|  | $1,828,000 | $2,882,000 |
| Work in Process, December 31 | 120,000 | 230,000 |
| Cost of Goods Manufactured | $1,708,000 | $2,652,000 |
| Finished Goods, Beginning Inventory | 240,000 | 560,000 |
|  | $1,948,000 | $3,212,000 |
| Finished Goods, Inventory End | 560,000 | 1,100,000 |
| Cost of Goods Sold | $1,388,000 | $2,112,000 |
| GROSS PROFIT ON SALES | $ 196,000 | $ 264,000 |
| **OPERATING EXPENSES:** | | |
| Selling Expenses | $ 44,000 | $ 85,000 |
| Financial Expenses | 30,500 | 47,500 |
| Executive Expenses | 25,000 | 41,500 |
| Corporate Expenses | 18,000 | 23,000 |
|  | 10,500 | 19,000 |
| Total Operating Expenses | $ 128,000 | $ 216,000 |
| Net Operating Profit | $ 68,000 | $ 48,000 |
| NON-OPERATING INCOME | 24,800 | 20,800 |
| Gross Income | $ 92,800 | $ 68,800 |
| NON-OPERATING EXPENSE | 31,000 | 53,600 |
| NET INCOME | $ 61,800 | $ 15,200 |

Figure 40.   Comparative Statement of Profit and Loss, with
Preliminary Estimate

are only 11 per cent of sales. This indicates that the estimated production cost of goods sold increases faster than the estimated sales price of sales. Or if falling prices are anticipated, it may be estimated that the sales price will fall faster than the production cost. This may be a situation which is unavoidable, but careful scrutiny should be made to determine some means by which it may be remedied. The tendency indicated by this comparison is a dangerous one, and one which is apt to occur if there is not close co-operation between sales and production departments.

### Ratio of Selling Expenses to Sales

The selling expenses are .027 of sales for the year 1921, but according to the estimated statement of profit and loss are to be .035 for the year 1922. This shows that though the sales are expected to increase, the proposed marketing plans are such that it will cost more to secure each dollar of sales than during the last year. An analysis of the sales expense will probably show that this increase is due to the estimated extra cost of salesmen's salaries and expenses and of advertising. It may be planned to incur these increased expenses to obtain additional business and build up good-will for the company. It may be proper to increase these, but the tendency for such expenses to increase faster than sales increase is a dangerous one, and care should be taken that it does not continue too long.

### Operating Expenses

The total operating expenses for 1921 are 8 per cent of sales, while for the year 1922, it is estimated that they will be 9 per cent. Although this increase is not large it shows an undesirable and a dangerous tendency, and a careful examination should be made to see if it is possible to change this condition before the budgets are approved,

## Net Operating Profit

The net operating profit for 1921 is 4 per cent of sales, while it is estimated to be but 2 per cent of sales for the year 1922. It is also estimated to be smaller in amount in 1922 than in 1921. This is the most discouraging information shown on the comparative statement of profit and loss. When it is estimated that the sales will increase 50 per cent, it is decidedly unsatisfactory to find an estimated decrease in net profit. It may of course be found that some of the expenses to be incurred during the coming year are expected to result in increased business during future years. If this be true, there may be some excuse for the unprofitable showing, but a careful examination should be made to ascertain if this is the situation.

## Non-operating Expense

It is estimated that there will be a large increase in the non-operating expenses for the year. This increase is probably due to the anticipated increase in interest resulting from the additional bonds and notes which are to be issued, and the increase in the amount of the mortgages payable.

## Net Income

The estimated net income for 1922 is approximately one-fourth of the net income for the year previous. This indicates that the proposed program for the year is not a proper one, since a 50 per cent increase in volume of business leads to a 75 per cent decrease in net income.

## Relation of Estimated Balance Sheet to Estimated Statement of Profit and Loss

If the comparative balance sheet given in Chapter XXI is studied in connection with the comparative statement of profit and loss shown in this chapter, a few significant indications are shown:

1. The comparative statement of profit and loss confirms the indications of the comparative balance sheet that a large increase in business is contemplated. It shows that the budgets are all based on a policy of expansion.

2. The comparative balance sheet shows a large anticipated increase in inventory of finished goods and an increase which is much larger proportionally than the anticipated increase in sales, as shown by the comparative statement of profit and loss. Whereas it is estimated that the sales will increase 50 per cent, it is estimated that the inventory of finished goods will increase almost 100 per cent. The comparative statement of profit and loss shows a decrease in the merchandise turnover. It is hard to conceive of conditions which would necessitate such a change in the rate of turnover in one year. These comparisons show rather conclusively that the proposed production program is out of harmony with the sales program and should be cut down.

3. The comparative balance sheet shows an estimated decrease in surplus of $104,000. The comparative statement of profit and loss shows a profit for the year of $15,200. It is evident, therefore, that it is planned to pay dividends which will necessitate the distribution of a considerable part of the accumulated surplus. The financial condition of the business, as shown by the comparative balance sheet, indicates that such a procedure would be unwise.

### Revision of Departmental Estimates

It is very probable that a study of the estimated balance sheet and the estimated statement of profit and loss would lead to a revision of the departmental estimates on which these statements are based. This revision is necessary for three reasons:

1. The estimated balance sheet shows that the contemplated program for the year will result in the firm's showing an unsatisfactory financial condition at the end of the year.
2. The estimated statement of profit and loss shows that the contemplated program will result in an unsatisfactory profit for the year.
3. The financial budget shows that the financial requirements of the proposed program would probably be larger than the firm could finance. As already pointed out, the financial condition of the firm, as shown by its estimated balance sheet, does not warrant the procurement of the quantity of loans for which the balance sheet calls.

## Some of the revisions which may possibly be made are:

1. The sales program will be scrutinized very carefully to determine if all the sales for which it calls can be made profitably. If not, those which are not profitable will be eliminated.
2. The sales program will also be examined to see if it is not possible to increase sales to be made on short-term credit and to reduce those made on long-term credit. Any possible changes will be made.
3. The estimated inventory of finished goods will be cut down to be in harmony with the sales program. This will result in a decrease in the production program, with a consequent decrease in labor, materials, and manufacturing expense cost.
4. If possible, the plant and equipment program will be cut down. This will be all the more possible because of the decrease in the production program.
5. The proposed dividend may be passed.
6. The operating expense estimates will be reduced, if possible, so that the ratio of operating expenses to sales will not be in excess of the previous year, and, if possible, so that it will be smaller.
7. Based on the foregoing revisions, the financial budget will be revised.

## Preparation of the Estimated Financial Reports

The preceding discussion has indicated the method by which the estimated balance sheet and statement of profit and loss are prepared and the manner in which they may be interpreted. In order to make the discussion as concrete as possible, assumed statements were taken and an interpretation of these made. It should be evident to the reader that such an interpretation may lead to erroneous conclusions when taken by itself. *The foregoing case is given to indicate the method by which statements should be analyzed rather than to emphasize the value of the particular conclusions drawn from the analysis.*

There may be a difference of opinion with reference to the placing of the responsibility for the preparation of the estimated statements. It is necessary to use the various departmental estimates in their preparation, and the executive in charge of the budgetary procedure is the only one to whom all these come automatically. A saving of time results, therefore, if this executive is held responsible for their preparation. After they are completed he may well submit them to the controller and the treasurer for consideration and suggestions.

The executive in charge of the budgetary procedure will prepare preliminary estimated financial statements and submit them to the budget committee at the time he submits the departmental estimates and the estimates of cash receipts and disbursements. After the budget committee has approved the departmental estimates, he will revise the estimated financial statements to give effect to the changes which have been made in the departmental budgets.

### Control of the Estimated Financial Statements

The estimated financial statements, like all other estimates, must be compared with results obtained at frequent intervals, if effective control is to be exercised over their use. Both the estimated balance sheet and the estimated statement of profit and loss should be compared at the end of each budget period with the actual balance sheet and actual statement of profit and loss as of that date. This comparison will be more significant if the actual financial statements at the beginning of the year are included.

| | Actual Dec. 31, 1921 | Estimated Dec. 31, 1922 | Actual Dec. 31, 1922 |
|---|---|---|---|
| **NATIONAL MANUFACTURING COMPANY** Actual and Estimated Balance Sheet as of the Dates Stated | | | |
| Current Assets | | | |
| Deferred Charges | | | |
| Fixed Assets | | | |
| Intangible Assets | | | |
| Total Assets | | | |
| Current Liabilities | | | |
| Fixed Liabilities | | | |
| Deferred Credits | | | |
| Total Liabilities | | | |
| Proprietorship | | | |
| Total Liabilities and Proprietorship | | | |

Figure 41. Comparison of Actual and Estimated Balance Sheets

A report showing proper comparisons for the balance sheet may be made in the form shown in Figure 41.

A similar report can be made on the statement of profit and loss in the form shown in Figure 42.

24

The reports shown in Figures 41 and 42 should be prepared by the executive in charge of the budgetary procedure and submitted to the budget committee at the time the other budget reports are transferred to it.

### The "General Budget"

Both practitioners and writers sometimes refer to the "general budget." The estimated balance sheet and estimated statement of profit and loss is the most convenient form in which to prepare the general budget. These statements show the effect of the proposed program, as expressed in the departmental estimates, on the financial condition and earnings of the firm, and this is the information which the executives and board of directors need in order to judge the advisability of the contemplated plans.

If the budget committee and the board of directors study carefully the financial budget and the estimated financial statements, together with departmental estimates which support these, they should have no difficulty in securing the information necessary for effective administrative control.

### Branch and Division Budgets

Where a business has branches, divisions, or subsidiary companies, it may desire to have separate budgets prepared for each. In this case separate sales estimates, production estimates, plant and equipment estimates, etc., may be prepared for each unit and these may be consolidated to form a financial budget and estimated financial statements for each.

The estimates of each unit will be submitted separately to the budget committee, and in addition they will be combined to form the estimates for the company as a whole. This procedure enables the budget committee and board of

## NATIONAL MANUFACTURING COMPANY

Actual and Estimated Statements of Profit and Loss as of the Dates Stated

|  | Actual 1921 | Estimated 1922 | Actual 1922 |
|---|---|---|---|
| GROSS SALES | | | |
| RETURNS AND ALLOWANCES | | | |
| NET SALES | | | |
| COST OF GOODS SOLD | | | |
| GROSS PROFIT ON SALES | | | |
| OPERATING EXPENSES | | | |
|   Selling Expenses | | | |
|   Financial Expenses | | | |
|   Executive Expenses | | | |
|   Corporate Expenses | | | |
|   Total Operating Expenses | | | |
| NET OPERATING PROFIT | | | |
| NON-OPERATING INCOME | | | |
| GROSS INCOME | | | |
| NON-OPERATING EXPENSE | | | |
| NET INCOME | | | |

Figure 42. Comparison of Actual and Estimated Statements of Profit and Loss

directors to judge better the contemplated program, since they can pass judgment on each unit separately. It also facilitates the enforcement of the estimates, since responsibility for the variations between the estimated and the actual can be definitely fixed.

## Summary

The purpose of the foregoing discussion is to explain and illustrate the use of the estimated balance sheet and estimated statement of profit and loss in business planning and administration. More particularly it attempts to show their relation to the general budgetary plans of the business. The development of the use of financial reports as a basis of management may be divided into three stages:

1. Business men learned to use the balance sheet which shows them *where they are* at a specific date.
2. They learned to use the statement of profit and loss which shows them *how they got to where they are.*
3. They are just now learning to use the estimated balance sheet and estimated statement of profit and loss which shows them *where they are going* and *how they are to get there.*

The slow growth of the use of the estimated balance sheet and estimated statement of profit and loss has no doubt been due in part to the attitude maintained by public accountants that the function of the accountant is to make statements showing the results of past operations, and not to prophesy as to what will happen in the future. This attitude is due probably to the realization that, since they are not connected with the business, they have no control over its future operations, and therefore cannot safely predict their result. They feel that such statements on their part might be used to mislead the public and this would react to their disfavor. Although the public accountant may be justified in this attitude because of the particular relations existing between him and his client, this in no way detracts from the value of the estimated financial statement as a basis of managerial control.

The bookkeeper has also failed to prepare estimated financial reports because he makes up his reports from the accounts, and the accounts do not reflect the decisions of the executives of the company with reference to results expected.

No doubt in the not distant future both the accountant and the business man will come to realize that all financial statements are but estimates, and although estimates of past results as shown by the standard balance sheet and statement of profit and loss may be more exact, estimates of future results may be equally useful.

# CHAPTER XXIII

## MANUAL OF BUDGETARY PROCEDURE

### Need for Manual

As shown by the discussion in the preceding chapters, the procedure involved in the preparation and execution of the various departmental budgets is a comprehensive and complex one. It requires the cooperation of the various functional executives, and a very definite coordination of the activities of the functional departments. The success of the budgetary program is dependent on this cooperation and coordination. If any part of the procedure fails, it disrupts the remainder.

For these reasons it is desirable that the budgetary procedure be very carefully worked out and reduced to written form, so that all executives and employees concerned may be fully cognizant of it. This can be most easily done by the preparation of a manual on budgetary procedure.

### Contents of Manual

The contents of a manual on budgetary procedure will vary from business to business, depending on the volume and nature of the operations performed and upon the organization by which the operations are carried on. In a manufacturing business it is usually desirable that the manual discuss the following:

1. Organization for Budgetary Control
2. The Sales Budget
3. The Production Budget
4. The Labor Budget
5. The Manufacturing Expense Budget

6. The Materials Budget
7. The Plant and Equipment Budget
8. The Expense Budgets
9. The Financial Budget
10. The Estimated Financial Statements

## Illustration of Manual

To show concretely the possible contents of a manual on budgetary procedure, there is given below the manual of a manufacturing company. The company has sales of about $6,000,000 a year. Part of the product of the company is sold direct to the consumer, while the remainder is sold to merchants. Branches are used to market part of the goods.

The president, who is also treasurer, does not reside in the city where the company is located but maintains an active interest in its affairs. The assistant treasurer is general manager; the other principal executives are the sales manager and works manager. The assistant to the general manager serves as office manager and head of the accounting and statistical departments. The company's accounting period is four weeks and its budget period is three accounting periods.

### I. ORGANIZATION FOR BUDGETARY CONTROL

#### 1. THE PRESIDENT

The President of the Company is to have direct control of all matters pertaining to the budgetary program. All officers to whom authority is delegated in this manual are acting as his agents and are responsible to him for the proper performance of the duties delegated to them. In all cases of disagreement between departments with reference to the coordination of estimates, the decision of the President will be final.

#### 2. THE GENERAL MANAGER

The General Manager will be the representative of the President in all matters pertaining to the budgetary program and will have such authority in connection therewith as the President may see fit to delegate to him.

In all matters so delegated, the decision of the General Manager will have the same authority as that of the President.

### 3. THE BUDGET COMMITTEE

The General Manager, the Works Manager, and the Sales Manager will constitute a Budget Committee which will have supervision of the budgetary program. The Assistant to the General Manager will be secretary of this committee.

Under the authority and direction of the President, the Budget Committee is to consider all departmental estimates and to make such changes and revisions as it may think desirable. No estimate is to be effective until it has received the approval of the Budget Committee. The Committee will receive all estimates from the Assistant to the General Manager and will transmit the estimates as approved by it to him. In case the Budget Committee cannot agree with reference to any estimate, the question in dispute is to be submitted to the President and his decision will be final.

In the consideration of the departmental estimates, the Budget Committee may call on departmental heads to explain the reasons for the variations in their estimates from the estimates of past periods.

The Committee will receive through the Assistant to the General Manager periodic reports showing comparisons of the performance for the past period with the estimated performance of that period. On the basis of these reports, it may make revisions in the budgets for the remainder of the budget period, if it deems such revisions necessary.

### 4. THE ASSISTANT TO THE GENERAL MANAGER

Under the authority and direction of the General Manager, the Assistant to the General Manager will have general control and supervision over the preparation and execution of the budgetary program. His general duties are outlined in the several sections of this manual.

These duties may be summarized as follows:

(1) To receive from the departmental heads the periodic estimates as provided for in this manual.

(2) To prepare from these estimates (a) estimate of cash receipts, (b) estimate of cash disbursements, (c) estimated balance sheet, and (e) estimated statement of profit and loss.

(3) To transmit all the estimates to the Budget Committee with such recommendations as he may think necessary.

(4) To receive from the Budget Committee the estimates as approved and to transmit these to the departmental heads.

(5) To receive periodic reports prepared by the operating departments or the accounting department showing the departmental performance for the month.

(6) To transmit the periodic reports to the Budget Committee showing the comparison between the estimated performance and the actual performance for the period for each department, and to make such recommendations as he may deem necessary.

(7) To transmit to departmental heads any revisions in the original estimates which have been made by the Budget Committee.

(8) To recommend to the General Manager and to the Budget Committee such changes in the budgetary procedure as he may deem desirable.

He has the implied authority to do all things which are necessary to the proper performance of these duties.

## 5. THE DEPARTMENTAL HEADS

The executive heads of the various departments are responsible for the preparation of the estimates of their departments at the time and in the manner prescribed in this manual. They are also responsible for the preparation of the reports called for in this manual. Any recommendations which any departmental executive desires to make with reference to changes in budgetary procedure will be transmitted in writing to the Assistant to the General Manager. It will be referred by him to the Budget Committee for consideration.

The responsibility for the preparation of the departmental estimate and the periodic report is in each case placed upon the head of the department. He may employ his assistants in their preparation at his discretion, but the responsibility rests on the executive head in each case.

## II. THE SALES BUDGET

## 1. PREPARATION OF SALES ESTIMATE

The Sales Manager will prepare for each budget period the estimate of the sales for that period. In the preparation of this estimate he will take into consideration:

(1) The sales of past periods

(2) The present market conditions

(3) The contemplated plans and policies of the business for future periods

### 2.  FORM OF ESTIMATE

The estimate of sales will be made in such form as to show the anticipated sales to:

(1)  Hospitals
(2)  Merchants

It will also show the anticipated sales of each principal grade of goods sold.   The first classification is necessary in order that the financial budget may be made, since the sales to hospitals are of different terms than the sales to merchants.   The second classification is necessary in order that production may be planned so as to have on hand the proper quantity of the different grades.   A form to be used in the submission of the sales estimate will be provided by the Assistant to the General Manager.

### 3.  WHEN SUBMITTED

The Sales Manager will transmit the sales estimate with his approval to the Assistant to the General Manager on or before the first day of the third week preceding the beginning of the budget period.

### 4.  PROCEDURE BY THE ASSISTANT TO THE GENERAL MANAGER

The Assistant to the General Manager will transmit a copy of the sales estimate to the Works Manager within two days after the receipt of the original estimate from the Sales Manager.   He will transmit the original estimate, together with all the other estimates called for in this manual, to the Budget Committee on or before the first day of the first week preceding the beginning of the budget period.

### 5.  APPROVAL BY THE BUDGET COMMITTEE

The Budget Committee will make such revisions as it thinks necessary in the sales estimate, and will transmit the revised estimate with its approval to the Assistant to the General Manager within two days after it receives this estimate.   In making its revisions the Budget Committee will make specific changes of particular amounts instead of making a percentage revision of the estimate as a whole.

### 6.  TRANSMISSION TO THE SELLING DEPARTMENT

The Assistant to the General Manager will transmit the revised estimate to the Sales Department immediately upon its receipts from the Budget Committee.   This estimate as revised and approved by the Budget Committee will constitute the budget of the sales department for the next budget period. Copies of this estimate should be sent by the Sales Department to the Manager of each branch, indicating the quota of the branch based on this estimate.

### 7. Periodic Report from the Statistical Department

At the end of each period the statistical department will send to the Assistant to the General Manager a report showing the sales made during the period. This report will be forwarded on or before the fifth working day of the period following the period for which it is made.

### 8. Periodic Report to the Budget Committee

On or before the tenth day of each period, the Assistant to the General Manager will transmit to the Budget Committee a report showing a comparison of the estimated and actual sales for the past period. He will accompany this report with any recommendations which he may think desirable.

### 9. Revision of Sales Budget by Budget Committee

On or before the twelfth day of the period, the Budget Committee will consider the report received from the Assistant to the General Manager, and will make such changes as it deems desirable in the sales budget for the remainder of the budget period. These changes will be communicated to the sales department by the Assistant to the General Manager on or before the fifteenth day of the period.

## III. The Production Budget

### 1. Estimate of Finished Goods

On or before the third day of the third week preceding the beginning of the budget period, the Works Manager will receive from the Assistant to the General Manager the estimate of sales prepared by the Sales Manager. Based on this estimate the Works Manager will prepare an estimate of the finished goods which must be produced in the next budget period to meet sales demands. In making this estimate the estimated inventory of finished goods on hand at the beginning of the period and the desired inventory of finished goods at the end of the period will be taken into consideration. The requirements of the sales department for the period plus the estimated inventory at the end of the period, minus the estimated inventory at the beginning of the period, will equal the estimated production of finished goods for the period.

### 2. Transmission to the Assistant to the General Manager

The Works Manager will transmit the estimate of production as prepared under the preceding section, to the Assistant to the General Manager within one week after the receipt of the sales estimate from the Assistant to the General Manager.

### 3. Approval by the Budget Committee

The Assistant to the General Manager will transmit the estimate of production to the Budget Committee on or before the first day of the first week preceding the beginning of the budget period. He may accompany this estimate with such suggestions or recommendations as he may think desirable. The Budget Committee will make such changes as it may deem desirable in the estimate, and return it with the Committee's approval to the Assistant to the General Manager within two days after its receipt by the Committee. The Assistant to the General Manager will immediately transmit it to the Works Manager.

### 4. Periodic Report from the Production Department

At the end of each period, the Works Manager will send to the Assistant to the General Manager a report showing the production for the period. This report will be forwarded on or before the fifth working day of the period following the period for which it is made.

### 5. Periodic Report to the Budget Committee

On or before the tenth day of each period, the Assistant to the General Manager will transmit to the Budget Committee a report showing a comparison of the estimated with the actual production for the past period. He will accompany this report with any recommendations which he may think desirable.

### 6. Revision of Production Budget by Budget Committee

On or before the twelfth day of the period, the Budget Committee will consider the report received from the Assistant to the General Manager and will make such changes as it deems desirable in the production budget for the remainder of the period. These changes will be communicated to the Works Manager by the Assistant to the General Manager.

## IV. The Labor Budget

### 1. Estimate of Labor Cost

On or before the tenth day preceding the beginning of the budget period, the Works Manager will send to the Assistant to the General Manager an estimate of the cost of factory labor for each month of the next budget period. This estimate will be based on the estimate of production which is prepared by the production department in the manner indicated in Section III of this manual. The Works Manager will be assisted by the Employment Department in the preparation of this estimate. The estimate of labor cost will be made on a form provided by the Assistant to the General Manager. It will have the following columnar headings:

(1) Department
(2) Same period last year
(3) Average for last four budget periods preceding the one during which the budget is prepared
(4) Estimated cost for this period
(5) Distribution:
    (a) First period
    (b) Second period
    (c) Third period

Columns (2) and (3) will be filled in by the Assistant to the General Manager prior to sending the form to the Works Manager.

2. APPROVAL BY THE BUDGET COMMITTEE

On or before the first day of the first week preceding the beginning of the budget period, the Assistant to the General Manager will transmit the estimate of labor costs as prepared by the Works Manager to the Budget Committee, with such recommendations as he may deem necessary. The Budget Committee will make such changes as it may deem expedient, and return the estimate with its approval to the Assistant to the General Manager within two days after its receipt by the Committee.

The Assistant to the General Manager will return the estimate of labor cost as approved by the Budget Committee, to the Works Manager immediately upon its receipt from the Committee.

3. PERIODIC REPORT ON LABOR COSTS

On or before the eighth day of each period, the Works Manager will send to the Assistant to the General Manager a report showing the cost of factory labor for the preceding period. The Assistant to the General Manager will supply the form for the submission of this report.

On or before the tenth day of the period, the Assistant to the General Manager will transmit a report to the Budget Committee showing a comparison between the estimated labor costs for the past period and the actual costs as reported by the Works Manager. If the Budget Committee desires to make any recommendations to the Production Department with reference to labor cost during the remainder of the budget period, these recommendations will be communicated to the Works Manager through the Assistant to the General Manager on or before the twelfth day of the period.

### V. Manufacturing Expense Budget

1. Estimate of Manufacturing Expense

On or before the tenth day preceding the beginning of the budget period, the Works Manager will send to the Assistant to the General Manager an estimate of manufacturing expense for each month of the next budget period. In preparing this estimate he will be assisted by the cost accounting department. This estimate will be based on the estimate of production which is prepared by the production department in the manner indicated in Section III of this manual. The estimate of manufacturing expense will be made on a form provided by the Assistant to the General Manager. It will have the following columnar headings:

(1) Department
(2) Same period last year
(3) Average for last four budget periods preceding the one during which the budget is prepared
(4) Estimated cost for this period
(5) Distribution:
    (a) First period
    (b) Second period
    (c) Third period

Columns (2) and (3) will be filled in by the Assistant to the General Manager prior to sending the form to the Works Manager.

2. Approval by the Budget Committee

On or before the first day of the first week preceding the beginning of the budget period, the Assistant to the General Manager will transmit the estimate of manufacturing expense as prepared by the Works Manager to the Budget Committee, with such recommendations as he may deem necessary. The Budget Committee will make such changes as it may deem expedient and return the estimate with its approval to the Assistant to the General Manager within two days after its receipt by the Committee.

The Assistant to the General Manager will return the estimate of manufacturing expense as approved by the Budget Committee to the Works Manager immediately upon its receipt from the Committee.

3. PERIODIC REPORT ON MANUFACTURING EXPENSE

On or before the eighth day of each period, the Accounting Department will send to the Assistant to the General Manager a report showing the manufacturing expense for the preceding period. The Assistant to the General Manager will supply the form for the submission of this report.

On or before the tenth day of the period, the Assistant to the General Manager will transmit a report to the Budget Committee showing a comparison between the estimated manufacturing expenses for the past period and the actual costs as reported by the Accounting Department. If the Budget Committee desires to make any recommendations to the Production Department with reference to manufacturing expense during the remainder of the budget period, these recommendations will be communicated to the Works Manager through the Assistant to the General Manager on or before the twelfth day of the period.

## VI. THE MATERIALS BUDGET

1. ESTIMATE OF COST OF PURCHASES

The Works Manager will prepare an estimate of the materials required for each budget period. This estimate will be based on the estimate of production prepared by the Works Manager as outlined in Section III of this manual. The Works Manager will transmit the estimate of materials required to the Assistant to the General Manager on or before the tenth day preceding the beginning of the budget period. The Assistant to the General Manager will transmit the estimate immediately to the General Purchasing Agent. On receipt of the estimate of raw materials requirements, the General Purchasing Agent will prepare an estimate of purchases to be made during the budget period. The General Purchasing Agent will make this estimate on the form supplied by the Assistant to the General Manager, which will contain the following columnar headings:

(1) Item
(2) First Period:
    (a) Estimated inventory at beginning of period
    (b) Estimated purchases
    (c) Estimated inventory at end of period
    (d) Estimated cash disbursements for purchases made during this period
    (e) Estimated cash disbursements for purchases made in previous periods

(3) Second Period:
- (a) Estimated inventory at beginning of period
- (b) Estimated purchases
- (c) Estimated inventory at end of period
- (d) Estimated cash disbursements for purchases made during this period
- (e) Estimated cash disbursements for purchases made during previous period

(4) Third Period:
- (a) Estimated inventory at beginning of period
- (b) Estimated purchases
- (c) Estimated inventory at end of period
- (d) Estimated cash disbursements for purchases made during this period
- (e) Estimated cash disbursements for purchases made in previous periods

The General Purchasing Agent will transmit this estimate to the Assistant to the General Manager on or before the last day of the second week preceding the beginning of the budget period.

## 2. APPROVAL BY THE BUDGET COMMITTEE

The Assistant to the General Manager will at once transmit the estimate of purchases to the Budget Committee. The Budget Committee will make any changes it may deem necessary, and return the revised estimate with its approval to the Assistant to the General Manager within two days after its receipt by the Budget Committee. The Assistant to the General Manager will send the estimate of purchases as approved by the Budget Committee to the Purchasing Agent immediately upon its receipt from the Budget Committee.

## 3. PERIODIC REPORT ON PURCHASES

At the end of each period, the Assistant to the General Manager will make a report to the Advisory Committee showing the actual purchases of the period compared with the estimated purchases and the actual inventory at the end of the period compared with the estimated inventory at the end of the period.

This report will be submitted to the Budget Committee on or before the tenth day of the period. If the Budget Committee desires to make any changes in the purchases budget for the remainder of the budget period, it will communicate its directions to the General Purchasing Agent through the Assistant to the General Manager on or before the twelfth day of the period.

## VII. Plant and Equipment Budget

### 1. Estimate of Plant and Equipment Cost

On or before the tenth day preceding the beginning of the budget period, the Works Manager will send to the Assistant to the General Manager an estimate of the expenditures for plant and equipment for each month in the next budget period. This estimate will be submitted on a form prepared by the Assistant to the General Manager.

### 2. Approval by Budget Committee

On or before the first day of the first week preceding the beginning of the budget period, the Assistant to the General Manager will transmit the estimate of plant and equipment expenditures as prepared by the Works Manager to the Budget Committee, with such recommendations as he may deem necessary. The Budget Committee will make such changes as it may deem expedient, and return the estimate with its approval to the Assistant to the General Manager within two days after the receipt of the estimate by the Committee. The Assistant to the General Manager will immediately transmit the estimate as approved by the Budget Committee to the Works Manager.

### 3. Periodic Report on Plant and Equipment Expenditures

On or before the eighth day of each period, the Accounting Department will send to the Assistant to the General Manager a report showing the expenditures for plant and equipment during the past period. The Assistant to the General Manager will supply the form for this report.

On or before the tenth day of the period, the Assistant to the General Manager will transmit a report to the Budget Committee showing a comparison between estimated plant and equipment expenditures for the past period and the actual expenditures as reported by the Accounting Department. If the Budget Committee desires to make any recommendations to the Production Department with reference to plant and equipment expenditures during the remainder of the budget period, these recommendations will be communicated to the Works Manager through the Assistant to the General Manager on or before the fifteenth day of the period.

25

### 4. Estimate of Furniture and Fixtures Required by General Offices

On or before the fifteenth day preceding the beginning of the budget period, the head of each department will submit to the General Manager an estimate of expenditures for Furniture and Fixtures during the next budget period. The General Manager after consultation with the General Purchasing Agent will make such revisions as he deems necessary and transfer the estimate with his approval to the Assistant to the General Manager on or before the tenth day preceding the beginning of the budget period.

### 5. Approval by the Budget Committee

On or before the first day of the first week preceding the beginning of the budget period, the Assistant to the General Manager will transmit the estimate of furniture and fixtures as required by the general offices to the Budget Committee with such recommendations as he may deem necessary. The Budget Committee will make such changes as it may deem expedient and return the estimate with its approval to the Assistant to the General Manager within two days after its receipt by the Committee.

The Assistant to the General Manager will return the estimate of furniture and fixtures to the heads of the various departments immediately upon its receipt by him from the Budget Committee.

### 6. Periodic Report on Furniture and Fixtures

On or before the tenth day of the period, the Assistant to the General Manager will transmit a report to the Budget Committee showing a comparison between the estimated expenditures for furnitures and fixtures for the general offices for the past period and the actual expenditures as submitted by the Accounting Department. If the Budget Committee desires to make any recommendations to the departmental heads with reference to furniture and fixture costs for the general offices for the remainder of the budget period, these recommendations will be communicated to the departmental heads through the Assistant to the General Manager.

## VIII.  The Expense Budgets

### 1. Control of Departmental Expense

In order to provide an effective control of the expenses of the various departments, as well as to provide the necessary data for the quarterly cash budget, the following procedure is prescribed for all departments and executive units of the business:

(1) Before the beginning of each budget period, an estimate will be prepared by the executive head of each department or unit showing the anticipated expenses of this department or unit for the next budget period, and sent to the Assistant to the General Manager.

(2) These estimates will be submitted by the Assistant to the General Manager to the Budget Committee and after being revised by it where deemed necessary, an appropriation will be made to meet the expenses called for by each estimate.

(3) The amount of the appropriations, as determined by the Budget Committee, will be communicated to the executive responsible for the original estimate by the Assistant to the General Manager.

(4) A monthly report will be made to the Budget Committee through the Assistant to the General Manager, showing the status of each of these appropriations.

(5) The original appropriation will not be exceeded without permission of the Budget Committee.

2. CLASSIFICATION OF DEPARTMENTS AND UNITS

For the purpose of expense control the various departments and units may be classified as follows:

A. Administration
    (1) General Manager's Office
    (2) Credit Department
    (3) Purchasing Department
    (4) Accounting Department
    (5) Statistical Department
    (6) Stenographic Department
    (7) Personnel Department

B. Selling
    (1) General Office
        (a) Office of the Sales Manager
        (b) Advertising and Sales Promotion
    (2) Direct Sales Units
        (a) Each Sales Office

C. Production
    (1) Office of the Works Manager
    (2) Subsidiary Production Departments

## 3. Procedure for the Preparation of Expense Budgets

The procedure to be followed in the preparation and control of the expense budgets of the various departments and executive units given in the foregoing outline will be as follows:

### Group A. Administration

#### (1) *Preparation of Estimate*

On or before the fifteenth day preceding the beginning of the budget period, the executive head of each of the departments listed under Group A will submit to the Assistant to the General Manager an estimate of the expenses of this department during the next budget period. The form to be used in the submission of the estimates will be provided by the Assistant to the General Manager and will contain the following columnar headings:

(1) Department
(2) Same period last year
(3) Average for last four budget periods preceding the one during which the budget is prepared
(4) Estimated cost for this period
(5) Distribution:
    (a) First period
    (b) Second period
    (c) Third period

Columns (2) and (3) will be filled in by the Assistant to the General Manager prior to sending the form to the executive head of each department.

#### (2) *Approval by the Budget Committee*

On or before the first day of the first week preceding the beginning of the budget period, the Assistant to the General Manager will submit the estimate of the expenses of the departments listed in Group A as prepared by the executive heads of the departments, to the Budget Committee with such recommendations as he may deem necessary. The Budget Committee will make such changes as it may deem necessary, and return the estimate with its approval to the Assistant to the General Manager within two days after the receipt of the estimate by the Committee.

The Assistant to the General Manager will return immediately the estimates as approved by the Budget Committee to the executive heads of departments listed under Group A.

### (3) *Periodic Report*

On or before the eighth day of each period the Accounting Department will send to the Assistant to the General Manager a report showing the expenses for the past period for each of the departments listed under Group A.   The Assistant to the General Manager will supply the form for the submission of this report.

On or before the tenth day of the month, the Assistant to the General Manager will transmit a report to the Budget Committee showing the comparison between estimated expenses for each of the departments under Group A for the past period and the actual expenses as submitted by the accounting department.   If the Budget Committee desires to make any recommendations to the executive heads of the departments with reference to their expenses during the remainder of the budget period, these recommendations will be communicated to the executive heads through the Assistant to the General Manager.

### Group B.   SALES

### (1) *Preparation of Estimates*

On or before the tenth day preceding the beginning of the budget period, the Sales Manager will transmit to the Assistant to the General Manager an estimate of the expenses of his department including:

    (a)  The expenses of himself and staff
    (b)  The expenses of the direct selling units
    (c)  The expenses of the advertising and sales promotion department

This estimate will be submitted on a form provided by the Assistant to the General Manager.

### (2) *Approval by the Budget Committee*

On or before the first day of the first week preceding the beginning of the budget period, the Assistant to the General Manager will submit the estimate of the expenses of the departments listed under Group B as prepared by the Sales Manager, to the Budget Committee with such recommendations as he may deem necessary.   The

Budget Committee will make such changes as it may deem necessary and return the estimate with its approval to the Assistant to the General Manager within two days after the receipt of the estimate by the Committee.

The Assistant to the General Manager will return immediately the estimates as approved by the Budget Committee, to the Sales Manager.

### (3) *Periodic Report*

On or before the eighth day of each period the Accounting Department will send to the Assistant to the General Manager a report showing the expenses for the past period for each of the divisions of the department listed under Group B. The Assistant to the General Manager will supply the form for the submission of this report.

On or before the tenth day of the period the Assistant to the General Manager will transmit a report to the Budget Committee showing the comparison between estimated expenses for each of the departments under Group B for the past period and the actual expenses as submitted by the Accounting Department. If the Budget Committee desires to make any recommendations to the Sales Manager with reference to the expenses of his department during the remainder of the budget period, these recommendations will be communicated to the Sales Manager through the Assistant to the General Manager.

### Group C. PRODUCTION

#### (1) *Preparation of Estimate*

On or before the tenth day preceding the beginning of the budget period, the Works Manager will submit to the Assistant to the General Manager an estimate of the expenses of his department. The expenses shown on this estimate will be exclusive of the expenses shown on the estimate of manufacturing expenses prepared as directed under Section V. This estimate will be submitted on a form provided by the Assistant to the General Manager.

#### (2) *Approval by the Budget Committee*

On or before the first day of the week preceding the beginning of the budget period, the Assistant to the General Manager will submit the estimate of the expenses of the Production Department as prepared by the Works Manager, to the Budget Committee with such recommendations as he may deem necessary. The Budget Committee will make such changes as it may deem necessary and return the estimate with its approval to the Assistant to the General Manager within two days after the receipt of the estimate by the Committee.

The Assistant to the General Manager will return immediately the estimate as approved by the Budget Committee to the Works Manager.

### (3) *Periodic Report*

On or before the eighth day of each period, the Accounting Department will send to the Assistant to the General Manager a report showing the expenses for the past period of the Production Department. The Assistant to the General Manager will supply the form for the submission of this report.

On or before the tenth day of the month, the Assistant to the General Manager will transmit a report to the Budget Committee showing the comparison between estimated expense for the Production Department for the past period and the actual expenses as submitted by the Accounting Department. If the Budget Committee desires to make any recommendations to the Works Manager with reference to the expenses of his department during the remainder of the budget period, these recommendations will be communicated to the Works Manager through the Assistant to the General Manager.

## IX. The Financial Budget

### 1. Preliminary Estimates of Cash Receipts and Cash Disbursements

The Assistant to the General Manager, working in conjunction with the Assistant Treasurer, will prepare a preliminary estimate of cash receipts and a preliminary estimate of cash disbursements for each budget period based on the following:

(1) The estimates submitted by the various departments.

(2) An estimate of the disbursements for taxes, insurance, and other items which are under the control of the Assistant Treasurer.

(3) Estimate of the collections from accounts receivable outstanding at the beginning of the period.

(4) Estimate of the disbursements on accounts payable outstanding at the beginning of the period.

The Assistant to the General Manager will transmit these preliminary estimates of cash receipts and cash disbursements to the Budget Committee on or before the first day of the first week preceding the beginning of the budget period. This will enable the Budget Committee to consider the financial requirements of the various estimates submitted to it.

### 2. REVISION OF PRELIMINARY ESTIMATES

After the departmental estimates have been approved by the Budget Committee, the Assistant to the General Manager will revise the preliminary estimates of cash receipts and cash disbursements giving effect to the revisions in the departmental estimate which were made by the Budget Committee. The revised estimates will be submitted to the Treasurer on or before the third day preceding the beginning of the budget period.

### 3. PERIODIC REPORTS

Periodic reports will be submitted to the Budget Committee showing a comparison between estimated receipts and actual receipts and estimated disbursements and actual disbursements. If the Budget Committee desires to revise other budgets because of the financial condition, these revisions will be submitted to the departments concerned by the Assistant to the General Manager. The revisions made in the financial budget will be communicated to the Treasurer.

## X. PRELIMINARY ESTIMATED FINANCIAL STATEMENTS

### 1. PRELIMINARY ESTIMATES OF FINANCIAL CONDITION AND RESULTS OF OPERATION

The Assistant to the General Manager will prepare from the departmental budgets an estimated balance sheet showing the estimated financial condition at the end of each accounting period during the budget period. He will also prepare in the same manner an estimated statement of profit and loss showing the anticipated results of the operations for each period.

The Assistant to the General Manager will transmit these preliminary estimates to the Budget Committee on or before the first day of the first week preceding the beginning of the budget period. This will enable the Budget Committee to consider these at the same time that it is considering the departmental estimates.

### 2. REVISION OF PRELIMINARY ESTIMATES

After the departmental estimates have been approved by the Budget Committee, the Assistant to the General Manager will revise the preliminary estimated financial statements giving effect to the changes made by the committee in the departmental estimates.

3. PERIODIC REPORTS

Periodic reports will be submitted to the Budget Committee by the Assistant to the General Manager, showing a comparison between the actual and the estimated financial statements. These reports will be submitted at the same time as the other budgetary reports.

## Comments on Manual—Manual Confined to Interdepartmental Procedure

It will be noticed that the manual is confined to the procedure involved in the interdepartmental relations arising from the budgetary program. It does not outline in detail the procedure to be followed by each department in the preparation of its estimate or the carrying out of its budget. Since the manual is to be placed in the hands of all of the executives, it is not thought worth while to encumber it with the detail of departmental procedures. It is thought better that these be issued as departmental orders.

## Central Control of Estimates

It is important to notice that the manual requires the estimates of *all* departments to be submitted to the budget committee at one time (on or before the first day of the first week preceding the beginning of the budget period); the consideration and approval of these estimates within two days after their receipt; and the return of the approved estimates to the departmental heads immediately upon their approval.

This enables the budget committee to have before it, at one time, the estimates of all the departments and units of the company, and provides a central control of all the activities of the business. The monthly reports which are to be submitted to the budget committee provide a means of control over the execution of the budgets.

## Authority of Budget Committee

It will be noted that the budget committee is given authority to pass on estimates. Although the manual does not so state, the financial budget and the estimated balance sheet and statement of profit and loss are submitted to the board of directors at the beginning of each budget period.

## Dates for Submission of Estimates and Reports

It will be noticed that particular attention is given to the dates on which reports and estimates are submitted. This is especially important, as otherwise there will be a lack of coordination in the budgetary procedure. For instance, the production department cannot prepare the finished goods estimate until it receives the sales estimate; the purchasing department cannot prepare the estimate of purchases until it receives the estimate of materials requirements; and the assistant to the general manager cannot prepare the estimated financial statements until he receives all the estimates. These illustrations show that if one department is tardy in the preparation of its estimate or report, the entire program is delayed as a consequence.

## Chart of Budget Procedure

A manual prepared in the form of the foregoing example contains a considerable amount of detail and it is somewhat difficult to obtain a comprehensive view of the procedure as a whole.

A chart prepared in the form shown in Figure 43, enables the executives to see the relationship between the various budgets and the duties of each executive with reference to each budget.

The chart is prepared from the manual given in this chapter with a few modifications. It will be noticed that the chart calls for a "stores purchased" budget and a "miscellaneous expense" budget, instead of a manufacturing expense budget and departmental expense budgets. It also omits the procedure for the preparation of the estimated financial statements.

# CHAPTER XXIV

## ADMINISTRATIVE REPORTS

### Need for Administrative Reports

The previous chapters have emphasized the need for the collection of data to serve

1. As the basis of formulating plans of operation, and
2. As the basis of enforcing plans which have been adopted.

This information is most serviceable when it is presented in a summarized and classified form by means of properly designed reports.

Reports should be used by all the executives and employees of a business. We usually think of reports in connection with the general officers, for their actions are based largely on reports and the reports which they receive are of a formal nature. Nevertheless, all employees except those engaged in routine manual tasks are receiving reports daily. These reports may come to them as business forms on which they perform certain tasks and then transmit them to others. They are nevertheless reports in the sense in which that term is used in this discussion.

### Classification of Administrative Reports

The reports used in administrative control may be classified broadly into the following groups:

1. Reports showing present financial condition. The standard form of balance sheet with its various subsidiary schedules is used for this purpose. This is the oldest and most widely used of administrative reports. The reasons for its origin and extensive use have been explained in a preceding chapter.

2. Reports showing the results of past operations in terms of expense and income. The various forms of expense and income analyses, and the standard form of statement of profit and loss, with subsidiary schedules, are used for this purpose. Next to the standard form of balance sheet, these are the reports most widely used. For internal control they are used more widely than the balance sheet and are decidedly more serviceable.

3. Reports showing pertinent information which is necessary for the daily actions of executives and employees. These reports may consist of a statement for the treasurer, showing the accounts payable falling due on a current day; of a report to the collection manager, showing accounts thirty, sixty, and ninety days past due; of a report to the sales manager, showing the slow-moving items of stock; and various other reports of a similar nature. These reports are not so widely discussed as the standard financial statements, yet they serve a very vital function in the internal administration of a business.

4. Reports showing anticipated results of future operations. These reports include estimates of sales, estimates of purchases, estimates of production, estimates of financial condition, estimates of income, expense, and net profit, and similar reports. These estimates serve as a basis for future plans in the manner explained in preceding chapters.

5. Reports showing a comparison between the actual performance and the estimated or standard performance. Such reports make possible the enforcement of budgets and provide data which serve as a means of revising the budgets when this is found necessary.

## Essentials of Executive Reports

In the foregoing discussion *administrative* reports have been defined broadly to include the reports used by all the executives and employees of a business. But in every business it is desirable to prepare some formal reports for the use of the principal executives only. In contradistinction to the broad group of *administrative* reports, these may be termed "executive" reports. During the remainder of this chapter we shall be concerned primarily with the latter group, although most of the discussion is equally applicable to the general group.

Since executive reports are intended to serve as a basis for the formulating of executive decisions, which in turn result in executive actions, it is expedient that they be made so as to present accurate and comprehensive information and to present it in such form that correct judgments can be formed with as little sacrifice of effort as possible. If this end is to be attained, executive reports must have the following characteristics:

First, they should present summarized information. Details should be eliminated as much as possible. Each report should show a few essential items of information. They should be constructed so as to show variations between the standard performance and the actual performance. In case of significant variations, the executive should receive an explanation of the cause from the controller or some other official designated for this purpose. If the executive receives a few condensed reports he will be able to study carefully each report. Details are of value only to explain variations. Many details serve only to confuse.

Second, executive reports should show the following:

1. Actual performance for the current period.
2. Comparison of the performance of the current period with the estimated or standard performance for the period.
3. Comparison of the current performance with the performance of past periods.
4. Comparison of the current performance with the results of the performance.

## Actual Performance

Each executive should know at frequent intervals what the performance has been of his own department and of each of the other departments the activities of which affect the activities of his own department. Reports presenting information of this kind have long been in use and little more need be said here with reference to them than to emphasize the following:

1. That care must be taken that these reports be made accurately.
2. That they be sufficiently comprehensive to serve as a basis for proper action.
3. That they should be made promptly.
4. That they are more effective if modified so as to include the comparisons indicated by the following discussion.

### Estimated Performance

Most if not all executives will admit the need of a statement of the current performance, but many do not realize the importance of establishing estimates of performance and comparing the actual with the estimated. The discussion in the preceding chapters has emphasized the importance of preparing budgets and using them as control devices. The reports which are used in preparing and controlling these budgets have been discussed in connection with each of them. In addition to these reports it is desirable that the effect of the budgetary program should be shown on all the executive reports. This can be done most easily by designing these reports so that they will show a comparison between the estimated and the actual performance.

By way of emphasis it is worth while to state the following benefits to be derived from the establishment of the estimates:

1. In order to make the estimates it will be necessary for the executives responsible for them to study past performance and to consider future possibilities. This study will undoubtedly increase the efficiency of these executives.

2. The estimates will set up a goal for attainment. They will constitute a "bogie" which the executives will try to

attain.   A comparison between the actual and the estimated will provide a check on the activities of the executives and will serve as an incentive towards the attainment of the estimated.

3. A study and comparison of the estimates will make possible a better coordination of the activities of the various functional departments, since each department can determine from the estimates the plans of other departments and guide its activities accordingly.

4. The preparation and use of the estimates will make possible the elimination of much detail in the reports to the executives.   Details instead of being presented for the consideration of the executives each month, will be presented in the original estimates when they are presented for executive approval.   After the estimates have been considered and approved, it will not be necessary for the executive to receive detailed reports during the period covered by the estimates.   If he receives a summary report which shows a comparison between the results attained and the estimate, it will be sufficient.   Executives should consider details with reference to operations *before* the operations take place rather than *after* they are performed.   Of course, if variations between the estimated and the actual are shown by the reports, they may ask for sufficient detail to explain the changes.

## Past Performance

Although past performance alone is not a satisfactory standard by which to judge current performance, a comparison between current performance and past performance is very useful in that it shows whether the *tendency* is desirable or undesirable.   If statistics with reference to past performance and current performance are compiled by means of reports for a considerable number of periods, very useful data will be available for use in making future estimates.

## Results of Performance

Whenever possible, a comparison should be made between performance and results. For instance, selling expense may be compared with sales; gross profits and net profits with sales; volume of production with cost of production; and various other comparisons which will occur to the reader. These comparisons should be shown not only for the current period but also for past periods, so that tendencies may be easily seen. Comparisons of this nature make it possible to obtain a true perspective of results. Obviously increased sales are desired only when increased profits will result.

## Illustration of Reports

It is obviously impossible to discuss and illustrate all the various reports which may be used in executive control. These will vary in number and form from business to business.

Some of these reports have been illustrated in previous chapters. For instance, in Chapters XXI and XXII the estimated balance sheet and estimated statement of profit and loss with the proper comparisons were illustrated. In earlier chapters reports showing a comparison between the actual and estimated performance were shown.

In the present discussion it is thought sufficient to illustrate a few of the reports which may be used in sales and production control. Using these as types and applying the the general principles given in the foregoing discussion, the reader should be able to design reports to fit any particular needs.

## Sales Reports

The reports which may be used in sales control are too numerous to mention. They will vary greatly from busi-

26

## MONTHLY REPORT OF SALES

MONTH OF _____ 192__

| SALES UNIT | THIS MONTH | Estimated This Month | Per Cent Increase or Decrease | LAST MONTH | Per Cent Increase or Decrease | TO DATE THIS YEAR | Estimated to Date This Year | Per Cent Increase or Decrease | TO DATE LAST YEAR | Per Cent Increase or Decrease |
|---|---|---|---|---|---|---|---|---|---|---|
| EASTERN DIVISION | | | | | | | | | | |
| WESTERN DIVISION | | | | | | | | | | |
| A BRANCH | | | | | | | | | | |
| B BRANCH | | | | | | | | | | |
| C BRANCH | | | | | | | | | | |
| D BRANCH | | | | | | | | | | |
| E BRANCH | | | | | | | | | | |
| F BRANCH | | | | | | | | | | |
| G BRANCH | | | | | | | | | | |

Figure 44.   Monthly Sales Report

## MONTHLY REPORT ON SELLING EXPENSE

MONTH OF _____ 192___

| SALES UNIT | THIS MONTH | Estimated This Month | Per Cent Increase or Decrease | Ratio Estimated Expense to Estimated Sales | Ratio Actual Expense to Actual Sales | Ratio Expense to Sales to Date This Year | Ratio Expense to Sales to Date Last Year |
|---|---|---|---|---|---|---|---|
| EASTERN DIVISION | | | | | | | |
| WESTERN DIVISION | | | | | | | |
| A BRANCH | | | | | | | |
| B BRANCH | | | | | | | |
| C BRANCH | | | | | | | |
| D BRANCH | | | | | | | |
| E BRANCH | | | | | | | |
| F BRANCH | | | | | | | |
| G BRANCH | | | | | | | |

Figure 45.   Monthly Selling Expense Report

ness to business depending on the volume of sales, nature of product sold, and method of marketing. But it is thought that in every business the principal executives of the business should have reports which show the following:

1. Volume of sales
2. Selling expenses
3. Net profits
4. Inventory of finished goods

Typical reports for each of these will be illustrated.

### Monthly Report on Volume of Sales

If a business markets its product through branches or divisions, this report will show the total sales of each selling unit for the current period compared with the estimated sales and the sales of previous periods. If the sales are all made from a central office, it may show the same comparisons for sales territories, or it may show the sales classified by groups, departments, or products. In any case the comparisons should be the same.

A typical form for this report is shown in Figure 44. This report is designed for the use of a manufacturing company marketing its product partly through division sales offices and partly through sales branches. This report shows useful comparisons for each selling unit and in addition provides a means of comparing the results attained by the different units.

### Monthly Report on Selling Expenses

If a business markets its product through divisions or branches, a monthly report should be made to show the total selling expense of each selling unit with a comparison of this expense with the sales obtained. If the sales are made from a central sales department, this report may show the same comparisons by territories. If selling expenses

MONTHLY REPORT ON NET PROFITS

MONTH OF _____ 192___

| SALES UNIT | THIS MONTH | Estimated This Month | Per Cent Increase or Decrease | LAST MONTH | Per Cent Increase or Decrease | SAME MONTH LAST YEAR | Per Cent Increase or Decrease | Ratio to Sales for This Year | Ratio of Estimated Profit to Estimated Sales | Ratio of Net Profit to Sales for Last Year |
|---|---|---|---|---|---|---|---|---|---|---|
| EASTERN DIVISION | | | | | | | | | | |
| WESTERN DIVISION | | | | | | | | | | |
| A BRANCH | | | | | | | | | | |
| B BRANCH | | | | | | | | | | |
| C BRANCH | | | | | | | | | | |
| D BRANCH | | | | | | | | | | |
| E BRANCH | | | | | | | | | | |
| F BRANCH | | | | | | | | | | |
| G BRANCH | | | | | | | | | | |

Figure 46. Monthly Net Profits Report

are allocated to lines of product, the report may be made to show the result of this allocation. In a department store it may show sales and expenses by departments. In this latter case judgment must be used in interpreting the report, for it is to be expected that the ratio of expense to sales will vary between departments which sell different kinds of goods.

A typical form for this report is shown in Figure 45. The report provides a means of:

1. Checking actual expenses against estimated expenses.
2. Comparing the ratio of expenses to sales during the current and past periods. This comparison is of especial importance, as increases and decreases in selling expenses are of significance only in comparison with the results obtained.
3. Comparing the ratio of expenses to sales in different selling units. This comparison is significant in judging the efficiency of branch executives.

## Monthly Report on Net Profits

This report may show net profits of selling units, territories, departments, or by lines of goods. In a business marketing its product through branches or division offices, it shows the net profits made by each selling unit and the ratio of net profits to sales with the proper comparisons.

A typical form for this report is shown in Figure 46. This report affords a means of:

1. Checking actual net profits against estimated net profits.
2. Comparing the ratio of net profits to sales during the current year with the same ratio for the past year. This comparison is a very important one, since it is not an increase of sales, but an increase of profits that is the goal.
3. Comparing the ratio of profits to sales in different selling units. This comparison is important in judging the efficiency of the management of the various units.

MONTHLY STOCK REPORT

MONTH OF_____ 192__

| CLASS or GROUP | INVENTORY | Estimated Inventory | Per Cent Increase or Decrease | SHIPMENTS | Estimated Shipments | Per Cent Increase or Decrease | Turnover This Quarter | Turnover Same Quarter Last Year |
|---|---|---|---|---|---|---|---|---|
| | | | | | | | | |
| | | | | | | | | |

Figure 47. Monthly Stock Report

# MONTHLY COMPARATIVE SUMMARY OF

## X WORKS

| GROUP | | THIS MONTH | | | | | | LAST MONTH | | | | | |
|---|---|---|---|---|---|---|---|---|---|---|---|---|---|
| | | Orders Received | Shipments | Production | Total Receipts into Stock | Cancellations | Unfilled Orders | Orders Received | Shipments | Production | Total Receipts into Stock | Cancellations | Unfilled Orders |
| 100 | Cast Iron | | | | | | | | | | | | |
| 200 | Iron Body | | | | | | | | | | | | |
| Total | | | | | | | | | | | | | |

## N WORKS

| | | | | | | | | | | | | | |
|---|---|---|---|---|---|---|---|---|---|---|---|---|---|
| 100 | Cast Iron | | | | | | | | | | | | |
| 200 | Iron Body | | | | | | | | | | | | |
| 300 | Brass | | | | | | | | | | | | |
| 500 | Walmanco | | | | | | | | | | | | |
| 600 | Nipples | | | | | | | | | | | | |
| 700 | Malleable | | | | | | | | | | | | |
| 1200 | Iron & Steel Pipe | | | | | | | | | | | | |
| X | Specialties | | | | | | | | | | | | |
| 1800 | Well | | | | | | | | | | | | |
| 1900 | Points | | | | | | | | | | | | |
| Total | | | | | | | | | | | | | |
| Total Both Works | | | | | | | | | | | | | |

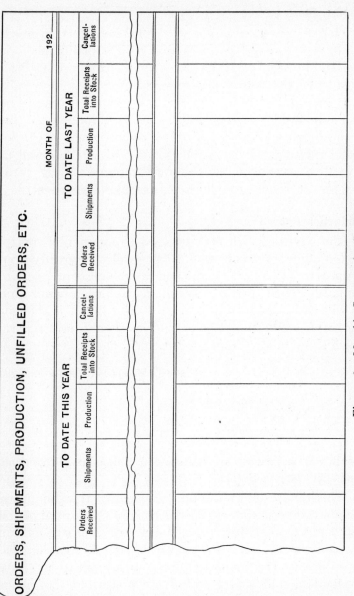

Figure 48. Monthly Comparative Summary

## Monthly Stock Report

This report should show the total inventory in stock classified according to the major groups maintained for sales and inventory. It should show the comparisons indicated by form in Figure 47.

It is desirable that a standard or estimated inventory be determined which can be used as a means of judging the size of the inventory on hand. It is important that careful consideration be given to turnover figures; so it is well to have them shown on the periodical reports. If the turnover for each quarter is shown this should be sufficient.

## Production Reports

The reports which may be used in production control are too numerous to mention. They will vary greatly from business to business, depending on the volume of production, the nature of the production process, and the organization by which the production is carried on. But it is thought that in every business the executives should have reports which show the following:

1. Summary of Orders Received, Shipments, Production, and Shortage or Surplus
2. Summary of Operations
3. Unit Costs
4. Factory Inventories

## Monthly Summary of Orders Received, Shipments, Production, and Shortage or Surplus

This report shows the orders received, the shipments, the production and the unfilled orders for the current period and for past periods, in such form that comparisons can be easily made. Each of these items will be classified according to the major groupings maintained for sales, production, and inventory. It is preferable that it be made in terms of physical units rather than in terms of value.

A typical form for this report is shown in Figure 48. As indicated by the illustration, totals are shown at the bottom of the form so that the totals of the groups can be compared. If a company has two or more factories a separate report will be made for each factory.

If desired, a separate report can be prepared for each of the items which appear on the combined report, that is, orders received, shipments, production, and unfilled orders. Each of these reports should show the following comparisons:

1. Group (name or number)
2. This month
3. Estimated this month
4. Per cent of increase or decrease
5. Last month
6. Per cent of increase or decrease
7. Same month last year
8. Per cent of increase or decrease
9. Total to date this year
10. Total to date last year
11. Per cent of increase or decrease

The additional information which these subsidiary reports provide is evident.

## Monthly Summary of Operations

It is desirable that both the production and other executives of the company should have a comprehensive picture of the factory operations for each period. A possible form for a report which will provide this is shown in Figure 49. The purpose of the data shown in this report is apparent.

In some cases the classification of cost elements shown in the first column will need to be changed. It can be made to suit the needs of each case.

## MONTHLY SUMMARY OF OPERATIONS

WORKS _____　　　MONTH OF _____ 192__

| ITEM | THIS MONTH | Estimated This Month | Per Cent Increase or Decrease | LAST MONTH | Per Cent Increase or Decrease | TO DATE THIS YEAR | TO DATE LAST YEAR | Per Cent Increase or Decrease |
|---|---|---|---|---|---|---|---|---|
| Direct Material | | | | | | | | |
| Direct Labor | | | | | | | | |
| Indirect Labor | | | | | | | | |
| Factory Supervision | | | | | | | | |
| Other Expense | | | | | | | | |
| Total Factory Cost | | | | | | | | |
| Less Increase in Work in Process Inventories | | | | | | | | |
| Less Increase in Plant and Equipt. Order Inventories | | | | | | | | |
| Add Decrease in Work in Process Inventories | | | | | | | | |
| Add Decrease in Plant and Equipt. Order Inventories | | | | | | | | |
| Less Plant and Equipment Charges | | | | | | | | |
| Factory Cost of Production | | | | | | | | |

Figure 49. Monthly Summary of Operations

## MONTHLY GROUP POUND COST

WORKS_____ MONTH OF_____192__

| NO. | GROUP NAME | | THIS MONTH | LAST MONTH | AVERAGE THIS YEAR | AVERAGE 19 | AVERAGE 19 | AVERAGE 19 |
|-----|------------|---|------------|------------|-------------------|------------|------------|------------|
| 100 | C. I. FITTINGS | Pounds Produced | | | | | | |
| | | Cost per Pound | | | | | | |
| 200 | IRON BODY VALVES | Pounds Produced | | | | | | |
| | | Cost per Pound | | | | | | |
| 300 | BRASS VALVES, ETC. | Pounds Produced | | | | | | |
| | | Cost per Pound | | | | | | |
| 400 | TOOLS | Pounds Produced | | | | | | |
| | | Cost per Pound | | | | | | |
| 500 | W. PRODUCT | Pounds Produced | | | | | | |
| | | Cost per Pound | | | | | | |
| 600 | NIPPLES | Pounds Produced | | | | | | |
| | | Cost per Pound | | | | | | |
| 700 | MALL. FITTINGS | Pounds Produced | | | | | | |
| | | Cost per Pound | | | | | | |
| 1800 | K. SPECIALTIES | Pounds Produced | | | | | | |
| | | Cost per Pound | | | | | | |
| 1900 | DRIVE WELL POINTS | Pounds Produced | | | | | | |
| | | Cost per Pound | | | | | | |

Figure 50. Monthly Group Pound Cost

## MONTHLY REPORT OF FACTORY INVENTORIES

MONTH OF _____ 192__

### X WORKS

| ITEMS | END OF THIS MONTH | | END OF LAST MONTH | | P. C. INCREASE OR DECREASE | | AVERAGE THIS QUARTER | | ESTIMATED AVERAGE THIS QUARTER | | P. C. INCREASE OR DECREASE | |
|---|---|---|---|---|---|---|---|---|---|---|---|---|
| | Pounds | Amount | Pounds | Amount | Lbs. | Amt. | Pounds | Amount | Pounds | Amount | Lbs. | Amt. |
| RAW MATERIALS | | | | | | | | | | | | |
| MISCELLANEOUS STORES | | | | | | | | | | | | |
| TOTAL | | | | | | | | | | | | |
| CASTINGS AND FORGINGS IN PROCESS | | | | | | | | | | | | |
| CASTINGS AND FORGINGS STORES | | | | | | | | | | | | |
| WORK IN PROCESS | | | | | | | | | | | | |
| PLANT AND EQUIPMENT IN PROCESS TOTAL | | | | | | | | | | | | |
| FINISHED STOCK | | | | | | | | | | | | |
| TOTAL X WORKS | | | | | | | | | | | | |

### Y WORKS

| ITEMS | END OF THIS MONTH | | END OF LAST MONTH | | P. C. INCREASE OR DECREASE | | AVERAGE THIS QUARTER | | ESTIMATED AVERAGE THIS QUARTER | | P. C. INCREASE OR DECREASE | |
|---|---|---|---|---|---|---|---|---|---|---|---|---|
| | Pounds | Amount | Pounds | Amount | Lbs. | Amt. | Pounds | Amount | Pounds | Amount | Lbs. | Amt. |
| RAW MATERIALS | | | | | | | | | | | | |
| MISCELLANEOUS STORES | | | | | | | | | | | | |
| TOTAL | | | | | | | | | | | | |
| CASTINGS AND FORGINGS IN PROCESS | | | | | | | | | | | | |
| CASTINGS AND FORGINGS STORES | | | | | | | | | | | | |
| WORK IN PROCESS | | | | | | | | | | | | |
| PLANT AND EQUIPMENT IN PROCESS TOTAL | | | | | | | | | | | | |
| FINISHED STOCK | | | | | | | | | | | | |
| TOTAL Y WORKS | | | | | | | | | | | | |
| TOTAL BOTH WORKS | | | | | | | | | | | | |

Figure 51. Monthly Factory Inventories Report

## Monthly Report on Unit Costs

This report shows the volume of production as well as the unit costs. The volume of production is significant in comparing unit costs, since the quantity produced may affect the unit costs.

A typical form for this report is shown in Figure 50. In the illustration the volume of production is stated in terms of tons, and pounds are used as the basis of stating unit costs. In many businesses it would be necessary to use other units for both of these.

## Monthly Report on Factory Inventories

This report shows the total inventories carried at the factory with appropriate comparisons. The classification of inventory will depend on the nature of the product manufactured, but should always indicate clearly the inventories of (1) raw materials, (2) work in process, and (3) finished goods. It should also show plant and equipment in process as a separate item. It is preferable that both the physical amount and the value of the inventories be stated.

A possible form of this report is shown in Figure 51.

## Varied Kind of Reports

It is desired to emphasize once more that the few reports illustrated in this chapter are intended to be suggestive only. These few are given primarily for the purpose of showing concretely the application of the principles discussed in the first part of this chapter. The reports needed for any particular business can be designed only after a careful study of its operations and of its organization and administrative methods.

# CHAPTER XXV

## ADVANTAGES AND LIMITATIONS OF BUDGETARY CONTROL

### ADVANTAGES OF BUDGETARY CONTROL

**Why Discussion Is Postponed**

In most texts on accounting, cost accounting, auditing, and similar subjects, the authors explain at the beginning of their texts the advantages to be derived from the application of the methods which they are to discuss. This undoubtedly is good propaganda, but it is the author's impression that the reader can better understand the advantages of any administrative procedure or device after he understands its nature and its method of operation. Consequently, he has deemed it expedient to postpone the discussion of the advantages of budgetary control until the end of the text. The advantages which are thought to be most significant will now be discussed.

**Coordination of Sales and Production**

Goods can be sold only when produced, and they should be produced only when they can be sold. To obtain sales orders which cannot be filled leads to loss in several ways, of which the following are the most apparent:

1. It causes the incurrence of unnecessary expenses in getting orders which cannot be filled.
2. It causes the expense of recording the orders when received.
3. It causes the expense of answering the inevitable complaints of the customers who fail to receive the goods when promised.

4. It causes the expense of reversing the entries made for the order when the customer finally cancels it.

5. It incurs the ill-will of the customer, which may result in the loss of his trade in the future when it may be needed.

On the other hand, the production of goods in excess of sales orders leads to even more undesirable results, of which the following are the most important:

1. It ties up capital in unsalable goods, with the consequent cost incurred in securing the capital.

2. It ties up capital which may be needed badly in carrying on other operations, and in some cases the loss of the use of this capital may result in serious financial embarrassments.

3. It results in the procurement of goods which may physically deteriorate or become obsolete before they can be sold.

If a sales estimate is prepared, and this estimate is approved by the production department and used as a basis of its program, these difficulties can in the main be eliminated. Any disagreement between the sales and production departments is settled by the budget committee, which is qualified to render impartial judgment.

What is said here with reference to the coordination of sales and production in a manufacturing business, applies equally to the coordination of sales and purchases in a mercantile business.

## Formulation of a Profitable Sales and Production Program

The sales department does not always desire to sell the goods which can be produced to the best advantage, and the production department does not always prefer to produce the goods for which there is the most ready and profitable market. If left to itself each department will follow the line of least resistance.

There has long been an argument as to whether the sales or production department should exercise the greater influence in deciding the commodities which a business produces and offers for sale. Production executives often contend that the production department should decide what it is best equipped to produce and that the sales department should then be instructed to find a market for these products. On the other hand, sales executives often contend that it is the function of the production department to serve the sales department and to produce the goods which the latter can sell.

A little consideration will show that neither of these views is correct. It is the function of each of these departments to serve the business as a whole to the end that as much profit as possible may be made. The hundred of idle factories in the country even in normal times is a testimonial to the fallacy of attempting to produce without a proper consideration of the market, and the many discarded machines of factories still operating, as well as the hundreds of items sold at a loss, is evidence of the impropriety of trying to change the production program to meet the passing whims of the sales department.

A proper coordination of sales and production, not only from the viewpoint of quantity, but also from the viewpoint of profit, is essential. The production equipment should be as flexible as possible so that changes can be made to meet market conditions, but a certain amount of standardization is essential to well-regulated production, and the sales department by proper effort can do much to increase the sales of those lines which can be produced most efficiently.

Although it is usually convenient for the sales department to take the first step in the budgetary process, the sales estimate must be gone over from the viewpoint of the production possibilities, profit potentialities, and financial requirements.

## Coordination of Sales and Production Programs with Finances

No sales and production program, regardless of its profit potentialities, is desirable if its financial requirements cannot be met by the particular firm under consideration. It is necessary that careful consideration be given to the financial requirements of all plans contemplated. As stated in Chapter II, a lack of coordination between sales and production will lead to a loss, but a lack of coordination between sales, production, and finance will lead to bankruptcy.

It must be remembered, however, that the capital possibilities of a firm may be materially affected by the length of time which is available for planning to meet requirements. If the financial requirements of the contemplated program are known for a sufficient length of time prior to its initiation, capital may be secured which would not be obtainable on short notice.

The budgetary program, therefore, is especially significant in financial planning and financial planning is the essence of financial administration.

## Proper Control of Expenses

A proper control of expenses is necessary to profitable operations. The purchase and sales prices of commodities are usually determined largely by competition. The difference between the expenses incurred and the gross profit determines the margin of net profit. To secure an effective control of expenses and yet not to affect the volume of profitable operations is one of the most important and difficult tasks of management.

If the estimated expenses of each department are submitted for the consideration of a central budget committee, composed of the principal executives of the company, and the departments are limited in their expenditures to the amount of the appropriations made by the budget committee after consideration of the departmental estimates, an effective method of control is available.

## Formulation of a Financial Program

The demand for capital is an imperative one. When funds are needed their procurement cannot be long delayed. To insure that it will be possible to secure them when needed, it is necessary to determine in advance the amount required and the time when required, so that plans may be made for their procurement.

It is possible to do this in a systematic way only when comprehensive and accurate statements of the plans of all the departments are available, so that estimates of cash receipts and disbursements which will result from these plans can be made and a program formulated for the procurement of any excess of disbursements over receipts.

## Coordination of All the Activities of the Business

The previous discussion has emphasized the close relationship between the activities of all the departments of a business. This relationship is so close that no one department can carry on its activities properly without a consideration of the activities of one or more of the other departments. Neither can the executives of a business judge properly the past or contemplated activities of any one department independently of the activities of the other departments.

To make possible the formulation of a well-balanced program for the business as a whole, it is essential that the plans of all the departments be presented for executive consideration and that the plans of the several departments be modified, if necessary, in order to bring about coordination. This can best be accomplished by the submission of formal estimates to a budget committee, and the formulation of these into a budgetary program, which will be enforced and controlled in some such manner as that discussed in the preceding chapters.

## THE LIMITATIONS OF BUDGETARY CONTROL

### Need for Consideration

It is as essential that the limitations of budgetary control be understood as that the benefits which may be derived from it be realized. Unless this be true the following results are apt to happen:

1. Too much will be expected from the budgetary program, and when it fails to fulfil expectations it may be thought useless and abandoned.
2. Too much reliance may be placed on its operation which may result in too little emphasis on other methods of administrative control.
3. It may be followed blindly which may bring results more detrimental than those which arise from its absence.

### Important Limitations

The most important and significant limitations of budgetary control are the following:

1. The budget program is based on estimates. Estimates cannot be made which are entirely accurate, and consequently they must be used with judgment and not followed arbitrarily. It is also necessary that provision be made for frequent revisions of these estimates as actual performance shows variations from the estimated performance.

2. Budgetary plans will not execute themselves. After budgets are prepared, every possible effort must be made to equal or exceed them. Detail plans must be made for their attainment and these plans must be enforced rigidly.

3. Budgetary control cannot take the place of admin-

istration.   It is not its purpose to deprive executives of the necessary freedom of action which is essential to progressive management.   Its purpose is to provide the information on which administrative decisions and administrative control are based.

4. Budgetary control cannot be perfected immediately. The procedure called for by the budgetary program is usually new to executives and it takes time to train them to make and use properly estimates of future operations.   Too much should not be expected at the beginning of budgetary control.   In many cases it is desirable to install budgetary control gradually so that the executives may be educated to its needs and purposes.

## Summary

The advantages to be derived from budgetary control may be stated in outline form as follows:

1. COORDINATION OF SALES AND PRODUCTION:
   (a) By estimating sales possibilities and planning production to produce the goods necessary to meet these possibilities.
   (b) By limiting the production to the amount necessary to meet probable sales demands as shown by the sales estimate, thus preventing an excess of inventory of finished product.

2. FORMULATION OF A PROFITABLE SALES AND PRODUCTION PROGRAM:
   (a) By determining the lines of goods most desirable for a well-rounded sales program and adapting production, in so far as is consistent with the following paragraph, to produce the necessary quantity of these lines.
   (b) By determining the lines of goods most desirable for a well-rounded production program and planning sales, in so far as is consistent with the preceding paragraph, to sell the amount of these lines necessary to secure economical production.

3. COORDINATION OF SALES AND PRODUCTION WITH FINANCES:

   (a) By considering the contemplated sales and production programs in terms of financial requirements and revising these programs, if necessary, to reduce the financial requirements to correspond to the financial program which is deemed possible and desirable.

   (b) By determining the financial requirements of the sales and production programs as revised in the manner prescribed in the preceding paragraph, and planning to secure funds to meet these requirements.

4. PROPER CONTROL OF EXPENDITURES:

   (a) By requiring the preparation by each department head of an estimate of the expenditures of his department during the budget period.

   (b) By requiring the submission of these estimates to the budget committee for consideration and approval.

   (c) By the prohibition of any expenditures in excess of the departmental estimates without the permission of the budget committee.

   (d) By requiring the submission of monthly reports showing a comparison between the actual expenditures for the month and the estimated.

5. FORMULATION OF A FINANCIAL PROGRAM:

   (a) By the estimating of cash receipts for each month based on the sales program and the estimate of collections.

   (b) By the estimating of cash disbursements for each month based on the production, purchasing, plant and equipment, and departmental expense budgets.

   (c) By determining the excess of disbursements over receipts and the preparation of a financial program which will secure funds to provide for this excess.

6. COORDINATION OF ALL THE ACTIVITIES OF THE BUSINESS:

   (a) By the preparation by each department of an estimate of its activities during the budget period.

   (b) By the study of these departmental estimates by the departmental executives and the budget committee.

    (c) By the modification of the activities of each department to the end that they coordinate with the activities of each other department.

    (d) By the preparation of an estimated balance sheet and an estimated statement of profit and loss showing the anticipated results of the operations provided for by the budgetary program.

    (e) By the formulation of plans and policies which will make possible the attainment of the estimated results as shown by the estimated financial reports prepared as directed in the preceding paragraph.

The limitations of budgetary control may be stated in outline form as follows:

1. The budgetary program is based on estimates.
2. Budgetary plans will not execute themselves.
3. Budgetary control cannot take the place of administration.
4. Budgetary control cannot be perfected immediately.

# CHAPTER XXVI

## BUDGETARY CONTROL FOR NON-COMMERCIAL ENTERPRISES

### Scope of Previous Chapters

The discussion in the preceding chapters has been confined to a consideration of the use of budgetary control in the administration of the commercial or profit-seeking enterprise. This has been done for the following reasons:

1. It is for such enterprises that budgetary control is most urgently needed at the present time.
2. The development of budgetary control in connection with such enterprises has been very slow and standard methods have not been formulated.
3. The literature dealing with the application of budgetary control of these enterprises is limited. There is considerable literature dealing with the various parts of the budgetary procedure, but so far as the author is aware this text is the first attempt to discuss the budgetary process as a whole. On the other hand, there is a considerable body of literature dealing with budgetary control of non-commercial enterprises.

For these reasons it is thought that this text will best serve its purpose by emphasizing the possible uses of budgetary control by the commercial enterprise and the possible methods by which its installation by such businesses may be effected. It is well to see, however, the other uses which may be made of it.

### Varied Uses of Budgetary Control

Budgetary control has long been practiced by governmental units, educational institutions, and similar organizations. Religious, social, and charitable institutions, such

425

as churches, Y. M. C. A.'s, and social service agencies, are accustomed to prepare budgets, although in some cases they are not carefully prepared nor rigidly enforced. There has been a considerable body of literature produced treating of its use for these purposes and this literature is readily available to the reader.

Although it is not thought worth while to enter into a detailed discussion of budgetary control for non-commercial enterprises, a brief description is given in this chapter of its use in connection with governmental units and educational institutions, with the hope that some benefit may be obtained by a comparison between the methods employed in these cases and those suggested for commercial enterprises in the preceding chapters.

### Budgetary Control for Governmental Units

A possible procedure to be followed in the formulation and execution of a budget for a city, state, or national government, stated in outline form, is as follows:

1. Some time before the beginning of the fiscal year each department prepares an estimate of its expenditures for the year. For instance, in a state government, the State Department, the Treasury Department, the Department of Justice, etc., will prepare such an estimate. The department head will base his estimate on the estimates submitted by the bureau chiefs within his department.

2. The head of the department will transmit this estimate with his approval to some official, usually the Treasurer, Comptroller, Director of Finance, or Director of the Budget, who is designated by the law to receive the separate estimates and formulate them into a combined estimate for all departments. For brevity, we shall refer to this executive as the Director of the Budget in the following discussion.

3. The Director of the Budget, prepares an estimate of

the revenue for the fiscal year. He then submits a report to the chief executive (the Mayor, Governor, or President) showing a comparison of the estimated expenditures with the estimated revenues.

4. The chief executive, and in many cases a Board of Review, Board of Estimate and Review, or Cabinet, consider the estimates received from the Director of the Budget. The departmental heads may be called into conference to give reasons for any increases requested by their departments.

5. If the estimated expenditures exceed the estimated revenues, one of the following must be done:

(a) Expenditures may be reduced. This involves a decrease in the estimates of one or more departments. The Chief Executive or his advisory board must decide which of the departmental estimates should be decreased.

(b) Revenue may be increased. This necessitates the devising of new methods of taxation or the increasing of the present rates of taxation.

(c) Additional funds may be secured from loans. This results in an increase of the indebtedness of the government.

6. The chief executive transmits the budget as approved by him to the legislative body responsible for transforming it into law. He may accompany it with recommendations with reference to methods of raising new revenue if this is necessary, or with reference to the decrease of taxes if this is possible.

7. The proposed budget is considered by the legislative body and such changes made as it deems fit. Usually the changes permitted are limited by law. In some cases the legislative body is given authority to decrease and strike out items, but cannot increase or add items.

8. When the budget is approved by the legislative body, it becomes the working program for all the departments for

the fiscal period.  No department is permitted to exceed its budget allowance without a special dispensation of the legislative body.  In some cases there is an "emergency fund" included in the budget and put at the disposal of the chief executive.  He may make allowances from this fund to departments which in his opinion are in need of additional funds.  The amount of this fund is usually small.

9.  Proper records are kept that all expenditures of each department may be charged against its budget or "appropriation."  Periodic reports are made to a representative of the chief executive, showing a comparison between estimated expenditures and actual expenditures.

It will be understood, of course, that the procedure stated in the foregoing outline is intended to be indicative only.  The procedure varies somewhat in different governmental units.

### Budgetary Control of the National Government

The "Budget and Accounting Act," which establishes budgetary control for the federal government, was approved by the President on June 10, 1921.  The complete act is given in Appendix A.  The most important features of this act for our purposes are the following:

1.  It places the final authority and responsibility for the preparation and enforcement of the budget in the President who is the chief executive of the administrative division of the government.

2.  It sets up a Budget Bureau which is responsible for the preparation and enforcement of the budgetary procedure. The executive head of this bureau is termed the Director of the Budget, and reports directly to the President.  In this sense he may be termed a staff assistant to the President. In so far as the President delegates to him authority in the

enforcement of the budget, he acts as an executive assistant instead of a staff assistant.

3. It sets up a budget officer in each bureau who is responsible for preparing the original estimate for his bureau. This results in placing the responsibility for initiating each budget on the unit which is responsible for its performance.

4. It prescribes that each bureau chief will consider the budget as prepared by his budget officer and after he has approved it transmit it to the department chief. The department head revises the estimates of the bureaus if he thinks this is necessary, and then combines these to make the estimate of his department.

5. It prescribes that each department head will transmit the estimates of his department to the Director of the Budget. The latter will revise the departmental estimates if necessary, and will then combine these to make the complete estimate on expenditures. He will transmit this together with the estimate of revenues to the President, who will make any changes which he thinks necessary and submit them with his approval to Congress.

6. It creates a Comptroller General who is responsible for the form of the records and the procedures of the various departments, and for exercising control over the disbursements made under the appropriations which are made in response to the budget.

It can be seen from the foregoing that the act sets up in general terms the procedure to be followed in the preparation and enforcement of the national budget.

### Budgetary Control of State Governments

The budgetary procedure of the several states varies to a considerable degree. The modern tendency is towards a more complete and comprehensive planning of financial operations than that formerly employed. In recent years there has been some tendency towards a classification of the administrative activities of the state on a functional basis, and the creation of functional departments to carry on these activities. In those few states which have followed this plan there is usually created a department of finance in which is vested *inter alia* the responsibility for the preparation and enforcement of the budget.

Appendix B gives an extract from the "Administrative Code" of the state of Ohio, which was approved by the Governor of the State on April 26, 1921. This extract shows the duties of the Department of Finance as defined in the law. This extract is interesting not only from the viewpoint of budgetary control, but also from the viewpoint of administrative control in general.

### Budgetary Control for Educational Institutions

Budgetary procedure will vary somewhat as between the small college and the large university, and it will be slightly different in the endowed institution from that of the institution supported by public funds.

To indicate briefly the principal considerations involved in the adoption of a procedure for an educational institution, a state university will serve our purpose.

### Budgetary Control for University

The president of the university is responsible for the preparation of the annual budget and its submission to the board of trustees for approval. In its preparation he may employ various subordinates. The subordinates which may be employed and the procedure which they may follow in performing their tasks may be understood better by considering separately (a) the estimate of income, and (b) the estimate of expenditures.

## The Estimate of Income

The income of a state university may be derived from the following sources:

1. United States land grants
2. Student fees
3. Departmental sales
4. Gifts
5. Appropriations

The income to be derived from United States land grants is not difficult to determine, for it is usually fairly uniform in amount. The income from student fees is dependent on the number of students enrolled. Since the attendance of a state university almost invariably increases each year, it is not difficult to determine the minimum amount of this item of income. It is, of course, impossible to determine the exact amount to be received from this source.

Departmental sales arise chiefly from sales of the school of agriculture, and the income from this source must be based on an estimate of the quantity of product and services offered for sale and the probable price to be obtained for them. Possible sales of all departments and colleges must be considered. The income from gifts is ordinarily not large and is usually restricted in its uses; so it has little effect on the general budget.

The income from appropriations cannot be determined until after the action of the legislature. The university ordinarily requests appropriations for sufficient amounts to meet the excess of disbursements over receipts as shown by its budget. In most cases more is requested than is obtained, and this necessitates a reduction in the original estimate of expenditures.

The business manager or comptroller can best make the estimate of income. He may consult other executives in its preparation. After its completion he will transmit it to the

president, who will combine it with the estimate of expenditures to form the budget which he submits to the board of
trustees.

## Estimate of Disbursements

The expenditures of a university may be grouped broadly
as follows:

1. General Administration, including the salaries of "business"
   employees and clerical and stenographic assistants in all departments.
2. Physical Plant Operation and Maintenance
3. Capital Additions
4. Teaching and Research
   (a) Library
   (b) Supplies
   (c) Instruction

## General Administrative Expenses

The estimate of general administrative expense will
be prepared by the controller. As a basis for this estimate
he will receive an estimate from each department and administrative unit. The controller will indicate such revisions as he thinks are necessary and transmit the combined
estimates to his superior officer, which may be the president
or the business manager. In any case the president will
make such revisions as he thinks are necessary and submit
the estimate with his recommendations to the board of
trustees.

## Physical Plant Operation and Maintenance

The superintendent of buildings and grounds will prepare the original estimate for expenditures for physical
plant operation and maintenance. In its preparation he
will be assisted by the purchasing agent, who will indicate
the cost of materials and supplies needed by the program.

If the university has a plant engineer he may also assist in the preparation of the estimate.

This estimate will be transmitted to the business manager who makes such revisions as he thinks necessary and transfers it to the president, who treats it likewise and submits it to the board of trustees.

## Capital Additions

The additions to property are usually made as the result of appropriations which are granted for the procurement or construction of specific property. Usually the president presents a building program to the board of trustees, and if it is adopted an attempt is made to secure appropriations for the construction of the buildings called for by the program.

In many cases the program covers a period of several years but indicates the buildings which are most urgent. Appropriations may be requested in the order indicated by the program. In presenting the program to the board of trustees and later to the legislature, it is necessary to show estimates of cost. These estimates may be prepared by the university architect in cooperation with the university engineer and the purchasing agent. In some cases outside counsel may be employed to make these estimates.

After appropriations are secured, contracts will be let for construction and the controller and business manager will supervise the expenditure of funds under the appropriation.

## Teaching and Research

The expenditures under this heading may be subdivided to show separately the cost of the following:

1. Maintenance of library
2. Supplies and equipment
3. Instruction

28

| SECTION I BUDGET OF COURSES | | | | | | | | | | | | | | | | | |
|---|---|---|---|---|---|---|---|---|---|---|---|---|---|---|---|---|---|
| FIRST QUARTER | | | | | | | SECOND QUARTER | | | | FOURTH QUARTER | | | | | | TOTAL |
| (1) | | (2) | (3) | (4) | (5) | (6) | (1) | | (2) | (3) | (1) | (2) | (3) | (4) | (5) | (6) | |
| Course | | Past Attend. | Est. Attend. | Section | Class Hours | Instructor | Course | | Past Attend. | Est. Attend. | | Past Attend. | Est. Attend. | Section | Class Hours | Instructor | |
| Number | Name | | | | | | Number | Name | | | | | | | | | |

Figure 52a. Departmental Salary Budget of a University (face of form)

| SECTION II BUDGET OF INSTRUCTOR'S TIME | | | | | | | | | | |
|---|---|---|---|---|---|---|---|---|---|---|
| INSTRUCTOR | | FIRST QUARTER | | SECOND QUARTER | | THIRD QUARTER | | FOURTH QUARTER | | TOTAL |
| (1) | (2) | (1) | (2) | (1) | (2) | (1) | (2) | (1) | (2) | |
| Name | Rank | Course | Class Hours | Course | Class Hours | Course | Class Hours | Course | Class Hours | |

Figure 52b. Departmental Salary Budget of a University (left half of reverse of form)

## SECTION III
## FINANCIAL BUDGET

| Rank of Instructor | FIRST QUARTER (1) No. | (2) Class Hours | (3) Cost | SECOND QUARTER (1) No. | (2) Class Hours | (3) Cost | THIRD QUARTER (1) No. | (2) Class Hours | (3) Cost | FOURTH QUARTER (1) No. | (2) Class Hours | (3) Cost | TOTAL |
|---|---|---|---|---|---|---|---|---|---|---|---|---|---|
| | | | | | | | | | | | | | |
| Total | | | | | | | | | | | | | |

## SECTION IV
## COMPARATIVE BUDGET

| Rank of Instructor | YEAR 1921-22 (1) No. of Instructors | (2) Cost | (3) Remarks | YEAR 1922-23 (1) No. of Instructors | (2) Cost | (3) Remarks | Increase or Decrease | Remarks |
|---|---|---|---|---|---|---|---|---|
| | | | | | | | | |
| Total | | | | | | | | |

## NOTES AND COMMENTS

Figure 52c. Departmental Salary Budget of a University (right half of reverse of form)

The director of the libraries will prepare an estimate of the cost of maintaining the library. He will also make an estimate of the cost of the necessary additions based on the requests of departments. In some cases there is a faculty committee which supervises such expenditures and passes on these requests. In some universities there are various other committees which pass on various kinds of expenditures.

After the estimate is prepared it will be transmitted to the president, who will submit it to the board of trustees for approval.

The estimate of supplies required by each department will be prepared by the head of each department and transmitted by him to the business manager, who will transmit it to the president, who will transmit it to the board of trustees.

In the preparation of the estimate of instruction cost for a university, a procedure similar to the following may be used:

1. An estimate will be prepared by each department showing the salaries recommended for each member thereof. A very useful form for the preparation of this estimate is shown in Figure 52.

2. The budget as prepared by the department will be forwarded by the head of the department to the dean of the college of which the department is a part.

3. The budget as approved by the dean of the college will be transferred to the budget committee. This committee may be composed of the deans of all the colleges. If the university has a functional organization, it will be composed of the staff officers in the office of the president. The president will be chairman of the committee.

4. The budget committee will consider carefully the budget of each department and of each college. When necessary it may call into conference the heads of departments and deans of the colleges. In the consideration of the separate budgets it will

have in mind the budget of the university as a whole, which it
will prepare from the separate budgets.

5. After the budget has been approved by the budget committee,
it will be transmitted to the president of the university. The
president will submit the budget to the board of trustees with
such recommendations as he may deem desirable.

6. If it is desired to make any revisions in the original budget, the
same procedure will be followed as in the making of the original
budget.

In the departmental salary budget (Figure 52a, b, c),
Section I is useful in that it shows the "class hours" required to carry the desired program. It serves as a basis
for estimating the required teaching staff. Column (5)
of this section must be equal to column (2) of Section II,
and column (2) of Section III. Section II is useful in
showing the disposition of instructors' time. If the budget
committee studies this section in connection with Section
I, it can judge intelligently the claims of departments for
additions to staff. Sections III and IV serve as a basis
for the preparation of the financial budget.

### Budgetary Procedure

A definite procedure should be established for the preparation of all the foregoing budgets, so that they will all reach
the president at the proper time and he can transmit them
to the board of trustees at the same time.

### Summary

No attempt has been made in this chapter to discuss a
complete procedure for the preparation and execution of
the budget of a non-commercial organization. To do this
would require a separate volume. Neither is it intended
to offer the procedures briefly outlined in this chapter as
those which can be adopted *in toto* by any particular organization, although the procedures given are adapted

from those with which the author is familiar. It is intended that this chapter be only suggestive of methods employed by non-commercial enterprises in seeking administrative control through the operation of a budgetary system.

# APPENDIX A

## THE BUDGET AND ACCOUNTING ACT

Following is the law, approved by the President June 10, 1921, which establishes budgetary control for the federal government.

An Act to provide a national budget system and an independent audit of Government accounts, and for other purposes.

### TITLE I—DEFINITIONS

SECTION 1. This Act may be cited as the "Budget and Accounting Act, 1921."

SEC. 2. When used in this Act—

The terms "department and establishment" and "department or establishment" mean any executive department, independent commission, board, bureau, office, agency, or other establishment of the Government, including the municipal government of the District of Columbia, but do not include the Legislative Branch of the Government or the Supreme Court of the United States;

The term "the Budget" means the Budget required by section 201 to be transmitted to Congress;

The term "Bureau" means the Bureau of the Budget;

The term "Director" means the Director of the Bureau of the Budget; and

The term "Assistant Director" means the Assistant Director of the Bureau of the Budget.

### TITLE II—THE BUDGET

SEC. 201. The President shall transmit to Congress on the first day of each regular session, the Budget, which shall set forth in summary and in detail:

(a) Estimates of the expenditures and appropriations necessary in his judgment for the support of the Government for the ensuing fiscal year; except that the estimates for such year for the Legislative Branch of the Government and the Supreme Court of the United States shall be transmitted to the President on or before October 15th of each year, and shall be included by him in the Budget without revision;

(b) His estimates of the receipts of the Government during the ensuing fiscal year, under (1) laws existing at the time the Budget is transmitted and also (2) under the revenue proposals, if any, contained in the Budget;

(c) The expenditures and receipts of the Government during the last completed fiscal year;

(d) Estimates of the expenditures and receipts of the Government during the fiscal year in progress;

(e) The amount of annual, permanent, or other appropriations, including balances of appropriations for prior fiscal years, available for expenditure during the fiscal year in progress, as of November 1 of such year;

(f) Balanced statements of (1) the condition of the Treasury at the end of the last completed fiscal year, (2) the estimated condition of the Treasury at the end of the fiscal year in progress, and (3) the estimated condition of the Treasury at the end of the ensuing fiscal year if the financial proposals contained in the Budget are adopted;

(g) All essential facts regarding the bonded and other indebtedness of the Government; and

(h) Such other financial statements and data as in his opinion are necessary or desirable in order to make known in all practicable detail the financial condition of the Government.

SEC. 202. (a) If the estimated receipts for the ensuing fiscal year contained in the Budget, on the basis of laws existing at the time the Budget is transmitted, plus the estimated amounts in the Treasury at the close of the fiscal year in progress, available for expenditure in the ensuing fiscal year, are less than the estimated expenditures for the ensuing fiscal year contained in the Budget, the President in the Budget shall make recommendations to Congress for new taxes, loans, or other appropriate action to meet the estimated deficiency.

(b) If the aggregate of such estimated receipts and such estimated amounts in the Treasury is greater than such estimated expenditures for the ensuing fiscal year, he shall make such recommendations as in his opinion the public interests require.

SEC. 203. (a) The President from time to time may transmit to Congress supplemental or deficiency estimates for such appropriations or expenditures as in his judgment (1) are necessary on account of laws enacted after the transmission of the Budget, or (2) are otherwise in the public interest. He shall accompany such estimates with a statement of the reasons therefor, including the reasons for their omission from the Budget.

(b) Whenever such supplemental or deficiency estimates reach an aggregate which, if they had been contained in the Budget, would have required the President to make a recommendation under subdivision (a) of section 202, he shall thereupon make such recommendation.

Sec. 204. (a) Except as otherwise provided in this Act, the contents, order, and arrangement of the estimates of appropriations and the statements of expenditures and estimated expenditures contained in the Budget or transmitted under section 203, and the notes and other data submitted therewith, shall conform to the requirements of existing law.

(b) Estimates for lump-sum appropriations contained in the Budget or transmitted under section 203 shall be accompanied by statements showing, in such detail and form as may be necessary to inform Congress, the manner of expenditure of such appropriations and of the corresponding appropriations for the fiscal year in progress and the last completed fiscal year. Such statements shall be in lieu of statements of like character now required by law.

Sec. 205. The President, in addition to the Budget, shall transmit to Congress on the first Monday in December, 1921, for the service of the fiscal year ending June 30, 1923, only, an alternative budget, which shall be prepared in such form and amounts and according to such system of classification and itemization as is, in his opinion, most appropriate, with such explanatory notes and tables as may be necessary to show where the various items embraced in the Budget are contained in such alternative budget.

Sec. 206. No estimate or request for an appropriation and no request for an increase in an item of any such estimate or request, and no recommendation as to how the revenue needs of the Government should be met, shall be submitted to Congress or any committee thereof by any officer or employee of any department or establishment, unless at the request of either House of Congress.

Sec. 207. There is hereby created in the Treasury Department a Bureau to be known as the Bureau of the Budget. There shall be in the Bureau a Director and an Assistant Director, who shall be appointed by the President and receive salaries of $10,000 and $7,500 a year, respectively. The Assistant Director shall perform such duties as the Director may designate, and during the absence or incapacity of the Director or during a vacancy in the office of Director he shall act as Director. The Bureau, under such rules and regulations as the President may prescribe, shall prepare for him the Budget, the alternative Budget, and any supplemental or deficiency estimates, and to this end shall have authority to assemble, correlate, revise, reduce, or increase the estimates of the several departments or establishments.

SEC. 208. (a) The Director, under such rules and regulations as the President may prescribe, shall appoint and fix the compensation of attorneys and other employees and make expenditures for rent in the District of Columbia, printing, binding, telegrams, telephone service, law books, books of reference, periodicals, stationery, furniture, office equipment, other supplies, and necessary expenses of the office, within the appropriations made therefor.

(b) No person appointed by the Director shall be paid a salary at a rate in excess of $6,000 a year, and not more than four persons so appointed shall be paid a salary at a rate in excess of $5,000 a year.

(c) All employees in the Bureau whose compensation is at a rate of $5,000 a year or less shall be appointed in accordance with the civil-service laws and regulations.

(d) The provisions of law prohibiting the transfer of employees of executive departments and independent establishments until after service of three years shall not apply during the fiscal years ending June 30, 1921, and June 30, 1922, to the transfer of employees to the Bureau.

(e) The Bureau shall not be construed to be a bureau or office created since January 1, 1916, so as to deprive employees therein of the additional compensation allowed civilian employees under the provisions of section 6 of the Legislative, Executive, and Judicial Appropriation Act for the fiscal years ending June 30, 1921, and June 30, 1922, if otherwise entitled thereto.

SEC. 209. The Bureau, when directed by the President, shall make a detailed study of the departments and establishments for the purpose of enabling the President to determine what changes (with a view of securing greater economy and efficiency in the conduct of the public service) should be made in (1) the existing organization, activities, and methods of business of such departments or establishments, (2) the appropriations therefor, (3) the assignment of particular activities to particular services, or (4) the regrouping of services. The results of such study shall be embodied in a report or reports to the President, who may transmit to Congress such report or reports or any part thereof with his recommendations on the matters covered thereby.

SEC. 210. The Bureau shall prepare for the President a codification of all laws or parts of laws relating to the preparation and transmission to Congress of statements of receipts and expenditures of the Government and of estimates of appropriations.   The President shall transmit the same to Congress on or before the first Monday in December, 1921, with a recommendation as to the changes which, in his opinion, should be made in such laws or parts of laws.

SEC. 211.   The powers and duties relating to the compiling of estimates now conferred and imposed upon the Division of Bookkeeping and Warrants of the office of the Secretary of the Treasury are transferred to the Bureau.

SEC. 212.   The Bureau shall, at the request of any committee of either House of Congress having jurisdiction over revenue or appropriations, furnish the committee such aid and information as it may request.

SEC. 213.   Under such regulations as the President may prescribe, (1) every department and establishment shall furnish to the Bureau such information as the Bureau may from time to time require, and (2) the Director and the Assistant Director, or any employee of the Bureau when duly authorized, shall, for the purpose of securing such information, have access to, and the right to examine, any books, documents, papers, or records of any such department or establishment.

SEC. 214.   (a) The head of each department and establishment shall designate an official thereof as budget officer therefor, who, in each year under his direction and on or before a date fixed by him, shall prepare the departmental estimates.

(b) Such budget officer shall also prepare, under the direction of the head of the department or establishment, such supplemental and deficiency estimates as may be required for its work.

SEC. 215.   The head of each department and establishment shall revise the departmental estimates and submit them to the Bureau on or before September 15 of each year.   In case of his failure so to do, the President shall cause to be prepared such estimates and data as are necessary to enable him to include in the Budget estimates and statements in respect to the work of such department or establishment.

SEC. 216.   The departmental estimates and any supplemental or deficiency estimates submitted to the Bureau by the head of any department or establishment shall be prepared and submitted in such form, manner, and detail as the President may prescribe.

SEC. 217.   For expenses of the establishment and maintenance of the Bureau there is appropriated, out of any money in the Treasury not otherwise appropriated, the sum of $225,000, to continue available during the fiscal year ending June 30, 1922.

## Title III—General Accounting Office

SEC. 301. There is created an establishment of the Government to be known as the General Accounting Office, which shall be independent of the executive departments and under the control and direction of the Comptroller General of the United States. The offices of Comptroller of the Treasury and Assistant Comptroller of the Treasury are abolished, to take effect July 1, 1921. All other officers and employees of the office of the Comptroller of the Treasury shall become officers and employees in the General Accounting Office at their grades and salaries on July 1, 1921, and all books, records, documents, papers, furniture, office equipment and other property of the office of the Comptroller of the Treasury shall become the property of the General Accounting Office. The Comptroller General is authorized to adopt a seal for the General Accounting Office.

SEC. 302. There shall be in the General Accounting Office a Comptroller General of the United States and an Assistant Comptroller General of the United States, who shall be appointed by the President with the advice and consent of the Senate, and shall receive salaries of $10,000 and $7,500 a year, respectively. The Assistant Comptroller General shall perform such duties as may be assigned to him by the Comptroller General, and during the absence or incapacity of the Comptroller General, or during a vacancy in that office, shall act as Comptroller General.

SEC. 303. Except as hereinafter provided in this section, the Comptroller General and the Assistant Comptroller General shall hold office for fifteen years. The Comptroller General shall not be eligible for reappointment. The Comptroller General or the Assistant Comptroller General may be removed at any time by joint resolution of Congress after notice and hearing, when, in the judgment of Congress, the Comptroller General or Assistant Comptroller General has become permanently incapacitated or has been inefficient, or guilty of neglect of duty, or of malfeasance in office, or of any felony or conduct involving moral turpitude, and for no other cause and in no other manner except by impeachment. Any Comptroller General or Assistant Comptroller General removed in the manner herein provided shall be ineligible for reappointment to that office. When a Comptroller General or Assistant Comptroller General attains the age of seventy years, he shall be retired from his office.

SEC. 304. All powers and duties now conferred or imposed by law upon the Comptroller of the Treasury or the six auditors of the Treasury Department, and the duties of the Division of Bookkeeping and Warrants of the Office of the Secretary of the Treasury relating to keeping the personal ledger accounts of disbursing and collecting officers, shall, so far as not inconsistent with this Act, be vested in and imposed upon the General Accounting Office and be exercised without direction from any other officer. The balances certified by the Comptroller General shall be final and conclusive upon the executive branch of the Government. The revision by the Comptroller General of settlements made by the six auditors shall be discontinued, except as to settlements made before July 1, 1921.

The administrative examination of the accounts and vouchers of the Postal Service now imposed by law upon the Auditor for the Post Office Department shall be performed on and after July 1, 1921, by a bureau in the Post Office Department to be known as the Bureau of Accounts, which is hereby established for that purpose. The Bureau of Accounts shall be under the direction of a Comptroller, who shall be appointed by the President with the advice and consent of the Senate, and shall receive a salary of $5,000 a year. The Comptroller shall perform the administrative duties now performed by the Auditor for the Post Office Department and such other duties in relation thereto as the Postmaster General may direct. The appropriation of $5,000 for the salary of the Auditor for the Post Office Department for the fiscal year 1922 is transferred and made available for the salary of the Comptroller, Bureau of Accounts, Post Office Department. The officers and employees of the Office of the Auditor for the Post Office Department engaged in the administrative examination of accounts shall become officers and employees of the Bureau of Accounts at their grades and salaries on July 1, 1921. The appropriations for salaries and for contingent and miscellaneous expenses and tabulating equipment for such office for the fiscal year 1922, and all books, records, documents, papers, furniture, office equipment, and other property shall be apportioned between, transferred to, and made available for the Bureau of Accounts and the General Accounting Office, respectively, on the basis of duties transferred.

SEC. 305. Section 236 of the Revised Statutes is amended to read as follows:

"SEC. 236. All claims and demands whatever by the Government of the United States or against it, and all accounts whatever in which the Government of the United States is concerned, either as debtor or creditor, shall be settled and adjusted in the General Accounting Office."

SEC. 306. All laws relating generally to the administration of the departments and establishments shall, so far as applicable, govern the General Accounting Office. Copies of any books, records, papers, or documents, and transcripts from the books and proceedings of the General Accounting Office, when certified by the Comptroller General or the Assistant Comptroller General under its seal, shall be admitted as evidence with the same effect as the copies and transcripts referred to in sections 882 and 886 of the Revised Statutes.

SEC. 307. The Comptroller General may provide for the payment of accounts or claims adjusted and settled in the General Accounting Office, through disbursing officers of the several departments and establishments, instead of by warrant.

SEC. 308. The duties now appertaining to the Division of Public Moneys of the Office of the Secretary of the Treasury, so far as they relate to the covering of revenues and repayments into the Treasury, the issue of duplicate checks and warrants, and the certification of outstanding liabilities for payment, shall be performed by the Division of Bookkeeping and Warrants of the Office of the Secretary of the Treasury.

SEC. 309. The Comptroller General shall prescribe the forms, systems, and procedure for administrative appropriation and fund accounting in the several departments and establishments, and for the administrative examination of fiscal officers' accounts and claims against the United States.

SEC. 310. The offices of the six auditors shall be abolished, to take effect July 1, 1921. All other officers and employees of these offices except as otherwise provided herein shall become officers and employees of the General Accounting Office at their grades and salaries on July 1, 1921. All books, records, documents, papers, furniture, office equipment, and other property of these offices, and of the Division of Bookkeeping and Warrants, so far as they relate to the work of such division transferred by section 304, shall become the property of the General Accounting Office. The General Accounting Office shall occupy temporarily the rooms now occupied by the office of the Comptroller of the Treasury and the six auditors.

SEC. 311. (a) The Comptroller General shall appoint, remove, and fix the compensation of such attorneys and other employees in the General Accounting Office as may from time to time be provided for by law.

(b) All such appointments, except to positions carrying a salary at a rate of more than $5,000 a year, shall be made in accordance with the civil-service laws and regulations.

(c) No person appointed by the Comptroller General shall be paid a salary at a rate of more than $6,000 a year, and not more than four persons shall be paid a salary at a rate of more than $5,000 a year.

(d) All officers and employees of the General Accounting Office, whether transferred thereto or appointed by the Comptroller General, shall perform such duties as may be assigned to them by him.

(e) All official acts performed by such officers or employees specially designated therefor by the Comptroller General shall have the same force and effect as though performed by the Comptroller General in person.

(f) The Comptroller General shall make such rules and regulations as may be necessary for carrying on the work of the General Accounting Office, including rules and regulations concerning the admission of attorneys to practice before such office.

SEC. 312. (a) The Comptroller General shall investigate, at the seat of government or elsewhere, all matters relating to the receipt, disbursement, and application of public funds, and shall make to the President when requested by him, and to Congress at the beginning of each regular session, a report in writing of the work of the General Accounting Office, containing recommendations concerning the legislation he may deem necessary to facilitate the prompt and accurate rendition and settlement of accounts and concerning such other matters relating to the receipt, disbursement, and application of public funds as he may think advisable. In such regular report, or in special reports at any time when Congress is in session, he shall make recommendations looking to greater economy or efficiency in public expenditures.

(b) He shall make such investigations and reports as shall be ordered by either House of Congress or by any committee of either House having jurisdiction over revenue, appropriations, or expenditures. The Comptroller General shall also, at the request of any such committee, direct assistants from his office to furnish the committee such aid and information as it may request.

(c) The Comptroller General shall specially report to Congress every expenditure or contract made by any department or establishment in any year in violation of law.

(d) He shall submit to Congress reports upon the adequacy and effectiveness of the administrative examination of accounts and claims in the respective departments and establishments and upon the adequacy and effectiveness of departmental inspection of the offices and accounts of fiscal officers.

(e) He shall furnish such information relating to expenditures and accounting to the Bureau of the Budget as it may request from time to time.

SEC. 313. All departments and establishments shall furnish to the Comptroller General such information regarding the powers, duties, activities, organization, financial transactions, and methods of business of their respective offices as he may from time to time require of them; and the

Comptroller General, or any of his assistants or employees, when duly authorized by him, shall, for the purpose of securing such information, have access to and the right to examine any books, documents, papers, or records of any such department or establishment. The authority contained in this section shall not be applicable to expenditures made under the provisions of section 291 of the Revised Statutes.

SEC. 314. The Civil Service Commission shall establish an eligible register for accountants for the General Accounting Office, and the examinations of applicants for entrance upon such register shall be based upon questions approved by the Comptroller General.

SEC. 315. (a) All appropriations for the fiscal year ending June 30, 1922, for the offices of the Comptroller of the Treasury and the six auditors, are transferred to and made available for the General Accounting Office, except as otherwise provided herein.

(b) During such fiscal year the Comptroller General, within the limit of the total appropriations available for the General Accounting Office, may make such changes in the number and compensation of officers and employees appointed by him or transferred to the General Accounting Office under this Act as may be necessary.

(c) There shall also be transferred to the General Accounting Office such portions of the appropriations for rent and contingent and miscellaneous expenses, including allotments for printing and binding, made for the Treasury Department for the fiscal year ending June 30, 1922, as are equal to the amounts expended from similar appropriations during the fiscal year ending June 30, 1921, by the Treasury Department for the offices of the Comptroller of the Treasury and the six auditors.

(d) During the fiscal year ending June 30, 1922, the appropriations and portions of appropriations referred to in this section shall be available for salaries and expenses of the General Accounting Office, including payment for rent in the District of Columbia, traveling expenses, the purchase and exchange of law books, books of reference, and for all necessary miscellaneous and contingent expenses.

SEC. 316. The General Accounting Office and the Bureau of Accounts shall not be construed to be a bureau or office created since January 1, 1916, so as to deprive employees therein of the additional compensation allowed civilian employees under the provisions of section 6 of the Legislative, Executive, and Judicial Appropriation Act for the fiscal year ending June 30, 1922, if otherwise entitled thereto.

SEC. 317. The provisions of law prohibiting the transfer of employees of executive departments and independent establishments until after service of three years shall not apply during the fiscal year ending June 30, 1922, to the transfer of employees to the General Accounting Office.

SEC. 318. This Act shall take effect upon its approval by the President: *Provided*, That sections 301 to 317, inclusive, relating to the General Accounting Office and the Bureau of Accounts, shall take effect July 1, 1921.

Approved, June 10, 1921.

# APPENDIX B

## ADMINISTRATIVE CODE FOR THE STATE OF OHIO

### DEPARTMENT OF FINANCE

SEC. 154–28. The department of finance shall have power to exercise control over the financial transactions of all departments, offices and institutions, except the judicial and legislative departments, as follows:

(1) By prescribing and requiring the installation of a uniform system of accounting and reporting, as to accruals of revenue and expenditures necessary in certifying that funds are available and adequate to meet contracts and obligations.

(2) By prescribing and requiring uniform order and invoice forms and forms for financial reports and statements, and by requiring financial reports and statements.

(3) By requiring itemized statements of expenditures proposed for any specified future period to be submitted to the department, and by approving or disapproving all or any part of such proposed expenditures.

(4) By requiring orders, invoices, claims, vouchers or payrolls to be submitted to the department, where such submission is prescribed by law or where the governor shall deem such submission necessary, and by approving or disapproving such orders, invoices, claims, vouchers or payrolls.

(5) By supervising and examining accounts, the expenditures and receipts of public money and the disposition and use of public property, in connection with the administration of the state budget.

(6) By prescribing the manner of certifying that funds are available and adequate to meet contracts and obligations.

(7) By prescribing uniform rules governing forms of specifications, advertisements for proposals, opening of bids, making of awards and contracts, governing purchases of supplies and performance of work.

(8) By reporting to the attorney general for such action, civil or criminal, as the attorney general may deem necessary all facts showing illegal expenditures of the public money or misappropriation of public property.

(9) By prescribing rules and regulations for carrying into effect any or all of the other powers herein granted.

No provision of law authorizing or requiring any department, office, or institution to keep accrual, encumbrance or cost accounts or to exercise fiscal management and control over or with respect to any institution, activity or function of the state shall be so construed as to exclude such department, office or institution from the control of the department of finance herein specified, but the power of the department of finance herein provided for shall apply and relate to such accounts and reports of all such departments, offices and institutions.

SEC. 154-29. As used in section 154-28 of the General Code:

"Order" means a copy of a contract or a statement of the nature of a contemplated expenditure, a description of the property or commodity to be purchased or service to be performed, other than services of officers and regular employes of the state, and per diem of the national guard, and the total sum of the expenditures to be made therefor if the same is fixed and ascertained, otherwise the estimated sum thereof.

"Invoice" means and includes estimates or contracts, or a statement showing delivery of the commodity or performance of the service described in the order, and the date of the purchase or rendering of the service, or a detailed statement of the things done, material supplied or labor furnished, and the sum due pursuant to the contract or obligation.

"Voucher" means the order and invoice as herein defined; and where-ever in the General Code the word "voucher" is used it shall be held to have the meaning herein defined.

"Public money" shall have the meaning defined in section two hundred and eighty-six of the General Code.

All orders and invoices shall specify the appropriation account from which they are payable.

SEC. 154-30. If any requirement of the department of finance respecting the submission of statements of proposed expenditures, or orders, invoices, claims, vouchers or payrolls is not complied with, or if any statement of proposed expenditures, or any order, invoice, claim, voucher or payroll is submitted to and disapproved in whole or in part by the department of finance, the department shall have authority to notify the auditor of state thereof, and such auditor shall not issue any warrants on the treasury in payment of such expenditure, claim or voucher.

The department of finance may certify to the auditor of state any order or statement of proposed expenditures approved by it, and direct the proper appropriation account or accounts to be charged therewith, or with the estimated amount thereof, in which event the sum so certified shall be a prior charge on such appropriation account or accounts, available only for the payment of invoices issued against such order, or expenditures within such statement, until the final invoice therefor is filed with the auditor of state, or until the department of finance shall certify that such order and the obligation recited therein have ceased to be an obligation against the state, or such proposed expenditures have been made or abandoned in whole or in part.

Whenever any commodity or service included in such order or statement so certified is delivered or performed, or whenever any payment is due upon any contract or obligation covered thereby, an invoice shall be filed with the auditor of state therefor. The total of all invoices issued against any such order shall not exceed the sum of such order or the estimated sum appearing on such order.

SEC. 154–31. The department of finance shall:

(1) Prepare and report to the governor, when requested, estimates of the income and revenues of the state, and devise new forms of revenue for the state;

(2) Prepare and submit to the governor biennially, not later than the first day of January preceding the convening of the general assembly, state budget estimates;

(3) Publish, from time to time, for the information of the several departments and of the general public, bulletins of the work of the department;

(4) Investigate duplication of work of the departments and the efficiency of the organization and administration of departments, and formulate plans for the further coordination of departments.

SEC. 154–32. In the exercise of any of the powers mentioned in section 154–28 of the General Code, the department of finance shall have the power to compel the attendance and testimony of witnesses, to administer oaths and to examine such persons as it may deem necessary, and compel the production of books and papers. The orders and subpoenas issued by the department in pursuance of the authority in it vested by this section may be enforced, on the application of the director of finance, by any court of common pleas by proceedings in contempt therein as provided by law.

SEC. 154–33. In the preparation of state budget estimates the director of finance shall, not later than the fifteenth day of September in the year preceding the regular session of the general assembly, distribute to all departments, offices and institutions of the state government, the blanks necessary for the preparation of budget estimates, which shall be in such form as shall be prescribed by the director of finance, to procure, among other things, information as to the revenues and expenditures for the two preceding fiscal years, and appropriations made by the previous general assembly, the expenditures therefrom, encumbrances thereon, and the amounts unencumbered and unexpended; an estimate of the revenues and expenditures of the current fiscal year, and an estimate of the revenues and amounts needed for the respective departments, offices, and institutions for the two succeeding fiscal years for which appropriations have to be made.    Each department, office and institution shall, not later than the first day of November, file in the office of the director of finance its estimate of receipts and expenditures for the succeeding biennium.    Such estimate shall be accompanied by a statement in writing giving facts and explanations of reasons for each item of expenditure requested.    The director of finance may in his discretion make further inquiry and investigation as to any item desired.    He may approve, disapprove or alter the estimates, excepting those for the legislative and judicial departments of the state government.    Such estimates as revised by him shall constitute the state budget estimates which the department of finance is required by this chapter to submit to the governor.

SEC. 154-34.    The governor shall, as soon as possible and not later than four weeks after the organization of the general assembly, submit a proposed state budget in the form of an appropriation bill or bills and a statement showing the amounts recommended by him to be appropriated to the respective departments, offices and institutions and for all other public purposes, the estimated revenues from taxation, the estimated revenues from sources other than taxation, and an estimate of the amount required to be raised by taxation.

SEC. 154-35.    Each department, office and institution of the state government, other than the legislative and judicial departments thereof, shall, before any appropriation to such department becomes available for expenditure, prepare and submit to the department of finance an estimate of the amount required for each specific purpose within the appropriation, or items of appropriation, as made by the general assembly, and accounts shall be kept and reports rendered to the department of finance showing the expenditure for each such purpose.    The department of finance shall exercise such control over items of appropriation accounts created by the general assembly, with respect to changes and adjustments therein within the general scope of a specific appropriation, as may be committed to it by any act making appropriations, and shall in general exercise such control over the expenditure of appropriations, in addition to that specifically provided for in this chapter, as may be so committed to it.

SEC. 154-36.    The papers, statements and copies thereof required by section 270–6 of the General Code to be filed in the office of the president of the "Sundry Claims Board" therein provided for shall be hereafter delivered to and filed in the office of the department of finance, and such department shall discharge all the duties provided for in said section of the General Code with respect to the filing, delivery and preservation of such papers, statements and copies thereof. The director of finance shall include all claims allowed by the "Sundry Claims Board" in the state budget estimates.

SEC. 154–37. The department of finance shall succeed to and exercise all powers and perform all duties vested by sections one thousand eight hundred and forty-six and one thousand eight hundred and forty-seven of the General Code jointly in the secretary of state and the auditor of state, which said powers are hereby transferred to and vested in said department.

The department of finance shall succeed to and exercise all powers of the state purchasing agent in the office of the secretary of state, and the secretary of state and auditor of state with respect to the purchase of supplies and equipment required for the use and maintenance of state officers, boards and commissions, the commissioners of public printing and the supervisor of public printing, and shall exercise all powers and perform all duties as to purchases heretofore vested in the Ohio board of administration under the provisions of section one thousand eight hundred and forty-nine of the General Code. Wherever powers are conferred or duties imposed upon any such departments, offices or officers with respect to the matters and things herein mentioned, such powers and duties shall be construed as vested in the department of finance. In addition to the powers so transferred to it, the department of finance shall have power to purchase all other supplies, material and equipment for the use of the state departments, offices and institutions, excepting the military department and institutions, administered by boards of trustees, and, excepting as to such department and institutions, to make contracts for and superintend the telephone and telegraph service for the state departments, offices and institutions. So far as practicable, the department of finance shall make all purchases under authority of this chapter from the department of public welfare in the exercise of the functions of said department in the management of state institutions.

SEC. 154–38. The tax commission of Ohio shall be a part of the department of finance for administrative purposes, in the following respects: The director of finance shall be ex officio the secretary of said commission, shall succeed to and perform all of the duties of the secretary of said commission, and shall exercise all powers of said secretary as provided by law; but such director may designate any employe of the department as acting secretary to perform the duties and exercise the powers of secretary of the commission. All clerical and other agencies for the execution of the powers and duties vested in said tax commission of Ohio shall be deemed to be in the department of finance, and the employes thereof shall be deemed to be employes in said department and shall have and exercise all authority vested by law in the employes of such commission. But the tax commission of Ohio shall have direct supervision and control over, and power of appointment and removal of, such employes whose positions shall be designated by the governor as fully subject to the authority of such commission.

# APPENDIX C

## A TRUST COMPANY BUDGET SYSTEM

By STUART H. PATTERSON, *Comptroller of the*
GUARANTY TRUST COMPANY OF NEW YORK

The Guaranty Trust Company has received a number of requests for an explanation of its budget system for expenses. Thinking that possibly other of its correspondents might desire to utilize this method, the following brief description of the system has been prepared.

The first step in this matter is to make a careful classification of the various expenses, so that it will be possible to locate readily any differences between the budget allowance and the actual expenditures. The second step is to estimate carefully the probable expenditure under each classification, by months, for the coming year; and after the estimates have been duly approved by the Executive Officers, to distribute them by months on an Appropriation Sheet, the notations being made thereon in pencil.

The purpose of preparing the Appropriation Sheet in pencil is to permit changes to be made from time to time during the year, either because of additional appropriations, or because some appropriation, say, for advertising, may not be expended until a later month than was anticipated, and consequently the appropriation should be carried along until such time as the expenditure actually takes place. The amounts should be distributed as well as possible over the probable months the expenditures will take place, with a notation on the budget to "carry along" such item, that is, to carry it along as an appropriation until required. As soon as a month is closed, the appropriations applicable to that month are inserted in ink.

Each month the appropriations are carried from the Appropriation Sheet to the Expense Statements, and entered opposite the actual expenditures under each classification.

The Expense Statements are divided into a Monthly Statement and a Cumulative Statement from January 1 to the end of the month just closed. The Cumulative Statement carries a memorandum column of the budget for the entire year for each classification. With this arrangement the statement shows at all times the amount each department or classification may spend, and, should the budget exceed its limit during one month, the leeway that exists for making up the deficiency in some other month.

456

The budget system is really very simple, but it is effective in indicating the probable expenses for a year before the expenditures are incurred, instead of giving an unsatisfactory review of them after the year is closed. This system also promotes economies which might otherwise be overlooked.

A copy of the instructions regarding the 1919 Budget, which were sent to Department Heads, follows:

### 1919 Budget

It is desired that the budget for conducting the business for the year 1919 shall be in the hands of the Managing Committee by December 1, 1918, and the Officers in charge of all departments are requested to have the figures carefully prepared by that date and delivered to Mr.———

In preparing the budget each department shall show separately by months the amounts of salaries, suppers, postage and stationery, and other items. They shall also show the details which go to make up the "other items."

An illustration of the budget form is as follows:

### BUDGET STATEMENT OF................DEPARTMENT

#### FOR YEAR 1919

|           | Salaries | Suppers | Postage | Stationery | Other Items |
|-----------|----------|---------|---------|------------|-------------|
| January........... | $ 1,950 | $ 5.00 | $ 40.00 | $ 80.00 | $ 35.00 |
| February......... | 1,950 | 5.00 | 40.00 | 80.00 | 35.00 |
| March........... | 1,950 | 10.00 | 40.00 | 80.00 | 35.00 |
| April............ | 1,950 | 5.00 | 50.00 | 80.00 | 35.00 |
| May............. | 1,950 | 5.00 | 40.00 | 80.00 | 35.00 |
| June............. | 1,950 | 10.00 | 50.00 | 80.00 | 35.00 |
| July............. | 1,950 | 5.00 | 40.00 | 80.00 | 35.00 |
| August.......... | 1,950 | 5.00 | 40.00 | 80.00 | 35.00 |
| September........ | 1,950 | 10.00 | 50.00 | 80.00 | 35.00 |
| October.......... | 1,950 | 5.00 | 40.00 | 80.00 | 35.00 |
| November........ | 1,950 | 5.00 | 40.00 | 80.00 | 35.00 |
| December........ | 1,950 | 10.00 | 50.00 | 80.00 | 35.00 |
|           | $23,400 | $ 80.00 | $520.00 | $960.00 | $420.00 |

#### DETAIL OF OTHER ITEMS

| | |
|---|---|
| Repairs to coin wrapping machine............................ | $ 60.00 |
| Rental of Telautograph machines............................ | 210.00 |
| Inspection of adding machines................................ | 12.00 |
| Photostatic expenses......................................... | 120.00 |
| Repairs to money truck...................................... | 12.00 |
| | $414.00 |

Each department should keep a copy of its budget, and if during the year it becomes necessary to expend money for some item not included in the budget, it should be the duty of the Officer in charge of such department to see that an additional appropriation be granted *before the expenditure is incurred.*

Requests for additional appropriations should be made to the Comptroller in writing on the form prepared for that purpose, together with a memorandum showing why the additional expense is necessary. The Comptroller has authority to grant such additional appropriations but should he decline to approve any appropriation either because he believes it to be unnecessary, or because he thinks the matter should have the attention of the Officers Meeting, it may be presented to the Officers Meeting through the Vice-President responsible for the operation of the department making the request.

| Guaranty Trust Company of New York | | | | | | | | SHEET No. 1 |
|---|---|---|---|---|---|---|---|---|
| Summary of Expenses for Month of | | | | | 192 | | | |
| | SALARIES | SUPPERS | POSTAGE AND STATIONERY | OTHER ITEMS | TOTAL EXPENSES | APPRO- PRIATIONS | PREVIOUS MONTH | SAME MONTH LAST YEAR |
| **EXPENSE OF SECURING BUSINESS** | | | | | | | | |
| New Business Department | | | | | | | | |
| See Sheet 2 | | | | | | | | |
| Publicity Department | | | | | | | | |
| See Sheet 2 | | | | | | | | |
| Bond Department | | | | | | | | |
| See Sheet 2 | | | | | | | | |
| 5th Ave. Office | | | | | | | | |
| See Sheet 5 | | | | | | | | |
| Madison Ave. Office | | | | | | | | |
| See Sheet 6 | | | | | | | | |
| 1. Officers' Salaries | | | | | | | | |
| 2.    "    Lunches | | | | | | | | |
| 3. Foreign Representatives | | | | | | | | |
| 4. General Traveling after Business | | | | | | | | |
| 5. General Entertaining | | | | | | | | |
| 6. Library | | | | | | | | |
| 7. Income Tax Dept. | | | | | | | | |
| 8. | | | | | | | | |
| 9. | | | | | | | | |
| **EXPENSE OF TRANS- ACTING BUSINESS** | | | | | | | | |
| CURRENT OPERATING | | | | | | | | |
| Main Office    See Sheet 3 | | | | | | | | |
| 5th Ave. Office   See Sheet 5 | | | | | | | | |
| Madison Ave. Office | | | | | | | | |
| See Sheet 6 | | | | | | | | |
| FIXED BY POLICY | | | | | | | | |
| Main Office    See Sheet 3 | | | | | | | | |
| 5th Ave. Office   See Sheet 5 | | | | | | | | |
| Madison Ave. Office | | | | | | | | |
| See Sheet 6 | | | | | | | | |
| OVERHEAD | | | | | | | | |
| Main Office *   See Sheet 4 | | | | | | | | |
| 5th Ave. Office   See Sheet 5 | | | | | | | | |
| Madison Ave. Office | | | | | | | | |
| See Sheet 6 | | | | | | | | |
| 310. Officers' Salaries | | | | | | | | |
| 311.    "    Lunches | | | | | | | | |
| NON PRODUCTIVE EXPENSES | | | | | | | | |
| Main Office    See Sheet 4 | | | | | | | | |
| 5th Ave. Office   See Sheet 5 | | | | | | | | |
| Madison Ave. Office | | | | | | | | |
| See Sheet 6 | | | | | | | | |
| **TOTAL EXPENSES** | | | | | | | | |

REMARKS

SHEET No. 2

Expenses of Securing Business    Month of    192

| | SALARIES | SUPPERS | POSTAGE AND STATIONERY | OTHER ITEMS | TOTAL EXPENSES | APPRO- PRIATIONS | PREVIOUS MONTH | SAME MONTH LAST YEAR |
|---|---|---|---|---|---|---|---|---|
| **NEW BUSINESS** | | | | | | | | |
| 30. Salaries | | | | | | | | |
| 31. Additional War Compensation | | | | | | | | |
| 32. Suppers | | | | | | | | |
| 33. Stationery & Supplies | | | | | | | | |
| 34. Postage | | | | | | | | |
| 35. Traveling Expenses N.Y. Men | | | | | | | | |
| 36. Telegrams & Telephone Tolls | | | | | | | | |
| 37. Entertainment | | | | | | | | |
| 38. Other Expenses | | | | | | | | |
| Out of Town Men | | | | | | | | |
| 39.    Salaries | | | | | | | | |
| 40.    Rent | | | | | | | | |
| 41.    Expenses | | | | | | | | |
| 42.    Traveling | | | | | | | | |
| 43. | | | | | | | | |
| 44. | | | | | | | | |
| 45. | | | | | | | | |
| Total | | | | | | | | |
| **PUBLICITY** | | | | | | | | |
| 60. Salaries | | | | | | | | |
| 61. Additional War Compensation | | | | | | | | |
| 62. Suppers | | | | | | | | |
| 63. Stationery & Supplies | | | | | | | | |
| 64. Postage | | | | | | | | |
| 65. Traveling Expenses | | | | | | | | |
| 66. Printing & Circulars | | | | | | | | |
| 67. Telegrams & Telephone Tolls | | | | | | | | |
| 68. Entertainment | | | | | | | | |
| 69. Other Expenses | | | | | | | | |
| 70. Advertising in Publications | | | | | | | | |
| 71. General Advertising & Publicity | | | | | | | | |
| 72. | | | | | | | | |
| 73. | | | | | | | | |
| 74. | | | | | | | | |
| Total | | | | | | | | |
| **BOND DEPARTMENT** | | | | | | | | |
| 100. Trading Div. | | | | | | | | |
| 101. Distributing Div. | | | | | | | | |
| 102. City Salesmen | | | | | | | | |
| 103. Outside Dealers | | | | | | | | |
| 104. Municipal Div. | | | | | | | | |
| 105. Special Sales Div. | | | | | | | | |
| 106. Correspondence Div. | | | | | | | | |
| 107. Executive Secretaries | | | | | | | | |
| 108. Corporation & New Business Div. | | | | | | | | |
| 109. Administration Accounting, &c. | | | | | | | | |
| 110. Undistributed Salaries | | | | | | | | |
| 111. | | | | | | | | |
| 112. | | | | | | | | |
| 113. Statistical | | | | | | | | |
| 114. Investigation Div. | | | | | | | | |
| 115. Outside Investigations & Examinations | | | | | | | | |
| 116. Out of Town Offices— Rent | | | | | | | | |
| 117.    Salaries | | | | | | | | |
| 118.    Private Wires | | | | | | | | |
| 119.    Traveling | | | | | | | | |
| 120.    Expenses | | | | | | | | |
| 121. | | | | | | | | |
| 122. | | | | | | | | |
| 123. | | | | | | | | |
| 124. Suppers | | | | | | | | |
| 125. Additional War Compensation | | | | | | | | |
| 126. Telephone Tolls—Telegrams & Cables | | | | | | | | |
| 127. Stationery & Supplies | | | | | | | | |
| 128. Circulars & Printed Matter | | | | | | | | |
| 129. Postage | | | | | | | | |
| 130. Traveling Expenses | | | | | | | | |
| 131. Entertainment | | | | | | | | |
| 132. Advertising | | | | | | | | |
| 133. Stock Ticker | | | | | | | | |
| 134. | | | | | | | | |
| 135. | | | | | | | | |
| 136. | | | | | | | | |
| 137. | | | | | | | | |
| 138. | | | | | | | | |
| Total | | | | | | | | |

| | | | | | | | | SHEET No. 3 |
|---|---|---|---|---|---|---|---|---|
| Expenses of Transacting Business—Main Office | | | | Month of | | | | 192 |
| | SALARIES | SUPPERS | POSTAGE AND STATIONERY | OTHER ITEMS | TOTAL EXPENSES | APPRO-PRIATIONS | PREVIOUS MONTH | SAME MONTH LAST YEAR |
| **CURRENT OPERATING DEPARTMENT** | | | | | | | | |
| 160. Accounting | | | | | | | | |
| 161. Analysis | | | | | | | | |
| 162. Auditing | | | | | | | | |
| 163. Archives | | | | | | | | |
| 164. Bookkeeping | | | | | | | | |
| 165. Collection | | | | | | | | |
| 166. Tellers | | | | | | | | |
| 167. Coupon | | | | | | | | |
| 168. Credit | | | | | | | | |
| 169. Chief Clerk's | | | | | | | | |
| 170. Emergency | | | | | | | | |
| 171. General Pages | | | | | | | | |
| 172. Filing | | | | | | | | |
| 173. Loan | | | | | | | | |
| 174. Mailing | | | | | | | | |
| 175. Messengers | | | | | | | | |
| 176. Reorganization | | | | | | | | |
| 177. Registration | | | | | | | | |
| 178. Securities | | | | | | | | |
| 179. Stenographers—General | | | | | | | | |
| 180. Secretaries—Executive | | | | | | | | |
| 181. Supply Dept. Operating | | | | | | | | |
| 182. Special Officers and Watchmen | | | | | | | | |
| 183. Stock Bookkeeping | | | | | | | | |
| 184. Transfer | | | | | | | | |
| Telephone, Telegraph & Cable | | | | | | | | |
| 185. Salaries Operators | | | | | | | | |
| 186. Service | | | | | | | | |
| 187. Undistributed Tolls | | | | | | | | |
| 188. Trust | | | | | | | | |
| 189. Vault | | | | | | | | |
| 190. Expressage & Mail Insurance | | | | | | | | |
| Foreign Department | | | | | | | | |
| 191. Salaries | | | | | | | | |
| 192. Suppers | | | | | | | | |
| 193. Travel | | | | | | | | |
| 194. Telegrams, Cables & Tel. Calls | | | | | | | | |
| 195. Postage & Express | | | | | | | | |
| 196. Stationery & Supplies | | | | | | | | |
| 197. Sundries | | | | | | | | |
| 198. | | | | | | | | |
| 199. | | | | | | | | |
| 200. | | | | | | | | |
| 201. | | | | | | | | |
| 202. | | | | | | | | |
| 203. | | | | | | | | |
| 204. | | | | | | | | |
| 205. | | | | | | | | |
| 206. | | | | | | | | |
| 207. | | | | | | | | |
| 208. | | | | | | | | |
| 209. | | | | | | | | |
| 210. | | | | | | | | |
| 211. | | | | | | | | |
| 212. | | | | | | | | |
| 213. | | | | | | | | |
| 214. | | | | | | | | |
| 215. | | | | | | | | |
| Total | | | | | | | | |
| **FIXED BY POLICY** | | | | | | | | |
| 230. Resident Attorney | | | | | | | | |
| 231. Legal & Professional Fees | | | | | | | | |
| 232. Directors & Committee Fees | | | | | | | | |
| 233. Examinations & Elections | | | | | | | | |
| 234. Insurance Liability & Fire | | | | | | | | |
| 235. Fidelity Bonds | | | | | | | | |
| 236. Dining Room | | | | | | | | |
| 237. Customers' Check Books Free | | | | | | | | |
| 238. | | | | | | | | |
| 239. | | | | | | | | |
| 240. | | | | | | | | |
| 241. | | | | | | | | |
| 242. | | | | | | | | |
| 243. | | | | | | | | |
| 244. | | | | | | | | |
| 245. | | | | | | | | |
| Total | | | | | | | | |

| | | | | | | | | | |
|---|---|---|---|---|---|---|---|---|---|
| SHEET No. 4 | | | | | | | | | |

**Expenses of Transacting Business—Main Office (Continued)** Month of 192

| | SALARIES | SUPPERS | POSTAGE AND STATIONERY | OTHER ITEMS | TOTAL EXPENSES | APPRO-PRIATIONS | PREVIOUS MONTH | SAME MONTH LAST YEAR |
|---|---|---|---|---|---|---|---|---|
| **OVERHEAD** Rent—140 Broadway | | | | | | | | |
| 260. Salaries | | | | | | | | |
| 261. Elec. Current | | | | | | | | |
| 262. Steam | | | | | | | | |
| 263. Materials & Repairs | | | | | | | | |
| 264. Taxes, Real Estate | | | | | | | | |
| 265. Water | | | | | | | | |
| 266. Burglar Alarm | | | | | | | | |
| 267. Other Items | | | | | | | | |
| 268. Postage & Stationery | | | | | | | | |
| 269. | | | | | | | | |
| 270. Rents Received | | | | | | | | |
| 271. Other N. Y. Rentals | | | | | | | | |
| 272. Stock & News Tickers | | | | | | | | |
| 273. Drinking Water & Ice | | | | | | | | |
| 274. Laundry & Towels | | | | | | | | |
| 275. Clearing House & Fed. Reserve Charges | | | | | | | | |
| 276. N. Y. & Other Banking Dept. Fees | | | | | | | | |
| 277. Furniture and Fixtures Repairs | | | | | | | | |
| Undistributed Items: | | | | | | | | |
| 278. Stationery & Books | | | | | | | | |
| 279. Supplies Other Than Stationery | | | | | | | | |
| 280. Postage | | | | | | | | |
| 281. Suppers | | | | | | | | |
| 282. Traveling Incident to Current Business | | | | | | | | |
| 283. Loss on Obsolete Stationery | | | | | | | | |
| 284. General | | | | | | | | |
| 285. New Furniture, Fixtures & Equipment | | | | | | | | |
| 286. Alterations | | | | | | | | |
| 287. | | | | | | | | |
| 288. | | | | | | | | |
| 289. | | | | | | | | |
| 290. | | | | | | | | |
| 291. | | | | | | | | |
| 292. | | | | | | | | |
| 293. | | | | | | | | |
| 294. | | | | | | | | |
| 295. | | | | | | | | |
| 296. | | | | | | | | |
| 297. | | | | | | | | |
| 298. | | | | | | | | |
| 299. | | | | | | | | |
| 300. | | | | | | | | |
| 301. | | | | | | | | |
| 302. | | | | | | | | |
| 303. | | | | | | | | |
| 304. | | | | | | | | |
| **Total** | | | | | | | | |
| **TOTAL TRANSACTING BUSINESS** | | | | | | | | |
| **NON PRODUCTIVE EXPENSES** | | | | | | | | |
| 320. Officers & Clerks on War Duty | | | | | | | | |
| 321. Pensions & Donations to Employees | | | | | | | | |
| 322. Educational | | | | | | | | |
| 323. Guaranty Club | | | | | | | | |
| 324. Subscriptions, Dues, etc. | | | | | | | | |
| 325. Welfare Dept. | | | | | | | | |
| 326. Medical Supplies & Examinations | | | | | | | | |
| 327. Liberty Loan Expenses | | | | | | | | |
| 328. Additional Compensation a/c War | | | | | | | | |
| 329. | | | | | | | | |
| 330. | | | | | | | | |
| 331. | | | | | | | | |
| 332. | | | | | | | | |
| 333. | | | | | | | | |
| 334. | | | | | | | | |
| 335. | | | | | | | | |
| 336. | | | | | | | | |
| 337. | | | | | | | | |
| 338. | | | | | | | | |
| 339. | | | | | | | | |
| 340. | | | | | | | | |
| **Total** | | | | | | | | |

| | | | | | | | | |
|---|---|---|---|---|---|---|---|---|
| **Guaranty Trust Company of New York** | | | | | | | | **SHEET No. 7** |
| Summary of Expenses for January 1st to | | | | | | | | 192 |
| | SALARIES | SUPPERS | POSTAGE AND STATIONERY | OTHER ITEMS | TOTAL EXPENSES | APPRO-PRIATIONS | TOTAL APPRO-PRIATIONS FOR YEAR | EXPENSES SAME PERIOD LAST YEAR |
| **EXPENSE OF SECURING BUSINESS** New Business Department       See Sheet 8 Publicity Department       See Sheet 8 Bond Department       See Sheet 8 5th Ave. Office       See Sheet 11 Madison Ave. Office       See Sheet 12 | | | | | | | | |
| 1. Officers' Salaries 2.  "  Lunches 3. Foreign Representatives 4. General Traveling after      Business 5. General Entertaining 6. Library 7. Income Tax Dept. 8. 9. | | | | | | | | |
| **EXPENSE OF TRANS ACTING BUSINESS** CURRENT OPERATING Main Office       See Sheet 9 5th Ave. Office  See Sheet 11 Madison Ave. Office       See Sheet 12 FIXED BY POLICY Main Office       See Sheet 9 5th Ave. Office  See Sheet 11 Madison Ave. Office       See Sheet 12 OVERHEAD Main Office       See Sheet 10 5th Ave. Office  See Sheet 11 Madison Ave. Office       See Sheet 12 | | | | | | | | |
| 310. Officers' Salaries 311.  "  Lunches | | | | | | | | |
| NON PRODUCTIVE EXPENSES Main Office       See Sheet 10 5th Ave. Office  See Sheet 11 Madison Ave. Office       See Sheet 12 | | | | | | | | |
| **TOTAL EXPENSES** | | | | | | | | |

REMARKS:

NOTE: Sheets 9, 10, 11 and 12 are the same as sheets 2 to 6, except that the columns are headed the same as sheet 7.

4·20　　　　　　　　　　　　　　　　　　　　　46·4·224

# Request for Appropriation

Authority is hereby requested for an increase of
$_____in the budget for the_____
Department, Classification No._____beginning
_____192  , for the following reasons:

Date_____192     Signed by_____

Request granted for $_____

_____
*Comptroller.*

Appropriation Sheet for Year 192

| | No. | | No. | | No. | |
|---|---|---|---|---|---|---|
| January | | | | | | |
| February | | | | | | |
| March | | | | | | |
| April | | | | | | |
| May | | | | | | |
| June | | | | | | |
| July | | | | | | |
| August | | | | | | |
| September | | | | | | |
| October | | | | | | |
| November | | | | | | |
| December | | | | | | |
| Total | | | | | | |

# INDEX

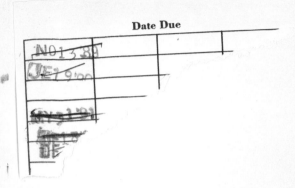